CUTTING AND CONNECTING

CUTTING AND CONNECTING
'Afrinesian' Perspectives on Networks,
Relationality, and Exchange

Edited by

Knut Christian Myhre

berghahn
NEW YORK · OXFORD
www.berghahnbooks.com

First published in 2016 by

Berghahn Books

www.berghahnbooks.com

© 2016 Berghahn Books

Originally published as a special issue of *Social Analysis*, volume 57, issue 3.

Library of Congress Cataloging-in-Publication Data

Names: Myhre, Knut Christian, 1971– editor.
Title: Cutting and connecting : 'Afrinesian' perspectives on networks, relationality, and exchange / edited by Knut Christian Myhre.
Description: New York : Berghahn Books, 2016. | "Originally published as a special issue of Social Analysis, volume 57, issue 3." | Includes bibliographical references and index.
Identifiers: LCCN 2016000490 (print) | LCCN 2016000846 (ebook) | ISBN 9781785332630 (pbk. : alk. paper) | ISBN 9781785332647 (ebook)
Subjects: LCSH: Social networks—Africa. | Social networks—Research—Methodology. | Social sciences—Network analysis—Methodology. | Ethnology—Melanesia. | Anthropology—Africa. | Anthropology—Comparative method.
Classification: LCC HM741 C88 2016 (print) | LCC HM741 (ebook) | DDC 302.3096—dc23
LC record available at http://lccn.loc.gov/2016000490

British Library Cataloguing in Publication Data

A catalogue record for this book is available from the British Library.

ISBN 978-1-78533-263-0 (paperback)
ISBN 978-1-78533-264-7 (ebook)

CONTENTS

INTRODUCTION
Cutting and Connecting—'Afrinesian' Perspectives on Networks, Relationality, and Exchange

Knut Christian Myhre

The notion of network has recently gained attention and significance, both in public parlance and the social sciences. In an era held to be marked by unprecedented mobility, networks envisage the movements and connections of persons and things through time and space, across boundaries and barriers. Information and communication technologies use 'network' to mean their operations and effects, which are claimed to bring about new kinds of behavior and actualize novel social forms (Anderson 2009). Both media and researchers herald the political potential of 'social networks' and ascribe to these phenomena pivotal roles in the recent Arab Spring and the Occupy and Indignados movements, as well as the alter-globalization protests that preceded them (Juris 2012; Mason 2012; Razsa and Kurnik 2012). The capacity of such 'liberation technology' to

Notes for this section begin on page 20.

"defend human rights, improve governance, empower the poor, promote economic development, and pursue a variety of other social goods" is explored at
the intersection between academic research and applied technology.[1] However,
'network' is also used to describe terrorist organizations that—along with drug
cartels, counterfeiters, and Internet fraudsters—exploit aspects of 'globalization' in a quest to undermine established institutional and political forms
(Gray 2003). Like 'flow' and 'circulation', 'network' seems a commonplace
in discourses that delineate phenomena on a 'global' scale (Ferguson 2006;
Tsing 2000, 2005).

Meanwhile, actor-network theory and assemblage theory are just two
approaches that employ the term with an aim to describe social complexity
without recourse to totalizing concepts that are claimed to have run their course
(DeLanda 2006; Latour 2005). As an alternative, these theories trace connections between heterogeneous elements that span different scales and levels to
reveal the hybrid character of social phenomena, which transcend analytical
divisions and domains (Latour 1993). According to these conceptions, networks
not only provide a means for describing and understanding contemporary social
phenomena, but also offer an opportunity to rethink the social itself and to
reconceive the logic and language of the political (Escobar 2008).

These approaches stress the need to develop new vocabularies of 'actor-
networks' and 'actants', or they redeploy familiar terms, such as 'assemblages',
'associations', 'articulation', and 'translation', with new meanings in order to
reveal the phenomena and processes in question. However, the emphasis on
novelty hampers reflection on the precursors to these concepts and ideas, as
well as their potential for refashioning more concrete and practical aspects to
the anthropological project. Marilyn Strathern (1996a), moreover, points out
that the concept of network entails an 'auto-limitlessness' that constitutes both
its analytical force and its weakness. It incites one to trace connections in every
direction without end, despite the fact that networks—like any action, analysis,
or interpretation—must have a point and therefore need to come to an end at
some definite place and time. In line with Strathern's (1988a, 1995, 1999, 2005)
idea that the relation simultaneously connects and divides, she argues that
attention should be directed toward the occasions, events, persons, or things
where connections are severed and networks cut in order to actualize specific
and definite forms. Cutting is the corollary of connecting: both are conceptual,
as well as pragmatic, requirements for any relationship.

Our concern with cutting and connecting in this volume seeks to extend
Strathern's insight in order to explore specific relational forms in contemporary
African settings with the aim of employing a novel form of anthropological
comparison. The chapters gathered here engage notions developed in recent
Melanesian ethnography to discuss the means by which, in different African
contexts, connections are cut and bonds severed in order to bring certain relations and social forms into being. As I argue below, this undertaking builds on
relationships between Africanist anthropology and Melanesian ethnography that
amount to debts of multifarious kinds, which enable elicitations of concepts
and concerns, analytics and approaches from one region for their deployment

in another. However, the ethnographies that these concepts and analytics afford go beyond these interpretive frames, allowing for their distortion and return in modified forms. The ethnographic explorations of the ways in which connections are cut thus allow for an exchange of anthropological analytics that severs the bonds between Africa and Melanesia to proportion the distance between them.

In this way, a historically informed notion of network that retrieves aspects of earlier forms of analysis enables a new form of comparative anthropology that reinvigorates specific legacies by extending them in novel ways to encompass new areas and domains. It contrives a conversation between past and present authorships to yield a 'trans-temporal' and 'disjunctive' comparison (Holbraad and Pedersen 2009; Lazar 2012) that 'bifurcates' (Strathern 2011) two of anthropology's formative regions. Simultaneously conceptual and empirical, this approach forms part of an 'ethnographic turn' (Fortun 2012) that adds to the heterogeneous and pluralist comparativism that Gingrich and Fox (2002) offer in response to the intellectual impasse and uncertainty occasioned by the crisis of representation.

Nordic and African Networks

Network analysis was spioneered in the post-war years by a group of researchers with close ties to Africanist anthropology. John Barnes, who had worked among the Ngoni of present-day Zambia and Malawi in the late 1940s, introduced the concept of network to anthropology in his study of Bremnes, a fishing and farming community on the west coast of Norway. Barnes (1954) was concerned with the operation of the class system in interpersonal relationships and the organization of collective action in a setting characterized by an emphasis on social equality. He used the notion of network to capture the relationships of kinship, friendship, and neighborhood that fell outside the territorial fields of settlement, cultivation, and administration, as well as the industrial system pertaining to the herring fisheries. In contrast to these fields, the network was marked by egality, and Barnes analyzed the manner in which this aspect shaped decision-making processes in the plethora of local formal associations. The analytical focus of Barnes's idea of network was thus on the character of social relationships in order to account for the behavior of those entangled in them. From this viewpoint, action became a function, or an effect, of social relations, which shifted the center of attention to the relations between relations and away from the characteristics of the persons partaking in those relations (Mitchell 1969a: 4).

The network described a relational order that was not accessible to structural concepts pertaining to the institutions of settlement and industry. In addition, the idea served to identify a kind of relationality that was different from that which anthropologists studied in other parts of the world. While it was deemed possible for anthropological analyses of 'simple societies' to aim for a comprehensive understanding of those societies as a whole, the diversity of interactional domains in 'complex societies' meant that one could feasibly study only one sector of these societies. Moreover, "[t]his limited area of detailed knowledge has then to be related, as best we can, to experience and information derived from other parts of society" (Barnes 1954: 39). The notion of network not only described a distinct relational order but moreover was a way of connecting the different domains of complex societies. Network analysis thus achieved an effect analogous, yet complementary, to that of conventional analytical frameworks. It made the network an addition to, rather than a replacement for, established modes of analysis (Mitchell 1974: 282).

Although early studies emphasized that the notion of network was best suited for complex societies (Bott 1957), Barnes (1954: 57) suggested that Bremnes could serve as a case study for the comparative analysis of the emergent administrative forms and nascent industrialization that pertained to processes of decolonization. A few years later, his concept was indeed deployed to study urban settings in central Africa (Mitchell 1969b) on the premise that the network was a device that could be used to explore social relationships in 'modern' settings. These studies built on research concerning urbanization and labor migration in South Africa (Mayer 1961; Pauw 1963) to investigate phenomena such as industrial relations, inter-ethnic politics, and urban social organization. Again, the strong point of network analysis proved to be the study of social forms that fell outside the purview of established approaches that relied upon notions such as 'structure' and 'system'.

The 'Point-Source'

Many of these studies were conducted by former colleagues of John Barnes from the Rhodes-Livingstone Institute of Central African Studies (RLI) and the Victoria University of Manchester, who were particularly well-placed to explore the concept of network and the mode of analysis it enabled. For them, the notion of network owed its attraction to two principal sources: "The first derives from a growing dissatisfaction with structural-functional analyses and the search, consequently, for alternative ways of interpreting social action. The second is in the development of non-quantitative mathematical ways of rigorously stating the implications entailed in a set of relationships among a number of persons" (Mitchell 1969a: 1). Before turning to anthropology, Barnes was trained in mathematics and was therefore able to appreciate the analytical potential of graph theory, which underpinned his vision of the network as "a set of points some of which are joined by lines" (1954: 43). Graph theory was claimed to hold great promise for the formal analysis and representation of social relationships, whose properties, it was argued, could be measured and modeled by various means (Mitchell 1969a: 34; 1974: 296).

Furthermore, these researchers were trained or influenced by Max Gluckman, whose directorship of the RLI and subsequent professorship at Manchester University fostered connections and cross-fertilization between these two institutions (Schumaker 2004: 121). In recognition of this, Mitchell's book *Social Networks in Urban Situations* (1969b) was dedicated to Gluckman, who was designated the "point-source of our network" (ibid.: ii). As a former student of A. R. Radcliffe-Brown and Isaac Schapera, and a close friend and one-time colleague of E. E. Evans-Pritchard and Meyer Fortes, Gluckman was hardly peripheral to the discipline's establishment. However, his vision for anthropology deviated in significant ways from the orthodoxy of British structural-functionalism. As Bruce Kapferer (2005a: 86) argues, Gluckman and his collaborators focused on issues that were outside the scope of the dominant paradigm to challenge its core concepts and theories. He developed an analysis that focused on the social, economic, and political conditions for the production of specific 'situations' that foregrounded process and temporality to enable a study of social complexity and change. This approach concerned specific persons and actual events in real time, rather than abstract reconstructions in the ethnographic present (Macmillan 1995: 47; Werbner 1984: 157), making history a closer ally than synchronic and static sociology.

Gluckman ([1940] 1958) explored situational analysis prior to his tenure at the RLI, and even then his approach matched the institute's mandate to contribute "to the scientific efforts now being made in various quarters to examine the effects upon native African society of the impact of European civilization" (Wilson 1940: 43). The RLI aimed to do this "by the formation in Africa itself of a center where the problem of establishing permanent and satisfactory relations between natives and non-natives—a problem of urgent importance where, as in Northern Rhodesia, mineral resources are being developed in the home of a primitive community—may form the subject of special study" (ibid.). Another institution that shared this concern was the International Institute of African Languages and Cultures (IIALC), which was founded in 1926 with Frederick D. Lugard as its first chairman. According to Lugard (1928: 2), the aim of the IIALC (later, the International African Institute, or IAI) was to bring about "a closer association of scientific knowledge and research with practical affairs." Its initial plan of research stated that the institute should provide "the exact knowledge that will assist in determining the right relations between the institutions of African society and alien systems of government, education, and religion" (IIALC 1932: 3). Questions concerning the effects of, and relationships between, colonial rule and African subjects were attenuated by indirect rule, whose conception and inception in large part stemmed from Lugard's tenure as governor of northern Nigeria and was subsequently formalized and extended throughout British colonial Africa (Perham 1965). The challenges posed by indirect rule became particularly acute in Northern Rhodesia, where the rapid development of the Copperbelt exacerbated the colonial contradiction between a desire to develop an export-led economy and a wish to limit social change and maintain institutions of political control (Brown 1979: 526).

Despite the similarities in the remits of these two institutes, however, Gluckman's conception diverged significantly from the 'practical anthropology' and 'the study of the changing native' that Malinowski (1929, 1930) devised on behalf of the IIALC. In particular, Gluckman (1947) objected to Malinowski's (1945) approach to colonial Africa as a situation of 'culture contact', where institutions that fulfill specific needs impact and impinge on one another. Gluckman

(1947: 112) argued that the presumption of 'culture' and 'institution' as the units of study committed Malinowski to the description of discrete realities, which blinded him to the similarities that cross-cut the differences. Moreover, it extroverted conflict and confined it to relations between cultures, whose internal relations in turn became marked by collaboration and integration. In such a light, 'contact' could only be accorded a destructive influence, which threatened 'African society' with disintegration (IIALC 1932: 32).

To overcome the analytical poverty of this perspective, Gluckman advocated the study of relations of collaborations and conflict within a single social field that included colonial agents and subjects in the same frame. This approach aimed to transform the putative differences and assumed similarities created by the notion of culture into processes and elements that would facilitate comparative analyses. It derived its impetus and urgency from the social problems connected to labor migration, which fostered the singular "Central African Society of heterogeneous culture-groups of Europeans and Africans" that Gluckman (1945: 9) aimed to address through the RLI's approach and research. Situational analysis therefore abandoned 'the tribe' as a unit of analysis in order to explore concepts of a finer grain than 'culture' and 'society' (Kapferer 2005b: 279; Schumaker 2004: 106). Network analysis accorded with these principles and therefore was one of the conceptual and methodological innovations—along with the extended case method (van Velsen 1967) and 'social drama' (Turner 1957)—that flourished around Gluckman's situational analysis, in response to conditions considered unsuited for concepts and analyses that simultaneously relied upon and created bounded and autonomous entities (Gluckman 1961).[2]

Melanesian Extensions

The highlands of Papua New Guinea became available for anthropological research shortly before the exploration of network analysis. At the time, Anglo-Saxon anthropological analysis was dominated by lineage or descent theory that was largely developed on the basis of studies conducted in Africa. In this respect, the publication of Fortes and Evans-Pritchard's *African Political Systems* (1940), under the auspices of the IAI, was especially significant due to the fact that its inauguration of political anthropology as a sub-discipline established kinship as the salient analytical context for the politics of stateless societies.

In the New Guinea Highlands, researchers encountered populations whose characteristics suggested useful comparison with the segmentary societies that had been described in Africa. The comparison was abetted by the fact that several of the early highland ethnographers were trained by Africanist anthropologists, whose commitment to lineage theory influenced the analysis of New Guinea social life (Barnes 2008: 279; Hays 1992: 33).[3] However, Barnes (1962: 5), who had relocated to Australia in the late 1950s, where he supervised several students working in the area, pointed out that mounting ethnographic evidence "weakened what we might call the African mirage in New Guinea."

Despite the fact that men in the highland communities apparently traced agnatic descent and that settlement patterns tended to be patrivirilocal, they did not constitute unilineal descent groups of the kind epitomized by the Nuer, Tallensi, and Tiv. Rather, the New Guinea Highlands were marked by multiple affiliations and allegiances, which enabled a proliferation of relationships on the level of the individual, rather than that of the group. Barnes argued that the situation was due to a greater range of choice and the widespread significance of ceremonial exchange, which contrasted New Guinea "network cohesion" and "unbounded affiliation" to the "group solidarity" and "bounded affiliation" of African sociality (ibid.: 8).

His institutional background and intellectual trajectory attuned Barnes to the problems posed by the structural-functionalist models derived from Africa and the alternative represented by the notion of network. The approaches developed at the RLI and the Manchester School struggled to overcome ontological commitments that opposed individual and society, part and whole, agency and structure (Evens 2005), where an emphasis on one element of the equation by necessity came at the expense of the other. However, the greatest significance and lasting impact of Barnes's text for Melanesianist anthropology does not lie in its promotion of individual choice and strategic manipulation at the expense of group structures. Its salient contribution rather consists in its self-consciousness regarding the heuristic nature of anthropological concepts and analytics.

Barnes (1962: 5) conceded that the African models of segmentary societies had enabled ethnographers to produce provisional accounts of the large, apparently patrilineal highland populations that lacked institutionalized forms of leadership. However, with time, the Africanist analytics threatened to overdetermine the highland ethnography and obscure its distinctiveness. Divergence from the models became a problem that required explanation, rather than a potential resource for anthropological reflection and theory. The solution to this quandary was to emphasize how the segmentary models had been heuristic devices for the analysis and representation of the experiences made by ethnographers. The pertinent issue was therefore not whether the people of central New Guinea had unilineal descent groups; rather, the key thing was how notions such as 'lineage', 'segmentation', and indeed 'group' shed light on their behavior.

The question raised by Barnes concerning the analytical effects of concepts for ethnographic representation and anthropological reflection gained great significance for a particular trend in regional anthropology that eventually was dubbed the New Melanesian Ethnography (Josephides 1991). Starting in the 1970s, scholars working in the New Guinea Highlands emphasized how anthropology consists of "a game of heuristic pretending" (Wagner 1974: 97) whereby concepts are adopted from one social context and applied to another in order to describe behavior in recognizable terms. Lineage theory, for instance, established analogies that enabled accounts of vernacular practice as if the Nuer and Tallensi have 'politics' and 'law', whose application as an analytical tool yielded groups of a specific kind.

However, Wagner (1974: 97) pointed out that the game of heuristic pretense is not played in isolation, but always takes place in relation to specific ethnographic material. Anthropological analytics therefore can—and must—be held to account by the material to which it is applied. This resulted in the realization that ethnography can be used to explore the assumptions that underpin anthropological concepts, including analytical staples such as 'culture', 'nature', 'gender', and 'society' (Wagner [1975] 1981; Strathern 1980, 1981, 1996b).[4] Ethnography can thus be used to chart the limits of analytical constructs in order to explore what they hide as well as what they reveal. It was furthermore maintained that this concern with the mutuality between revelation and concealment is shared with New Guinea Highlanders, who employ and enact similar processes in myth, ceremonial exchange activities, and initiation rituals (Strathern 1988a; Wagner 1978; Weiner 1988). These claims and alignments confound the distinction between theory and argument in a manner that recognizes simultaneously how analytics pre-forms ethnography and the way in which ethnographic phenomena may constitute conceptual resources for anthropological reflection.

In this perspective, analysis consists of a double move, whose effect results from the parallel deployment and retention of specific concepts. As Reed (2003: 11) points out, in *The Gender of the Gift* Strathern (1988a) deliberately hides certain organizing conceptual oppositions in order to make visible an alternative analytic. This move does not amount to a simple substitution but rather a mode of concealment that assumes the form of an eclipse, where an interposition enables the contours of an obscured object to be traced. Strathern's notion of 'the relation' thus occludes the opposition between society and individual to render visible the otherwise hidden or tacit operations of anthropological knowledge practices. Her use of certain analytical 'fictions' thereby reworks Melanesian ethnography to highlight the operations of anthropology with the effect of dissolving their distinction. Several entities are thus simultaneously brought into view, albeit with different modalities.

Aspects of these moves were anticipated by the early network analysts, even though the concepts they deployed and retained differed from those of Strathern. Barnes, for instance, stressed the analytical, rather than metaphorical, character of the network notion and endeavored to characterize and define its heuristic utility (Mitchell 1969a: 2). These early analysts moreover recognized that 'structure' and 'network', as distinct relational orders, involved different modes of abstraction made on the basis of divergent assumptions from the same observed behavior (Mitchell 1969a: 10; 1974: 284). Networks were hence the effects of a particular concept and the outcome of the analysis, rather than entities in the world. The point was not that people *have* networks; rather, the notion allows for events to be described *as if* social life is constituted in a particular way.

Indeed, G. Kingsley Garbett (1970: 216) revealed that Gluckman's situational analysis shared the same analytical perspective: "When a situation is treated as a unit of analysis, the events contained within its temporal and spatial boundaries are arbitrarily and heuristically circumscribed … in terms of some theoretical perspective." It is moreover held in common with more recent actor-network theory: "Thus, the network does not designate a thing out there that would have roughly the shape of interconnected points, much like a telephone, a freeway, or a sewage 'network'. It is nothing more than *an indicator of the quality of a text* about the topics at hand" (Latour 2005: 129; original emphasis). In this conception, 'network' forms part of a mode of apprehension and description that renders the world in a specific form which differs from that yielded by other analytical concepts.

However, network analysis did not simply consist in the application of an analytical concept; it also involved the subtraction of other notions. Thus, Barnes (1954: 43) argued: "For our present purposes ... I want to consider, roughly speaking, that part of the total network that is left behind when we remove the groupings and chains of interaction which belong strictly to the territorial and industrial systems. In Bremnes society, what is left is largely, though not exclusively, a network of ties of kinship, friendship, and neighbourhood." In Barnes's account, the network owed its appearance as much to the removal of the effects of certain analytical concepts as to his use of an alternative notion. In a similar way, Latour (2005: 221) argues that actor-network theory "is a negative, empty, relativistic grid that allows us *not* to synthesize the ingredients of the social in the actor's place." By pre-empting a specific sense of 'the social', Latour creates the space for an alternative to deploy itself, which brings forth a heterogeneity of actors that surpasses the homogeneous networks envisaged by Barnes and his colleagues, whose nodes tended to consist solely of individuals.[5] Latour's conception furthermore makes room for a notion of agency as a property of networks of relations, which resolves the equivocation between the structural and transactional perspectives on networks (Mitchell 1974: 284ff.) that mirrored a deeper ambivalence among the members of the Manchester School (Englund 2002: 29) and arguably contributed to the demise of network analysis. Despite their differences, however, all these authors acknowledge and explore how analysis creates its effect by bringing one concept to bear at the same time that other concepts are withdrawn. Melanesianist anthropology may have been dominated by 'tribal concerns' (Knauft 1999: 203; see also Reed, below), but its theoretical and analytical perspectives owe something to the notion of network, which was instrumental in subverting 'the tribe' in Africanist anthropology. En route to Melanesia, however, the social and political urgency that drove and characterized situational analysis and its offshoots became displaced onto the plane of anthropological representations and theorization.[6]

Cutting Connections to Make Relations and Networks

Strathern's account of Melanesian exchange activities involves a further debt to the notion of network, which moreover constitutes a resource for its conceptual development. In the classic conception, the obligations of exchange entail that the presentation of a gift is an instigation of a relationship between two persons by means of a material object (Mauss [1925] 1990). According to Strathern (1988a), however, what appears as the donor's voluntary bestowal is in fact the recipient's elicitation on the basis of a debt relationship. The gift is not a means for establishing a relationship, but an objectification of the relationship that already exists between the parties involved. The gift does not connect the giver and the receiver; instead, it differentiates them as giver and receiver by making visible the aspect under which one is able to elicit something from the other. Thus, "[t]he constitution or capability of one person becomes externalized by he or she drawing out of another a counter condition" (Strathern 1988a: 173). In this way, the exchange separates the persons involved by making visible the conditions that connect and constitute them in the form of an object. Persons and things are thus the reified effects of social relationships that are manipulated in different kinds of exchange with the aim of extending, furthering, or fostering relations. Social relations are the object of concern and engagement in a world where relations can only be turned into, or made to stand for, other relations.

Strathern's conception of exchange radicalizes the network notion that a social phenomenon is a function—and thus effect—of a particular relationship, along with its corollary that salience pertains to the relations between relations.[7] However, her endeavor to grant primacy and priority to the relation displaces the individual and his or her impetus to connect, which allows exchange to emerge as simultaneously a means of separation and connection. In turn, this enables an expansion of the concept of the relation to include processes by which connections are severed, in order to make relations of a specific kind. Building on Wagner's (1977) heuristic analysis of relationality as a flow of similarity that must be interrupted in order to differentiate and make relationships of specific kinds, Weiner (1993: 292) points out that "[i]n a world such as that of the Foi or the Melpa that is relationally based, the task confronting humans is not to sustain human relationship. The very bodily compulsions of life—appetite, sexuality, anger, conflict—do that themselves. What people must do is place a limit on relationship, on this 'form-enhancing force'; they must restrict its extension." Cutting is a corollary of connection and a condition for the existence of relations.

Indeed, the notion of network confronted its early analysts with the same conundrum. Barnes (1954: 43–44) argued that "[a] network of this kind has no external boundary, nor has it any clear-cut internal divisions," but the notion threatened consequently to engulf the entirety of social life. Mitchell (1969a: 40) therefore pointed out that "[c]ertain difficulties arise … in identifying the limits or extent of a personal network." He realized, though, that "[c]learly, some limit must be put on the number of links to be taken as definitive for any specific network; otherwise it would be co-extensive with the total network" (ibid.). The problem arose because the analytical effort was devoted solely to connections and their character, without a view for how their limits are drawn: "The majority, so far, have concentrated on the nature of the links among people in the network as being the most significant feature" (ibid.: 10). Strathern (1996a) points out that actor-network theory faces a similar problem: if unchecked, its notions of network and hybridity facilitate narratives without end and the pursuit of networks within networks that are as extensive and entangled as one may wish. Like the term itself, actor-network theory acquires a hyphenated character, as its concern for chains of association and the effort required to sustain processes of translation and maintain assemblages generate descriptions of phenomena as series of connected nouns (Law 2012). A view that sees only connections, without a concern for distinctions, expands the network without limitation, at the same time that it restricts the concept of the relation.

The problem of delimitation in early network analysis was compounded by its failure to realize that the analysis imposes its own limits on the network. Or, rather, unease at the thought that the analytical severance does not accord with the limits of the vernacular network occasioned theoretical and conceptual developments to facilitate congruence between the two. Mitchell (1974: 279) pointed out that such elaborations came at the expense of empirical studies and precipitated a proliferation of concepts and terms, which in turn undermined the comparative ambition (Barnes 1969: 53). Furthermore, this development induced a combination of conceptual deliberation, on the one hand, and an empirical emphasis on small-scale personal networks, on the other, which made the mode of analysis simultaneously highly abstract and intensely specific. Network analysis thus yielded the middle ground that is occupied by the bulk of anthropological research (Knauft 2006). Latour's (2005: 221) call for increased theoretical abstraction, in combination with the myopic tracing of connectors and mediators, enables and inhabits a similar analytical space. It is a curious consequence of a concern with the correspondence between resultant and factual networks, which neglects the analytical nature of the concept, whose effect and value reside in its ability to reveal something and to contribute to a given material. As Riles (2001) argues, a correspondence between analytical and vernacular notions of network poses particular problems that require alternative analytical moves besides the application of a concept to a material for an effect.

In contrast, Strathern's idea that the relation simultaneously combines and divides accentuates the requirement to cut the network in order to render it into a particular form. In an apparent paradox, a focus on how connections are cut enables an expansion of the analytical concept of network. Strathern's attention to processes of separation, substitution, detachment, and decomposition thus is in marked contrast to the actor-network theory's logic of addition, which accords a different dynamic and directionality to both social life and theory.[8] As actor-network theory hones in on how elements are combined to produce something new, its conceptualization and theorization take the form of an addition or expansion in which concepts dilate to include ever more phenomena. In contrast, Strathern's concern for separation allows for an alternative form of abstraction—one where concepts simultaneously cut and are cut to reveal specific aspects of the world (Holbraad and Pedersen 2009), thus allowing for a view of how the concept of network itself cuts and combines phenomena in particular ways to present the world in a certain way.

Claiming Debts and Cutting Networks

The chapters presented here result from a two-day workshop held at the Nordic Africa Institute in Uppsala, Sweden, that was entitled "Explorations of 'Afrinesia': Experimental Approaches to Legal and Political Anthropology in Africa." Its initial impetus was the increased interest in Africanist anthropology with regard to notions such as globalization, democratization, and postcolonialism, which locate Africa within larger transnational dynamics that dissolve the boundaries of the anthropological field site and extend the reach of social processes. These developments raise questions regarding the salience of social phenomena, the manner in which they relate to each other, and the relevant contexts for their study, which allow for inquiries into the form and nature of received analytical domains. In this respect, the advances of the New Melanesian Ethnography were considered relevant, so the workshop aimed to explore new approaches to political and legal anthropology in Africa in terms of concepts and ideas developed about Melanesia. The focus was restricted to these domains partly due to their historical significance for Africanist anthropology, but mainly because they appeared to be the ones most affected by the new developments and seemed most vulnerable to the presuppositions and conceptions called into question by Melanesianist anthropology.

However, during our proceedings in Uppsala, we realized that this endeavor had several problematic implications. A straightforward application of Melanesianist models on Africanist ethnography would simply invert the earlier relationship between these regions to little effect beyond reversing the arrow of influence. It would moreover frame Africanist ethnography as raw material to be refined by means of anthropological resources and processes supplied from elsewhere, and thus create an intellectual analogy to the colonial economies with whose effects the RLI and the IIALC were set up to engage. Indeed, it would instantiate the logic of indirect rule, as notions and practices from one place would be generalized for their application elsewhere. Most gravely, however, it risked reiterating the moves made by the early students of the New Guinea Highlands by treating ethnographic divergences from these models as phenomena that require explanation, rather than exploration. Raised explicitly in Thomas Yarrow's workshop contribution, and sharpened through persistent and systematic inquiry by Yarrow and our discussant Adam Reed, the key question that emerged during the workshop was how to treat ethnographic material that exceeds the Melanesianist perspectives and approaches.

As it turns out, the history and development of the notion of network offer a solution to this question and provide a basis for a novel form of comparison between Africa and Melanesia. The personal, intellectual, and institutional connections between early network analysis and Melanesianist anthropology described above reveal how concepts and approaches that were pioneered in Nordic and African contexts were imported and improved upon in Melanesia. They show that Melanesianist anthropology is indebted to perspectives that were developed elsewhere and may be regarded as the effect of relations from a distance. These regions and perspectives are therefore already related, so the task in confronting them is not to sustain relations, but rather to place limits on them. One way to do this is to enact an analogy of Melanesian gift exchange and activate these debt relations to elicit concepts, concerns, procedures, and forms from Melanesianist anthropology in order to utilize them in African contexts, where they may be modified before they are sent back. The heuristic analogy of gift exchange thus affords a traffic in analytics that differentiates the two regions by making visible the aspect through which they relate to each other. 'Africa' and 'Melanesia' are then not distinct entities between which connections must be fostered, but the effects of endeavors to cut the bonds between them.

On this basis, our solution to the question raised by our workshop is to appropriate Strathern's idea of cutting the network and redirect our efforts to explore how relationships are gathered, severed, docked, blocked, or turned around at strategic points in concrete cases concerning contemporary African ethnography. In the follow-up to the workshop, the authors were asked to give particular consideration to the manner in which the processes of cutting unfold, and how they serve to bring certain relations into view and give them distinct form. As the chapters testify, this focus enables engagement with a wide range of ethnographic phenomena and theoretical concerns and allows for a reconsideration of the topic of relationality.

The concern with how networks are cut to enable and reveal different relational forms motivates Isak Niehaus's comparison of HIV/AIDS in South Africa and kuru in Melanesia. Certain significant similarities between these epidemics afford a comparative view, but Niehaus is not concerned with devising a universal framework. Instead, he deploys 'culpability' as a mediating term to demonstrate how different discourses bring "certain modes of relationality into view [while], at the same time, occluding others." The history of kuru shows how biomedical researchers, local people, and anthropologists engaged in exchange relationships, where bodies and their fluids were donated in anticipation of a cure. However, the network it created connected kuru to cannibalism, framing the Fore as a disreputable 'other', who in turn cut their engagement with the researchers to resume sorcery discourses that confined the matter to particular social relations. Both the medical and vernacular discourses involved the extraction of bodily substances, but their divergent configurations of culpability cut and connected people in different ways to render dissimilar relational forms. In an analogous way, South African health workers linked HIV/AIDS to sexual promiscuity, which stigmatized and isolated sufferers, while witchcraft accusations were "bids to affect relational forms" that involved alternative networks. As a heuristic, 'culpability' thus discloses how divergent and contested discourses of various interlocutors form part of multiple networks that are cut in different ways to bring about alternative relational forms.

Two of the contributions explore processes and phenomena that call into question the appositeness of cutting as a relational operation altogether. Niklas Hultin investigates the sharing and non-sharing of legal information in urban Gambia, where the law is marked by "indeterminacy … vagueness, ambiguity, and remoteness." Hultin terms this 'opacity', which does not mean non-transparency but instead designates an incompleteness or partiality that enables specific social forms. Where the law is known about, but not known, the circulation of legal information may be considered a form of exchange that instantiates a mode of sociality, as a reiteration of the transactors' concerns. Conversely, non-sharing does not entail the absence of a connection; rather, it involves a relation of disinterest and condemnation that is attempted to be remedied through an amendment of law or supplement of legal information. Unlike elsewhere in Africa, the opacity of the law therefore results not in disengagement but in an aspiration for perfect legality. It does not simply cut and combine people in specific ways, but affords a dynamic and an impetus to social interaction that is constitutive of particular political communities. Opacity is therefore neither a hindrance for relations nor a provision that people establish in order to create relations. It is a condition and premise for a relation, as it defines what may count as information and hence what amounts to a relation through its sharing or non-sharing.

Tone Sommerfelt, meanwhile, describes marriage exchanges in rural Gambia, where the majority of unions take place between close relatives. Her account of the manner in which bridal trousseaus are acquired and assembled shows how money as a medium of exchange neither diminishes nor homogenizes the plethora of prestations, but enables their multiplication and the mobilization of wider networks of people. In turn, the redistribution of trousseau items materializes and makes visible a specific relationship between the bride and the other women in the marital homestead to whom she is already related in several different yet overlapping ways. In the redistribution, these multifarious connections are eclipsed in favor of the emergent relationship between co-wives. In line with accounts from Melanesia, the redistribution is thus not an effort to connect unrelated persons, nor is it a straightforward matter of separating people by placing limits on their connections. Rather, it accentuates certain connections and aspects, while allowing others to drift from view. This involves a mode of disclosure that departs from Melanesian ceremonial exchanges, where agents detach and transact gendered components in order to make visible and manipulate social relationships. Instead, in the Gambian context, certain relationships are allowed to stand forth against a background of receding relations that are erased from view. The distribution of the trousseau thus 'fades' certain connections to shape networks of relations as degrees of similarity and difference. In this way, the progressive receding of connections establishes gradual distinctions of proximity rather than categorical divisions between bounded units, thus rendering 'fading' a more apt term than 'cutting'.

Other contributors explore forms of connectivity that distort the notion of relationality developed in the Melanesian accounts. In her chapter, Daivi Rodima-Taylor considers the kinds of freedoms and constraints enabled and entailed by voluntary associations and collectivities among the Kuria of Tanzania that blur the distinctions of political and legal theory. She combines Gluckman's notion of relational rights with Munn's and Strathern's work on indigenous relational forms to explore how women's credit associations and mutual help groups extend particular social forms, where persons exert and expand their influence by engaging and multiplying exchange partners and debt relations.

Like Sommerfelt, Rodima-Taylor thus investigates how money and other material means augment and distend claims and obligations, making it necessary to contain and limit them. It furthermore allows her to show how freedom, independence, and sovereignty are the effects of engagements and entanglements in various associational forms, whose connections are cut to yield the figure of the autonomous business woman. Kuria ethnography is in this way suitable for exploration by means of Melanesian analytics, but Rodima-Taylor's account of the person in terms of the notion of *omooyo* challenges the 'partible person' concept described by Strathern. Whereas the latter is composed of gendered elements that are elicited and manifested in specific events, *omooyo* is a passageway or "vessel of flow and movement" that allows certain combinations and disconnections to emerge and take place. *Omooyo* renders the person neither partible nor permeable (Busby 1997) but rather a momentary gathering of heterogeneous elements that are funneled into a specific form. In turn, this has consequences for Kuria relational forms, whose public and political potential differ from the dynamics described in Melanesian accounts.

Like Rodima-Taylor, Richard Vokes queries Strathern's notion of the partible person, which is shown to have heuristic value for ethnographic evidence from southwestern Uganda concerning the constitutive character of the flows of bodily substances. Furthermore, the curtailments of these flows may be considered socially productive ways of cutting the network that controls and directs the currents of substances in generative ways. Melanesian analytics thus allows for and brings forth phenomena that Vokes considers "the primary dynamics of everyday social life," but that Africanist anthropologists have tended to consider in negative terms as 'blockages'. At the same time, however, the Ugandan emphasis on flows points out the limits of the unit-based forms that recur in accounts of Melanesian transactions and allows for an 'intensive quantification', where the 'swelling' of the person indexes the character and gradual shifts in the currents of substances. As with the Kuria, the person assumes the character of a vessel or conduit that enables certain connections and separations, whose effects are registered in its form and appearance. This perspective moreover allows Vokes to reconsider the social significance of cattle, whose greater quantities of the same crucial bodily substances afford them a role in amplifying the dynamics of swelling and quantification. In this way, Vokes is able to further extend and distort Melanesian analytics by demonstrating the implication of animals in these exchanges and the significance of non-human agents for human personhood.

Livestock also feature prominently in Knut Christian Myhre's exploration of how animals are butchered and their meat shared among the Chagga-speaking people of Tanzania. When the analytic of 'sacrifice' is deliberately hidden, butchering can be considered an event and process in which specific relationships are cut from the animal's body and revealed in the form of the different shares of meat. Seen in this light, butchering is a mode of differentiation where "people are distinguished and constituted as persons of specific kinds by virtue of the social relationships that are intrinsic to their personhood." Each share of meat enfolds a relationship between multifarious entities, which butchering unfolds as a network. Myhre shows how dynamics similar to those in Melanesian reports may be revealed in this particular African context, but only after the vernacular language use that surrounds and pertains to butchering is taken into consideration. The Chagga ethnography thematizes the significance of language for processes of elicitation and decomposition, which is 'muted' in Strathern's account. On this basis, Myhre shows how the Chagga cut and combine language and life in a way that can serve to place the ethnographic description and anthropological analysis on the same scale and level as vernacular statements. The case of how animals are butchered in Kilimanjaro thus cuts the expanse of social life to conjoin and divide vernacular and analytical concepts in a different way. The emphasis on language expands the modality of disclosure described from Melanesia to recombine and recast the relation between theory and argument.

Harri Englund and Thomas Yarrow explore the relationship between ethnography and theory to problematize the connection between generality and particularity in anthropological thinking. Strathern's insights into the dynamics between theory and place require a heightened reflexivity and an increased concern for the origins of theoretical propositions, which preclude a simplistic application of ideas between contexts. The same point applies to Strathern's own theorizations, whose limits are thus traced by her own approach. Inspired by this, Englund and Yarrow explore how the multiple origins and constitution of 'relational rights' entail that this notion cannot be conveniently localized but must be recognized as the conceptual outcome of comparison. Meanwhile, the divergent trajectories and recent inversion of the notion of network support their broader point that the deliberate confusion of theory and evidence implies that analytical concepts are not a means for connecting and comparing distinct places. Rather, both concepts and places are effects of comparison that enable reflexive engagement with epistemological assumptions to delimit and reorder anthropological concepts by way of ethnographic artifacts. In an analogue to Myhre's move regarding the relationship between language and life, Englund and Yarrow's exploration of Strathern's thinking as a self-limiting device cuts and combines the connection between ethnography and anthropology to recast the relationship between theory and place. In this approach, place becomes a heuristic and arbitrary entity, whose analytical construction and usefulness should not be mistaken as a geographical counter to, or as an origin of, theory.

'Afrinesian': The Comparison of Concepts and Relationships

Unlike the early researchers of the New Guinea Highlands, we do not look on ethnographic surfeits as curiosities and artifacts that need to be explained; rather, we treat them as potentialities for modifying, extending, or distorting the notions and approaches developed elsewhere. The chapters gathered in this volume trace the limits of Melanesian-based relationalist perspectives and highlight the contributions that material and perspectives from African contexts make to anthropological theorizations. In this way, our considerations of how networks are cut in different ethnographic situations and contexts 'cuts' Melanesianist perspectives in relation to the various African localities we explore. The focus on the limitations of Melanesianist perspectives for Africanist ethnography reveals how, where, and the extent to which the anthropological relationship between Africa and Melanesia may be severed. The regard for how connections are cut in specific ethnographic contexts thus cuts the anthropological perspectives, whose connections have brought them into existence. Like the Melanesian gift, the elicited concepts and concerns objectify the conditions under which Africa and Melanesia already connect, and, as theoretical gifts that we extract and receive, they are employed and modified before they are returned.

The tangled origins and effects of the notion of network make its cutting a superb basis for a comparative project between Africa and Melanesia, under the auspices of a Nordic research institute, whose results appear in a journal intended to extend the ideas of the Manchester School (Kapferer 2006: 5). Furthermore, it enables engagement with aspects of Melanesianist anthropology that differ from other attempts at deploying its concepts for comparative purposes. Where we focus on cutting the network, along with the relational forms and modes that this entails and effects, other researchers concentrate on notions and practices concerning personhood, embodiment, and gender (Busby 1997; Gregor and Tuzin 2001; Keen 2006; Lambek and Strathern 1998; McCallum 2001; Mosko 2010; Piot 1999; Vilaça 2011). Our concern with networks moreover draws on different elements of the RLI and Manchester legacy compared to other recent attempts to explore its potential and significance for contemporary anthropological theory. Where they concentrate on the relevance of situational analysis and the extended case method for practice theory and other poststructuralist social philosophies (Evens and Handelman 2005; Kapferer 2010), our agenda concerns the contribution of an expanded notion of the network for relationalist perspectives. Hence, our efforts to trace, cut, and theorize the network of 'network' make a distinct contribution to other attempts at engaging related concepts and discourses.

Recognizing and reiterating the recursive relationship between Africa and Melanesia moreover averts the localization of concepts that commonly accompanies their movement from one place to another (Strathern 1988b, 1990). Or, rather, it effectuates a different form of localization, one that does not depend upon the negative strategy of inversion. The analytical debt relationship entails that the elicited conceptual gifts are not exogenous imports, whose negation brings forth indigenous resources that in turn may be exported. Instead, the mutual implication of Africa and Melanesia destabilizes the distinction between the external and the internal, bringing into view the ways in which they contain or permeate each other. As Englund and Yarrow demonstrate, this enables a co-theorization of Africa and Melanesia that ruptures the association between theory and place, which equates particular concepts with specific parts of the world.

A consequence of this is that the relationalist perspectives are 'demoted' and no longer appear as high theory, which is to be employed on African ethnography. Indeed, the relationship skirts the analytical move whereby concepts are applied or added to a material held to be of a different epistemological status and character in order to evade the analytical colonization of one region by another.[9] Instead, our move recognizes the endeavor on the part of Strathern, Wagner, and their collaborators to borrow analytics from ethnography. These analytics do not derive from Melanesia in a simple manner but owe something to Africanist and Nordic ethnography, as well as the anthropological canon. Melanesian, African, Nordic, and theoretical constructs are on a par with each other and of the same character to facilitate their comparison. However, this mode of comparison does not presume the existence of discrete contexts or entities among which the ethnographer connects and translates, in order to document their similarities and differences. Rather, it assumes an analytical similarity, which allows for explorations of the differences that bound and delimit it. The comparative exercise elicits specificity, rather than subsuming difference under a general term. Keeping in mind the contingent and heuristic character of the enabling similarity unsettles the distinction between fieldwork and writing to relativize the basis for comparison and reveal the relational character of knowledge production (Bruun Jensen 2011; Strathern 1999). It ensures that the mode of comparison remains what Vokes, citing Herzfeld (2001: 261), describes as "reflexively reflexive." The analogy of gift exchange thus enables a heuristic comparison of heuristics that levels theory and argument, anthropology and ethnography, comparison and fieldwork. It achieves a flat conception that locates anthropology, Africa, and Melanesia at the same latitude to trace a topography of multiplicities that differs from that of other modes of comparison (Strathern 1988b).

It is in this respect that the notion of 'Afrinesian' is of significance. A deliberate riff on the idea of 'Melazonia', developed in a comparative project of Melanesia and Amazonia (Gregor and Tuzin 2001), we originally envisaged an exploration of 'Afrinesia', which then shifted to a concern for 'Afrinesian'. Instead of an imaginary place, 'Afrinesian' is a supposed language whereby heterogeneous regions, notions, and phenomena can engage in dialogue. In an attempt to make explicit the indebtedness described above, this language consists equally of analytical concepts and vernacular notions derived from both Africa and Melanesia. 'Afrinesian' realizes Strathern's (1988b: 95; 1990: 212) idea of an analytical vocabulary that acts as an explicit voice and is capable of mediating an encounter between alien interlocutors. It facilitates a comparison of concepts and relationships, rather than regions or places, and is therefore simultaneously conceptual and empirical. At the same time, efforts to trace the limitations of these concepts and relationships accentuate their lack of identity and congruence, thus exposing the basis for this comparison and its inadequacy for representing one in terms of another. 'Afrinesian' is therefore an artificial language that aims for comparison while keeping the non-comparability of phenomena in mind. Through the vernacular and analytical concepts it engages, 'Afrinesian' furnishes its own subversion to achieve a 'controlled equivocation' (Viveiros de Castro 2004) that allows the differences between Africa and Melanesia to emerge.[10]

The origins and extensions of the notion of network thus involve a multitude of debts and connections, which enable a novel mode of comparison that retrieves and expands analytics from the anthropological past and conjoins these with contemporary concepts and concerns to chart a possible disciplinary future. At a time when the notion of network is gaining currency, it is important to recognize the long history, complex afterlife, and perambulatory capacities of this analytical construct. The attempt to trace relations that separate contributes to an understanding of the longtime and ongoing relationship between Africa and Melanesia, which has been cut in different ways at various moments in time. 'Afrinesian' thus speaks of an exchange relationship that not only allows two regions that have been formative for anthropology to emerge as mutually constitutive and constituted terms, but also provides theoretical gifts that may circulate beyond anthropology where the notion of network is currently in vogue.

Acknowledgments

The workshop that occasioned this volume was held in March 2010 at the Nordic Africa Institute in collaboration with Africa Network Norway. I am grateful to Carin Norberg, Fantu Cheru, Kjell Havnevik, Bjørn Erring, and Sigrid Damman for making this event possible, as well as to Tania Berger, Ingrid Andersson, and Caroline Kyhlbäck for logistical and administrative support. I thank Gerhard Anders, Amrik Heyer, Ruth Prince, James Williams, and Sita Zougouri for presenting papers at the workshop and regret that they could not be included in this publication. I also thank Mats Utas and Tea Virtanen for chairing sessions and contributing to the discussions along with Per Brandström and Sten Hagberg. A particular debt of gratitude is owed to Harri Englund for his invaluable advice before and after the workshop and for reading and commenting on a draft of this introduction. I am also thankful to Adam Reed, Kathleen Marie Jennings, and two anonymous readers for their detailed, incisive, and encouraging remarks on an earlier draft of this text.

Knut Christian Myhre is a researcher attached to the ERC-funded project entitled "Egalitarianism: Forms, Processes, Comparisons" in the Department of Social Anthropology at the University of Bergen. Recent publications include articles in *American Ethnologist*, *Anthropological Theory*, *Journal of the Royal Anthropological Institute*, and *Social Analysis*. He previously held research positions at the University of Oslo, the Nordic Africa Institute, and the Norwegian University of Science and Technology (NTNU).

Notes

1. See http://liberationtechnology.stanford.edu/ (accessed 16 June 2011).
2. This argument is underscored by Mitchell's (1969a: 32) point that several of the contributors to *Social Networks in Urban Situations* combined situational and network analysis or deployed them at different stages during the research process.
3. Marilyn Strathern, for instance, was supervised as a doctoral student by Esther Goody, who had research experience from West Africa. Her student days at Cambridge in the early 1960s moreover coincided with Fortes's tenure as William Wyse Professor and the ascendancy of Jack Goody as his eventual successor. Edmund Leach, meanwhile, was arguably a significant non-Africanist influence (cf. Gell 1999).
4. Anticipating Strathern (1996b) to some extent, Gluckman (1961: 14) argued that "it may well be that we shall have to abandon the concept of society altogether, and speak of 'social fields.'"
5. As such, network analysis presupposed a concept of the individual and a relational form that Strathern undermines by means of the notion of the relation. However, it should be emphasized that although the early network analysts mainly considered networks consisting of connections between individuals, they did not restrict the notion to such links, leaving open the option for the inclusion of other entities (Barnes 1962: 5). Indeed, in Elizabeth Bott's (1957) account, the nodes of the network consisted of conjugal couples, whose relationship to each other was a function of the density of their relations to other couples.
6. In light of the debts that the New Melanesian Ethnography owes to the concepts and approaches of the RLI and the Manchester School, it is appropriate and fitting that Marilyn Strathern eventually succeeded Max Gluckman as Professor of Social Anthropology at Manchester University.
7. The focus on exchange activities represents a further commonality with the work of the early network analysts. While they maintained that the notion of network did not commit one to any particular theory of action, Kapferer (1973) argued that exchange theory was the most appropriate basis for network analysis.
8. I am grateful to an anonymous reviewer for this point.
9. As such, the project bears affinities with the complex relationship between ethnography and anthropology, case material and concept formation, implicit in Gluckman's situational analysis (Evens and Handelman 2005: 1; Kapferer 2010: 5).
10. It thus accords with the orientation toward the "internal destabilization of interpretation" that Kapferer (2010: 4) identifies with the Manchester School.

References

Anderson, Chris. 2009. *The Longer Long Tail: How Endless Choice is Creating Endless Demand.* Rev. ed. London: Random House Business.

Barnes, John A. 1954. "Class and Committees in the Norwegian Island Parish." *Human Relations* 7, no. 1: 39–58.

Barnes, John A. 1962. "African Models in the New Guinea Highlands." *Man* 62, no. 1: 5–9.

Barnes, John A. 1969. "Networks and Political Process." Pp. 51–76 in Mitchell 1969b.

Barnes, John A. 2008. *Humping My Drum: A Memoir.* Raleigh, NC: Lulu Press.

Bott, Elizabeth. 1957. *Family and Social Network.* London: Tavistock.

Brown, Richard. 1979. "Passages in the Life of a White Anthropologist: Max Gluckman in Northern Rhodesia." *Journal of African History* 20, no. 4: 525–541.

Bruun Jensen, Casper. 2011. "Comparative Relativism: Symposium on an Impossibility." *Common Knowledge* 17, no. 1: 1–12.

Busby, Cecilia. 1997. "Permeable and Partible Persons: A Comparative Analysis of Gender and Body in South India and Melanesia." *Journal of the Royal Anthropological Institute* 3, no. 2: 261–278.

DeLanda, Manuel. 2006. *A New Philosophy of Society: Assemblage Theory and Social Complexity.* London: Continuum.

Englund, Harri. 2002. *From War to Peace on the Mozambique-Malawi Borderland.* Edinburgh: Edinburgh University Press for the International African Institute.

Escobar, Arturo. 2008. *Territories of Difference: Place, Movement, Life, Redes.* Durham, NC: Duke University Press.

Evens, T. M. S. 2005. "Some Ontological Implications of Situational Analysis." *Social Analysis* 49, no. 3: 46–60.

Evens, T. M. S., and Don Handelman. 2005. "Introduction: The Ethnographic Praxis of the Theory of Practice." *Social Analysis* 49, no. 3: 1–11.

Ferguson, James. 2006. *Global Shadows: Africa in the Neoliberal World.* Durham, NC: Duke University Press.

Fortes, Meyer, and E. E. Evans-Pritchard, eds. 1940. *African Political Systems.* London: Oxford University Press for the International African Institute.

Fortun, Kim. 2012. "Ethnography in Late Industrialism." *Cultural Anthropology* 27, no. 3: 446–464.

Garbett, G. Kingsley. 1970. "The Analysis of Social Situations." *Man* (n.s.) 5, no. 2: 214–227.

Gell, Alfred. 1999. *The Art of Anthropology: Essays and Diagrams.* London: Athlone Press.

Gingrich, Andre, and Richard G. Fox, eds. 2002. *Anthropology, by Comparison.* New York: Routledge.

Gluckman, Max. [1940] 1958. *Analysis of a Social Situation in Modern Zululand.* Manchester: Manchester University Press for the Rhodes-Livingstone Institute.

Gluckman, Max. 1945. "Seven-Year Research Plan of the Rhodes-Livingstone Institute of Social Studies in British Central Africa." *Human Problems in British Central Africa* 4: 1–32.

Gluckman, Max. 1947. "Malinowski's 'Functional' Analysis of Social Change." *Africa* 17, no. 2: 103–121.

Gluckman, Max. 1961. "Ethnographic Data in British Social Anthropology." *Sociological Review* 9, no. 1: 5–17.

Gray, John. 2003. *Al Qaeda and What It Means to Be Modern.* London: Faber & Faber.

Gregor, Thomas A., and Donald Tuzin, eds. 2001. *Gender in Amazonia and Melanesia: An Exploration of the Comparative Method.* Berkeley: University of California Press.

Hays, Terence E. 1992. "A Historical Background to Anthropology in the Papua New Guinea Highlands." Pp. 1–36 in *Ethnographic Presents: Pioneering Anthropologists in the Papua New Guinea Highlands,* ed. Terence E. Hays. Berkeley: University of California Press.

Herzfeld, Michael. 2001. "Performing Comparisons: Ethnography, Globetrotting, and the Spaces of Social Knowledge." *Journal of Anthropological Research* 57, no. 3: 259–276.

Holbraad, Martin, and Morten Axel Pedersen. 2009. "Planet M: The Intense Abstraction of Marilyn Strathern." *Anthropological Theory* 9, no. 4: 371–394.

IIALC (International Institute of African Languages and Cultures). 1932. "A Five-Year Plan of Research." *Africa* 5, no. 1: 1–13.

Josephides, Lisette. 1991. "Metaphors, Metathemes, and the Construction of Sociality: A Critique of the New Melanesian Ethnography." *Man* (n.s.) 26, no. 1: 145–161.

Juris, Jeffrey S. 2012. "Reflections on #Occupy Everywhere: Social Media, Public Space, and Emerging Logics of Aggregation." *American Ethnologist* 39, no. 2: 259–279.

Kapferer, Bruce. 1973. "Social Network and Conjugal Role in Urban Zambia: Towards a Reformulation of the Bott Hypothesis." Pp. 83–110 in *Network Analysis: Studies in Human Interaction*, ed. Jeremy F. Boissevain and J. Clyde Mitchell. The Hague: Mouton.

Kapferer, Bruce. 2005a. "Situations, Crisis, and the Anthropology of the Concrete: The Contribution of Max Gluckman." *Social Analysis* 49, no. 3: 85–122.

Kapferer, Bruce. 2005b. "Coda: Recollections and Refutations." *Social Analysis* 49, no 3: 273–283.

Kapferer, Bruce. 2006. "In Memoriam: G. Kingsley Garbett, 1935–2006." *Social Analysis* 50, no. 1: 3–5.

Kapferer, Bruce. 2010. "Introduction: In the Event—toward an Anthropology of Generic Moments." *Social Analysis* 54, no. 3: 1–27.

Keen, Ian. 2006. "Ancestors, Magic, and Exchange in Yolngu Doctrines: Extensions of the Person in Time and Space." *Journal of the Royal Anthropological Institute* (n.s.) 12, no. 3: 515–530.

Knauft, Bruce. 1999. *From Primitive to Post-Colonial in Melanesia and Anthropology*. Ann Arbor: University of Michigan Press.

Knauft, Bruce. 2006. "Anthropology in the Middle." *Anthropological Theory* 6, no. 4: 407–430.

Lambek, Michael, and Andrew Strathern. 1998. "Introduction: Embodying Sociality: Africanist-Melanesianist Comparisons." Pp. 1–28 in *Bodies and Persons: Comparative Perspectives from Africa and Melanesia*, ed. Michael Lambek and Andrew Strathern. Cambridge: Cambridge University Press.

Latour, Bruno. 1993. *We Have Never Been Modern*. Trans. Catherine Porter. Cambridge, MA: Harvard University Press.

Latour, Bruno. 2005. *Reassembling the Social: An Introduction to Actor-Network Theory*. Oxford: Oxford University Press.

Law, John. 2012. "Notes on Fish, Ponds and Theory." *Norsk Antropologisk Tidsskrift* 23, no. 3–4: 225–236.

Lazar, Sian. 2012. "Disjunctive Comparison: Citizenship and Trade Unionism in Bolivia and Argentina." *Journal of the Royal Anthropological Institute* (n.s.) 18, no. 2: 349–368.

Lugard, Frederick D. 1928. "The International Institute of African Languages and Cultures." *Africa* 1, no. 1: 1–12.

Macmillan, Hugh. 1995. "Return to Malungwana Drift—Max Gluckman, the Zulu Nation and the Common Society." *African Affairs* 94, no. 1: 39–65.

Malinowski, Bronislaw. 1929. "Practical Anthropology." *Africa* 2, no. 1: 22–38.

Malinowski, Bronislaw. 1930. "The Rationalization of Anthropology and Administration." *Africa* 3, no. 4: 405–430.

Malinowski, Bronislaw. 1945. *The Dynamics of Cultural Change: An Inquiry into Race Relations in Africa*. New Haven, CT: Yale University Press.

Mason, Paul. 2012. *Why It's Kicking Off Everywhere: The New Global Revolutions*. London: Verso.

Mauss, Marcel. [1925] 1990. *The Gift: The Form and Reason for Exchange in Archaic Societies*. London: Routledge.

Mayer, Philip. 1961. *Townsmen or Tribesmen: Conservatism and the Process of Urbanization in a South African City*. Cape Town: Oxford University Press.

McCallum, Cecilia. 2001. *Gender and Sociality in Amazonia: How Real People Are Made.* Oxford: Berg.

Mitchell, J. Clyde. 1969a. "The Concept and Use of Social Networks." Pp. 1–50 in Mitchell 1969b.

Mitchell, J. Clyde, ed. 1969b. *Social Networks in Urban Situations.* Manchester: Manchester University Press.

Mitchell, J. Clyde. 1974. "Social Networks." *Annual Review of Anthropology* 3: 279–299.

Mosko, Mark. 2010. "Partible Penitents: Dividual Personhood and Christianity Practice in Melanesia and the West." *Journal of the Royal Anthropological Institute* (n.s.) 16, no. 2: 215–240.

Pauw, Berthold A. 1963. *The Second Generation.* Cape Town: Oxford University Press.

Perham, Margery. 1965. "Introduction." Pp. xxvi–xlix in Frederick D. Lugard, *The Dual Mandate in British Tropical Africa.* London: Frank Cass.

Piot, Charles. 1999. *Remotely Global: Village Modernity in West Africa.* Chicago: University of Chicago Press.

Razsa, Maple, and Andrej Kurnik. 2012. "The Occupy Movement in Žižek's Hometown: Direct Democracy and a Politics of Becoming." *American Ethnologist* 39, no. 2: 238–258.

Reed, Adam. 2003. *Papua New Guinea's Last Place: Experiences of Constraint in a Postcolonial Prison.* New York: Berghahn Books.

Riles, Annelise. 2001. *The Network Inside Out.* Ann Arbor: University of Michigan Press.

Schumaker, Lyn. 2004. "The Director as Significant Other: Max Gluckman and Team Fieldwork at the Rhodes-Livingstone Institute." Pp. 91–130 in *Significant Others: Interpersonal and Professional Commitments in Anthropology,* ed. Richard Handler. Madison: University of Wisconsin Press.

Strathern, Marilyn. 1980. "No Nature, No Culture: The Hagen Case." Pp. 174–222 in *Nature, Culture and Gender,* ed. Carol MacCormack and Marilyn Strathern. Cambridge: Cambridge University Press.

Strathern, Marilyn. 1981. "Culture in a Netbag: The Manufacture of a Subdiscipline in Anthropology." *Man* (n.s.) 16, no. 4: 665–688.

Strathern, Marilyn. 1988a. *The Gender of the Gift: Problems with Women and Problems with Society in Melanesia.* Berkeley: University of California Press.

Strathern, Marilyn. 1988b. "Concrete Topographies." *Cultural Anthropology* 3, no. 1: 88–96.

Strathern, Marilyn. 1990. "Negative Strategies in Melanesia." Pp. 204–216 in *Localizing Strategies: Regional Traditions of Ethnographic Writing,* ed. Richard Fardon. Edinburgh: Scottish Academic Press.

Strathern, Marilyn. 1995. *The Relation: Issues in Complexity and Scale.* Cambridge: Prickly Pear.

Strathern, Marilyn. 1996a. "Cutting the Network." *Journal of the Royal Anthropological Institute* (n.s.) 2, no. 3: 517–535.

Strathern, Marilyn. 1996b. "The Concept of Society Is Obsolete: For the Motion." Pp. 60–66 in *Key Debates in Anthropology,* ed. Tim Ingold. London: Routledge.

Strathern, Marilyn. 1999. *Property, Substance and Effect: Anthropological Essays on Persons and Things.* London: Athlone Press.

Strathern, Marilyn. 2005. *Kinship, Law and the Unexpected: Relatives Are Always a Surprise.* Cambridge: Cambridge University Press.

Strathern, Marilyn. 2011. "Binary License." *Common Knowledge* 17, no. 1: 87–103.

Tsing, Anna L. 2000. "The Global Situation." *Cultural Anthropology* 15, no. 3: 327–360.

Tsing, Anna L. 2005. *Friction: An Ethnography of Global Connection.* Princeton, NJ: Princeton University Press.

Turner, Victor W. 1957. *Schism and Continuity in an African Society: A Study of Ndembu Village Life*. Manchester: Manchester University Press.

van Velsen, Jan. 1967. "The Extended-Case Method and Situational Analysis." Pp. 129–149 in *The Craft of Social Anthropology*, ed. A. L. Epstein. London: Tavistock.

Vilaça, Aparecida. 2011. "Dividuality in Amazonia: God, the Devil, and the Constitution of Personhood in Wari' Christianity." *Journal of the Royal Anthropological Institute* (n.s.) 17, no. 2: 243–262.

Viveiros de Castro, Eduardo. 2004. "Perspectival Anthropology and the Method of Controlled Equivocations." *Tipití: Journal of the Society for the Anthropology of Lowland South America* 2, no. 1: 3–22.

Wagner, Roy G. 1974. "Are There Social Groups in the New Guinea Highlands?" Pp. 95–122 in *Frontiers of Anthropology: An Introduction to Anthropological Thinking*, ed. Murray J. Leaf. New York: Van Nostrand.

Wagner, Roy G. 1977. "Analogic Kinship: A Daribi Example." *American Ethnologist* 4, no. 4: 623–642.

Wagner, Roy G. 1978. *Lethal Speech: Daribi Myth as Symbolic Obviation*. Ithaca, NY: Cornell University Press.

Wagner, Roy G. [1975] 1981. *The Invention of Culture*. Chicago: University of Chicago Press.

Weiner, James F. 1988. *The Heart of the Pearl Shell: The Mythological Dimension of Foi Sociality*. Berkeley: University of California Press.

Weiner, James F. 1993. "Anthropology Contra Heidegger Part 2: The Limit of Relationship." *Critique of Anthropology* 13, no. 3: 285–301.

Werbner, Richard. 1984. "The Manchester School in South-Central Africa." *Annual Review of Anthropology* 13: 157–185.

Wilson, Godfrey. 1940. "Anthropology as a Public Service." *Africa* 13, no. 1: 43–61.

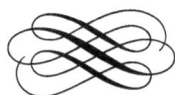

Chapter 1

KURU, AIDS, AND WITCHCRAFT
Reconfiguring Culpability in Melanesia and Africa

Isak Niehaus

> I almost wish cannibalism is more prevalent than it is.
>
> — Carleton Gajdusek, Nobel laureate

The emergence of AIDS has prompted researchers to consider the social con-figurations of epidemics (Herring and Swedlund 2010; Jonsen and Stryker 1993; Lindenbaum 2001). Rosenberg (1992) observes that epidemics follow a common dramatic pattern of increased revelatory tension, a move toward crisis, and a drift toward closure. Epidemics, he argues, are social 'sampling devices', disrupting once stable modes of social reproduction and stripping life bare, revealing ideas, structural inequalities, and conflicts that are kept subdued in less critical times.

Notes for this chapter begin on page 38.

These studies emphasize the attribution of blame and culpability. Throughout the history of epidemics, diverse actors have stigmatized disease carriers and other 'scapegoats'. Foreigners were singled out for blame during epidemics in Renaissance Italy, untouchables in India, and Jews in Europe (Herring and Swedlund 2010). Likewise, the AIDS epidemic has spawned various 'geographies of blame' (Farmer 1992). In the global North, epidemiologists designate 'disreputable' populations—such as intravenous drug users, gay men, and immigrants—as 'risk groups'. This contributes to various forms of discrimination. Competing discourses flourished in the global South. Popular conspiracy theories posited that the American military deliberately created AIDS as a means of biological warfare or as a strategy of discouraging black people from procreating. There were also claims that European sex tourists introduced HIV. Within village communities, elders blame the youth, and men blame 'free women' for the AIDS epidemic (Farmer 1992; Schoepf 2001; Weiss 1993).

In this chapter, I investigate the spate of witchcraft accusations that AIDS has unleashed in Southern Africa. Sufferers, their kin, diviners, and Christian healers often interpret as evidence of witchcraft the very same symptoms that are diagnosed by physicians as AIDS. Ashforth (2002) shows how residents of Soweto see common symptoms of AIDS as those of slow poisoning, called *isidliso*. They allege that witches insert a small creature into the gullet of their victims, which gradually devours them from the inside. *Isidliso* covers literally anything that affects the lungs, stomach, and digestive tract and leads to a slow, wasting illness. Ashforth finds the association of AIDS with witchcraft to be particularly plausible in contexts of inequality and insecurity. Other parts of Southern Africa have witnessed a resurgence of witch-finding and witch-cleansing movements (Andersson 2002; Probst 1999; Schoepf 2001; Yamba 1997).

A similar situation can be found in Impalahoek, a village in the Bushbuckridge municipality of South Africa's Mpumalanga Province,[1] where I have conducted intermittent fieldwork. Starting in 1990, I visited Impalahoek for a period of at least one month each year, doing participant observation and conducting open-ended interviews on topics such as witchcraft beliefs and accusations, politics, sexuality, and the AIDS epidemic. Villagers did not believe that witches actually sent AIDS, but they were of the opinion that witches manufactured sicknesses that mimicked its symptoms. In this manner, witches took advantage of the epidemic and used AIDS as a shield to disguise their nefarious activities (Niehaus 2013: 155–157). Researchers often see the framing of AIDS in terms of witchcraft as a matter of indigenous belief obstructing effective health seeking (Pronyk 2001).

To gain deeper, intercontextual insight into the significance of witchcraft accusations during the AIDS epidemic in Bushbuckridge, I have utilized theoretical insights from Melanesian anthropology, notably studies of the kuru epidemic in Papua New Guinea. Certain similarities between AIDS and kuru enable a comparative analysis. Like AIDS, kuru is an incurable disease—a slow infection that can remain dormant in the human body for years before its first symptoms appear. As with AIDS, the host population also invoked mystical explanations, blaming sorcerers for the kuru epidemic.[2]

I am particularly drawn to the work of Warwick Anderson (2000, 2008), who analyzes the labeling of kuru in terms of multiple networks of relatedness, interaction, and exchange. His use of 'network' is considerably broader than that of Thornton (2009: 413–414), who has fruitfully investigated the nature of 'sexual networks' as "intricate social structures constituted primarily by sexual relationships" in South Africa and in Uganda. Anderson treats networks as comprising a broad range of human and non-human actors that are involved not only in the transmission of disease (pathogens, bodies, corpses), but also in the articulation of illness (sick people, their caretakers and kin, diviners and healers whom they consult, medical technologies, physicians and scientists). He shows how the labeling of kuru by diverse actors was an intensely political act, involving the allocation of blame and culpability. It constituted persons and networks in particular ways, bringing certain modes of relationality into view and, at the same time, occluding others. The allocation of blame involved the construction of boundaries, the 'cutting of networks' (Strathern 1996), and also the strengthening of existing configurations.

Anderson (2000, 2008) documents how the biomedical and scientific fraternity first interacted closely with the South Fore in labeling kuru and searching for a responsible agent, but then, in its readiness to connect kuru to the cannibalistic consumption of dead humans, set the South Fore apart on the basis of a disreputable alterity. By attributing kuru to the sorcery of affines and neighbors, the South Fore countered victim blaming and reconfigured culpability. Through his analysis of this complex series of transactions, Anderson enables us to transcend the conventional view that sorcery is simply a matter of attachment to local belief. His research is particularly pertinent to Bushbuckridge, where health workers and educators played a central role in labeling AIDS as an incurable condition that resulted from sexual promiscuity. Such framing stigmatized villagers and contributed to the exclusion of people living with AIDS from networks of social intercourse. In a bid to shift culpability onto different sets of networks, and in order to reinforce the relations that AIDS threatened to disrupt, accusations of witchcraft followed in the wake of this victim blaming.

Kuru in the New Guinea Highlands

As Anderson (2000, 2008) shows, the labeling of kuru arose from a complex series of interactions within a broad network, comprising Australian patrol officers, medical scientists, anthropologists, and the South Fore. These interactions involved the global circulation of scientific valuables, including biomedical technologies, pathogens, and corpses.

Operating from a post at Okapa, Australian patrol officers made contact with the South Fore in the eastern highlands of New Guinea during the late 1940s. A group of about 14,000 slash-and-burn horticulturalists, the South Fore cultivated sweet potato, taro, yam, corn, sugar cane, and bananas. They kept pigs and hunted small mammals, cassowaries, other birds, and reptiles. South Fore men accompanied the patrol officers to witness the operations of government in Port Moresby, learning how to build roads and to cultivate new crops such as potato, tomato, and coffee (Anderson 2000: 718).

In 1953, a patrol officer noticed a South Fore girl sitting by a fire. She shivered violently, her head jerking from side to side. Unable to eat, she died within a few weeks. This was the first recorded case of kuru (lit., 'trembling' or 'fear') in medical literature. With the discovery of new cases, medical orderlies discovered that the symptoms of kuru were remarkably uniform. As a 'slow infection', it could remain invisible for incubation periods of up to several decades. The disease began with a failure of muscle coordination and a tremor involving the extremities and the head. After a few months, speech became unintelligible, and the afflicted person could no longer walk or stand. The victim then became progressively incapacitated, being unable to eat, urinate, or defecate. Death was inevitable and followed the first clinical signs by about three to five months (Lindenbaum 1979: 10).

Medical scientists in Port Moresby initially described kuru as 'acute hysteria' in otherwise healthy adults. The anthropologists Ronald and Catherine Berndt elaborated upon this perception. They observed that the Fore attributed kuru to sorcery and hypothesized that the disease was a manifestation of stress and emotional insecurity, occasioned by European contact. Following Cannon's (1942) well-known essay on 'voodoo death', the Berndts reasoned that fears provoked by the threat of sorcery could have far-reaching psychosomatic effects (see Berndt 1954). This suggestion influenced colonial practice. A patrol officer called together the villagers, made a great bonfire, and asked them to burn all of the items that they might use in sorcery. Sorcery accusations declined, but kuru deaths did not abate (Anderson 2008: 14).

A careful review of ethnographic evidence suggests that while the South Fore did attribute kuru to sorcery, they also explored alternative mystical explanations for the onset of the disease. They believed that sorcerers harmed their intended victims by burying items of their clothing, along with sorcery bundles, in swampy land. Diviners cooked food in a number of bamboo containers, each representing a particular village. Food that did not cook properly showed which village housed the responsible sorcerers. Should diviners be able to retrieve the buried clothing, they believed, the victim would recover (Beasley 2006: 187). But the South Fore also identified kuru as 'cassowary disease' (i.e., foolishness resulting from assaults by anthropomorphic spirits) and as a manifestation of 'ghost winds'. They fed the sufferers bark from casuarinas trees, whose swaying resembled tremors of the body. The South Fore saw ghost winds as a sign that the arrival of cargo was imminent. On these occasions, they placed human skulls in villages and filled newly built home with stones, wood, and leaves. After anointing the items with pig blood, they awaited their transformation into paper, knives, and rifles (Berndt 1954: 226).

Henceforth, scientific discourses increasingly medicalized kuru and also the South Fore themselves. After spending 20 days among the South Fore in 1956, Vin Zigas, a medical officer, began to suspect that kuru might well be an example of encephalitis. Zigas collaborated with Carleton Gajdusek, an American specialist in biophysical chemistry and child development working at the Hall

Institute in Melbourne who was often described as an erratic and irritating colleague, but one who worked with great enthusiasm. In 1957, Gajdusek began to study kuru from a base camp at Okapa, and he, too, became convinced that kuru would turn out to have a biological cause. But he viewed the disease in the broadest possible perspective, considering the interactions of biochemistry, culture and society, and the lived realities of people's lives. He actively sought the collaboration of other biomedical scientists, anthropologists, and the South Fore, participating in exchanges, building networks, and negotiating relations.

Gajdusek first compiled a census of the entire Fore region, mapping out the distribution of kuru. He determined that the epidemic was concentrated among the South Fore, noting fatalities of up to 10 percent in some hamlets. He also reported that kuru entered the South Fore area during the late 1920s and reached a peak between 1957 and 1960, when it claimed about 200 deaths per annum. Although the vast majority of adult victims were women, kuru affected boys and girls with about equal frequency. At the height of the epidemic, life expectancy for a South Fore woman was little more than 20 years, leaving men without wives and infants without mothers. However, in subsequent years, the age at which the first clinical signs appeared increased.

In search of the infectious agent, Gajdusek urged the South Fore to donate samples of their blood, spinal fluid, and urine for chemical analysis and the corpses of their loved ones for medical autopsies. He dissected the bodies on his dining room table, preparing them for scientific examination, and then air-freighted them to metropolitan laboratories for microbiological analysis (Anderson 2000: 725). Gajdusek plied kuru sufferers with virtually every drug that biomedicine had to offer, including vitamins, anti-convulsants, tranquilizers, anabolic steroids, and corticosteroids. He treated mundane infections, tended to wounds, and distributed soap, blankets, and clothing. Microbiological analysis showed pathological changes to the central nervous system and neurological deterioration of brain tissue. But it failed to identify the toxic element.

Bennett et al. (1958) theorized that kuru might be a hereditary disorder, determined by a single autosomal gene, dominant in females but recessive in males. Scientists cautiously accepted this suggestion as the best available hypothesis. To prevent the spread of the genetic trait, some even urged the government to create a kuru reserve from which no emigration would be allowed. However, this eugenics policy was not practically enforceable (Anderson 2008: 128).

In 1959, the veterinary pathologist William Hadlow provided Gajdusek with a new model for the transmission of kuru. Hadlow observed that the brain tissue of kuru victims resembled sheep brains with scrapie, a degenerative infectious disease. There were characteristic vacuoles between the cells, giving the tissue a spongy appearance. Veterinary scientists had successfully transferred the disease to healthy sheep and goats, suggesting that a 'slow virus' was responsible. In 1963, Gajdusek and his co-workers inoculated chimpanzees intracerebrally with diseased material from deceased kuru victims. Two years later, the primates began to develop neurological disorders akin to kuru.

If a rare slow virus was indeed responsible for kuru, how then was it transmitted among the South Fore? To answer this question, attention shifted from laboratories back to the field. During 1961 and 1962, the anthropologists Robert Glasse and Shirley Lindenbaum studied the social aspects of kuru. By gathering information on kinship, they were able to reject a purely hereditary interpretation of transmission. They noted that many kuru victims were kin in a social, non-biological sense. The recentness of kuru also made a hereditary explanation hard to defend. Glasse and Lindenbaum began to suspect that the unidentified agent for kuru might be transmitted by endo-cannibalism: "When a body was considered for human consumption, none of it was discarded except the bitter gall bladder ... [M]aternal kin dismembered the corpse with a bamboo knife and stone axe. They first removed the hands and feet, then cut open the arms and legs to strip the muscles ... After severing the head, they fractured the skull to remove the brain. Meat, viscera and brain were all eaten. Marrow was sucked from cracked bones, and sometimes the pulverized bones themselves were cooked and eaten with green vegetables" (Lindenbaum 1979: 20).

The consumption of the flesh of deceased relatives explained the concentration of kuru among certain families and also its sex and age distribution. Glasse and Lindenbaum wrote that men claimed prior rights to pork to compensate for the depletion of wild game. Women supplemented their lesser allotment of pork with small game, insects, and dead humans, and young children ate whatever their mothers gave them. A woman's brain (the most significant body matter in the transmission of the disease) was given to the wives of her brothers and sons. According to Glasse and Lindenbaum, children who grew up after the suppression of cannibalism by missionaries did not succumb to the disease. The epidemic slowly abated, and by the 1990s there were hardly any deaths (Lindenbaum 2001: 368).

Anderson (2008) and Beasley (2009) describe the growing anger and bitterness expressed by the South Fore toward health workers and scientists, whom they saw as taking without giving. Grief stricken by the loss of kin, South Fore men desperately desired a cure. They had already been exposed to the successes of medical treatment in the case of yaws, and initially saw it as their responsibility to accompany the Australian medical orderlies on their dangerous missions. The men assisted in providing basic treatment for dying relatives, translated conversations for the orderlies, helped collect biological specimens, and witnessed medical examinations and autopsies. But the South Fore gradually lost confidence in medical explanations for kuru.

Existing histories do not make this clear, but the change in attitude of the South Fore seems to have been a response to the manner in which scientists and health workers pathologized local culture by blaming the kuru epidemic on sorcery beliefs and cannibalism. Although outsiders almost universally accepted the thesis of the cannibalistic transmission of kuru, critics found little evidence to support it. They contended that the Fore might plausibly have spread kuru through the handling of decomposing corpses in pre-Christian mortuary rituals (Arens 1979; Steadman and Merbs 1982).[3] The South Fore themselves were not convinced by the suggestion that cannibalism might be responsible for kuru. When anthropologists raised this hypothesis, they responded with 'uncertainty'. This was true even in 2008, after missionaries had proselytized for half a century and current generations had rejected the behavior of their ancestors as incompatible with Christianity (Lindenbaum 2010: 324).

Scientists gradually departed from Papua New Guinea. In 1976, Gajdusek won a Nobel Prize for discovering a new disease etiology.[4] But thereafter scientific interventions became more detached and less beneficial to the South Fore. During the 1990s, Stanley Prusiner determined that a pathogenic protein, called 'prion', rather than any virus, was the cause of kuru. Prions are "small proteinaceous infectious particles" that "resist inactivation by procedures that modify nucleic acids" (Lindenbaum 2001: 366). This discovery earned Prusiner, too, a Nobel Prize. However, unlike Gajdusek's research, Prusiner's work was confined to high-tech laboratories, and his interactions were largely with California's lucrative biochemical industry (Anderson 2008: 192–198). None of the research ever led to a cure. Yet kuru became crucial for understanding other pathologies, such as Creutzfeldt-Jakob disease (CJD), Alzheimer's, and HIV/AIDS.

Since kuru withstood all biomedical cures, the South Fore no longer accepted that it might be a 'sickness' (*sik malaria*). By the 1990s, they refused to be hospitalized and turned down five out of every six medical requests for autopsies. Many bodies were not available for any price. One man refused to allow a scientist to draw his wife's blood, saying, "You are just wasting your time. Kuru is due to sorcery" (Anderson 2008: 178).

Sorcery now became the hegemonic explanation for kuru. It accounted for the resilience of kuru against biomedical interventions and, at the same time, countered victim blaming. Accusations of sorcery also rendered certain local modes of relationality more visible. Among the South Fore, networks of kin and affines stretched across different village settlements, which created a situation of competing loyalties. In this context, accusations of sorcery helped define group boundaries. They led to the complete severing of alliances between the Wanitabe and Nabu, two parish segments that had previously collaborated in activities such as arranging marriage payments (Lindenbaum 1979: 118–119). The accusations also cut the intimacy between different affinal groups resident within common neighborhoods, leading them to keep each other at a distance. The accused sorcerers were nearly always widowers who had in the past aspired to be great men (ibid.: 121–125). The South Fore never located enemies within their own patrilineages. They policed the boundaries of their hamlets more firmly than they had done before, closing all gates and posting sentries at night (ibid.: 28). Hope lay in locating and destroying sorcery bundles.

AIDS in Bushbuckridge, South Africa

Anderson's (2000, 2008) emphasis on broad networks of interaction and exchange involved in the labeling and articulation of kuru offers insights that can help us transcend the view that the attribution of AIDS to witchcraft is purely a matter of attachment to indigenous cosmology. As in the case of sorcery during the kuru epidemic, the invocation of witchcraft was a means to counter victim blaming in health propaganda about AIDS and a bid to recon-figure culpability by shifting blame onto different sets of networks.

In 1982, a white, gay male air steward was the first South African to be diag-nosed HIV positive. He had possibly contracted the virus in New York. By 1987, several black South African mine workers tested positive for HIV antibodies, and by 1990 it was clear that the epidemic was mainly heterosexually transmitted. Infection was rapid, given diffusion across South Africa's long, permeable north-ern border and the very high prevalence of labor migration. By 2003, 5.3 mil-lion citizens were infected with HIV, and the South African AIDS epidemic had become the fastest growing epidemic in the world (Iliffe 2006: 45). The disease reached Bushbuckridge fairly late but then spread rapidly. Between 1995 and 2005, AIDS became the predominant cause of death in all age groups. Antenatal seroprevalence at the local Tintswalo Hospital increased from 2 percent in 1992 to 25 percent in 2007 (MacPherson et al. 2009).

Unlike in the case of kuru, the medical establishment did not primarily use rural areas as laboratories to learn about the virology of AIDS and other factors that might facilitate its transmission. During the 1960s, the science of kuru, slow viruses, and prions was at a 'revolutionary stage', when previously estab-lished paradigms were being challenged, contested, and overturned. During the 1990s, the science of HIV/AIDS was at a 'normal stage', when established biomedical paradigms were being defended with a great deal of confidence (Kuhn 1962). In a global epidemic there was very little to be learned from local settings: the facts were known and had to be proselytized.

Thus, public health educators played a crucial role in labeling and allocat-ing blame for AIDS in Bushbuckridge. The relations between them and vil-lagers comprised asymmetrical pedagogical interactions, marked by unequal exchanges. Residents of Bushbuckridge learned about HIV/AIDS from health propaganda well before they could identify people suffering from its symptoms. The scale and urgency with which non-governmental organizations (NGOs) and the public health fraternity undertook AIDS-awareness education vastly exceeded efforts connected to any previous public health campaigns, such as those targeting malaria, tuberculosis, and family planning. In 1992, the Health Systems Development Unit and Reproductive Health Groups Project launched sexual health programs. Staff members gave regular talks on sexual hygiene to police, clergy, headmen, diviners, and youth at local schools. The organizations also trained teachers as sex educators. In 2000, a LoveLife youth center was built only 6 kilometers from Impalahoek. The NGO aimed to promote a positive lifestyle based on romantic love, being faithful, abstaining from sex, and using condoms. It hosted motivational workshops, dancing, studio broadcasting, computer training, drama, basketball, and volleyball (Wahlström 2000).

AIDS awareness became an important component of life-orientation classes in local schools. Each quarter, teachers at Impalahoek Primary divided the stu-dents into three groups. Teachers did not mention sex to the youngest learners, but they warned the children not to play with scissors, razors, and pins; not to touch bleeding friends; and not to inflate balloons (i.e., condoms) that they found lying around. The teachers demonstrated safe sex to the older learners using stage props such as artificial penises and different kinds of condoms. AIDS activists addressed students at secondary schools as often as twice a week. Young people told me that they felt overburdened by constantly having to listen to these messages about AIDS.

As in the case of kuru, interventions by the medical community were for a long time non-therapeutic. By focusing on prevention rather than care, these campaigns created the impression that AIDS was a fatal, incurable, and untreatable disease. 'Groundbreakers' at the LoveLife youth center used scare tactics. During one workshop they showed attendees videocassettes of Ethiopians dying of AIDS-related diseases. The only message they gave about treatment was that those who ate fruit and vegetables might prolong their lives.

During the tenure of President Thabo Mbeki, the South African government stalled the provision of anti-retroviral drugs (ARVs).[5] A network of 3 hospitals, 7 health centers, and 57 clinics in Bushbuckridge merely screened pregnant women for seroprevalence, provided voluntary counseling and testing, and treated opportunistic infections. In 1999, the Rixile ('rising sun' in XiTsonga) HIV Clinic was established at Tintswalo Hospital, within walking distance of Impalahoek. The clinic monitored CD4 counts, hosted support groups, and assisted people in applying for disability grants. Yet only in 2005 did Rixile begin to supply highly active anti-retroviral therapy (HAART) to patients who registered a CD4 count of below 200.

HAART proved very effective in suppressing viral replication and drastically reduced morbidity and mortality (MacPherson et al. 2009: 5).[6] By December 2008, 6,638 patients had enrolled at Rixile. Yet the clinic's services reached only 20 percent of those in need within its catchment area, and the pedagogical emphasis remained. All patients were required to attend treatment literacy classes, where facilitators lectured them on how to live productive lives with ARVs while lambasting the masculine pursuits of drinking, smoking, and engaging in sex with multiple partners (Mfecane 2010: 109–110).

Ethnographic evidence shows that, by blaming the spread of HIV on promiscuous and unsafe sexual intercourse, the messages of health educators stigmatized both the host populations and the sick people themselves. By labeling AIDS as fatal, early public health campaigns also contributed to the perception that HIV-positive persons were tainted with death. But there was another, perhaps more important way in which stigma was created. Because HIV has such a long incubation period, identifying someone as HIV positive frequently amounts to an accusation that he or she had (in all likelihood) spread the disease to past and present sexual partners and was therefore responsible for their pending deaths. Much like the claims about South Fore cannibalism, these assertions set villagers of Bushbuckridge apart on the basis of a disreputable alterity.

These messages profoundly shaped local perceptions of AIDS. Residents of Impalahoek identified HIV-positive persons as 'dead before dying' and symbolically located them in the liminal domain between life and death. Their bodies, like those of biblical lepers, were seen as comprising an anomalous mixture of living and dead flesh. This conception raised the uncomfortable possibility of pollution that they might represent to outsiders (Niehaus 2007). Such labeling contributed to the rejection of HIV-positive people from networks comprising sexual partners, kin, and neighbors. Among the first recognized victims of AIDS in Impalahoek were two young women who had sought their fortunes in Johannesburg but returned to their natal homesteads in a severe state of ill health. At their funerals, mourners gossiped that they had worked as prostitutes on the city's streets.

Villagers perceived HIV-infected persons as extremely polluting and generally secluded them indoors, keeping them from public view. This was done as much to protect vulnerable sick people from others as to protect others from them. Adults sometimes delegated the tasks of care to younger men, such as cousins and nephews. There were also cases of severe neglect. An extreme example is the case of George Bila, a construction worker. In 1988, George developed severe diarrhea and became extremely thin. After a few months, lesions appeared on his legs, and he soon was unable to walk. His parents confined him to a small, one-roomed building in their backyard, where he lay on the floor on a mattress. George's family had given up all hope that he might recover. His brothers brought him food and water, and his sister occasionally washed him, but George's room was often filthy. He was delirious, and neighbors frequently heard him call out at night, screaming for water. George's funeral was a bitter occasion, attended by very few mourners.

At times, testing HIV positive has been a source of bitter conflict between husbands and wives and, on at least one occasion, has even been a pretext for homicide. In December 2004, the chair of a local community police forum (CPF) told me of a most horrible killing. Ferris Dube returned from his workplace in Johannesburg after a long period of absence. He suffered from a persistent cough and consulted a general practitioner. Ferris's wife accompanied him, and on the way back home she screamed at him, saying that he had merely returned to Bushbuckridge to infect her with the 'dreaded disease'. The next day, neighbors reported that they had heard the couple arguing throughout the night and saw smoke coming from the windows of their home in the morning. Members of the CPF broke down the door, but they were too late. They discovered that Ferris had tied his wife to their bed with an electric cord, doused her with petrol, and burned her to death. He then committed suicide by setting himself on fire. Although Ferris had left a suicide note, nobody could decipher its meaning.

Silence was a common strategy to avoid antagonisms and conflicts that might cut intimate social relations and tear households apart. For example, orators at funerals in Impalahoek hardly ever mentioned AIDS as the cause of death (Durham and Klaits 2002; McNeill and Niehaus 2010; Stadler 2003). Villagers spoke of AIDS only in backstage domains and even then avoided using the words 'HIV' and 'AIDS' directly. Instead, they would employ euphemisms, saying that people suffered from the 'three letters' (*maina a mararo*) or from the 'fashionable disease' (*lwetši bja gona bjalo*).

During the first 15 years of the epidemic, few people chose to be tested for HIV antibodies, saying that knowledge of a positive result would cause unbearable stress, hastening rather than delaying their deaths. Those who chose medical testing and treatment tended to view it as a last resort. Pronyk (2001) calculates a mean delay of 10 weeks from the onset of tuberculosis (the most prominent AIDS-related disease) and the commencement of treatment among 298 patients at Tintswalo Hospital. In some cases, the delay exceeded a year. The use of medical facilities increased greatly after HAART became available, yet patients were still reticent about therapeutic consultations and often visited the clinic under the cover of darkness. They complained of unbelievably long waiting lines, saying that they would arrive at 6:45 AM and would not be seen by a doctor until 3:00 PM. Patients also described conditions in hospitals, such as those prevailing in the tuberculosis wards, as extremely spartan. They told me that they were fed only in the morning and at tea time and that their mattresses sometimes smelled of urine.

Occasionally, silence and concealment gave way to more direct forms of resistance, such as when residents of Impalahoek contested and challenged the messages contained in health propaganda. As elsewhere in South Africa, men saw multiple sexual partners as a sign of success, rather than a source of shame (Delius and Glaser 2005; Hunter 2005). However, they were extremely sensitive to the manner in which outsiders attached negative connotations to 'African sexuality'. Indeed, President Mbeki's denial of the sexual mode of transmission of HIV was, in part, a reaction to racist renditions of Africans as "promiscuous carriers of germs" who display "uncontrollable devotion to the lust of sin" (Posel 2005: 127). My research interviewees condemned the eagerness of AIDS activists to scrutinize the sexuality of others and disapproved of their lack of discretion in discussing sex with youngsters. Given the profound stigma, they found it inconceivable that the activists would encourage people to reveal their HIV status in public.

Much like the questionable thesis of cannibalistic transmission of kuru, the notion that sexual promiscuity is responsible for the rapid spread of HIV stands on shaky grounds. Recent evidence suggests that the key difference between Southern Africa and regions with lower rates of infection is not sexual behavior per se, but rather the concurrency of relations with different sexual partners (Epstein 2007) and the diffuse nature of sexual networks. Thornton (2009: 413) convincingly links vulnerability to HIV infection to individuals maximizing "their social capital by extending the diversity and density of their sexual networks."

Popular conspiracy theories deflected the culpability from local sexual networks and relocated it onto powerful external actors, such as the government, the business community, and even the medical fraternity itself. There were widespread rumors in Impalahoek that Wouter Basson, the cardiologist who had been the head of the old apartheid government's chemical weapons program, had actually manufactured AIDS as a means of reducing South Africa's black population. Two men told me that South Africa's new government purposefully withheld a cure for AIDS because it benefited financially from taxes and bribes paid by the funeral industry and by those involved in the clandestine transnational trade in organs harvested from deceased people (Niehaus and Jonsson 2005). There were also widespread rumors that government-issued condoms had actually been laced with 'HIV worms' (McNeill 2009).

It was easier to identify the source of witchcraft accusations than of conspiracy theories. In Impalahoek, particular cases of sickness and death usually provoked fierce disagreement. Whereas outsiders were more inclined to mention AIDS, especially when gossiping in backstage domains, insiders such as kin were more likely to identify witchcraft as the cause. During fieldwork, I recorded details of 126 deaths that villagers attributed to AIDS. In 27 of these, insiders declared that witches were actually responsible. These claims, like the conspiracy theories, were a reaction to the victim blaming inherent in medical discourses about AIDS. They reconfigured culpability, absolved sufferers from being responsible for their own sickness and from potentially having infected sexual partners, and shifted blame onto outsiders. In this way, witchcraft accusations were bids to affect relational forms (Myhre 2009): they drew boundaries that cut certain networks and, at the same time, strengthened others that the stigma of AIDS threatened to disrupt.

Here, different patterns are apparent. In 13 cases, household members accused non-kin, such as neighbors, colleagues, Christian preachers, diviners, or unnamed outsiders. These accusations were bids to reinforce the boundary between kin and non-kin and also to bolster the solidarity of domestic units. This is apparent in the case of Elphas Shokane, who developed skin lesions, experienced severe abdominal pains, and lost his appetite soon after he started work as a gardener at an electricity supply depot. A diviner told Elphas and his parents that a neighbor had bewitched him in the hope that he would resign so that her son could be appointed to his position. Elphas remarked: "I think it was an old woman. She saw me carrying groceries home to my parents and asked me for a cold drink." In this instance, the accusation of witchcraft drew attention to Elphas's contribution to his parents' household before he became sick.

In another four cases, household members blamed spouses of the sick persons. These accusations were bids to cut relations constituted through bride wealth and thereby strengthen the ties between cognates. They were also an attempt to reverse the arrow of culpability. This is apparent in the example of Moses Chiloane. Starting in 1992, when Moses lost his position as a truck driver, his wife, Lerato, had supported him from the salary she earned as a teacher. She bought him a van and gave him sufficient money to purchase beer every day. According to rumors, Moses contracted HIV when he cheated on Lerato with younger women. However, when Moses first became severely ill in 2002, his sister alleged that Lerato had doctored him with 'love potions' (korobela). She even threw stones at Lerato's car, breaking the rear window. These allegations resurfaced after Moses died. His cognates now claimed that when Lerato's aunt came to pray for Moses, she actually placed herbs underneath his mattress to hasten his death. Outside observers told me that, in making these accusations, Moses's cognates were staking a claim to inherit his estate.

Eleven accusations were made against senior members of the same domestic unit, most often fathers. These accusations expressed intergenerational tensions that had become pronounced since the 1990s. In South Africa, ideologies of national liberation that accompanied the end of apartheid posited a progressive process of increased status and prosperity through time. In these ideologies, children were expected to be improved versions of their parents (Ferguson 2006: 176–193). But the actual experiences of young men who entered the labor market during an era of deindustrialization and high unemployment contradicted the visions of the future that these discourses provided. Sons were often quick to learn that their fathers actually enjoyed greater economic security, had attained virtually unchallenged authority in domestic units, and were, in many cases, destined to outlive them.

In accounting for the misfortunes of their own generation, some younger people pointed to the continued status and power of elders, which they attributed to witchcraft. They alleged that when their fathers worked as migrant laborers in South Africa's centers of industry and mining during the 1980s, they purchased witch familiars in order to secure promotions and earn good salaries. But once their fathers retired in Bushbuckridge, the familiars caused havoc and claimed the blood of their children. In this manner, fathers inadvertently sacrificed their children's futures for their own prosperity. For example, Jabulani Mashile retired from working in the gold mines to take up residence with his family in Impalahoek. Within a few years, his wife and five of his children had passed away. Jabulani's remaining descendants claimed that he had bewitched the members of his own family, giving some of them the appearance of AIDS-like symptoms so as not to arouse too much suspicion. Such accusations were bids to sever ties with elders, who frequently blamed AIDS on the unscrupulous sexual conduct of the younger generation, and to construct new relations of intergenerational solidarity, or to reinforce old ones, particularly among siblings.

Conclusions

In this chapter, I have attempted to show how a focus on networks, as elaborated in Anderson's (2000, 2008) analysis of the kuru epidemic in Papua New Guinea, can offer valuable analytical insights into witchcraft accusations in Bushbuckridge, South Africa. Anderson exhorts us not to view the labeling and the allocation of blame for kuru as a matter of indigenous cosmology, but rather to see it in terms of multiple networks of interaction and exchange. This approach calls for reflexivity and challenges us to consider the manner in which the biomedical and public health fraternities pathologize certain patterns of behavior among host populations. Allegations of cannibalism are a profound marker of primitive exoticism at the frontiers of colonial rule (Obeyesekere 2005). Yet the impact of these allegations on the South Fore is yet to be fully explored, particularly as it pertains to likely contestations between Christians and pagans. It remains unclear whether Christianity generated any new understandings of the body and of death that led to the abandonment of traditional funeral rites and to the refusal of the Fore people to provide corpses for medical autopsies. In the South African lowveld, it is only now that the stigmatizing effects of two decades of AIDS-awareness campaigns, which have highlighted the fatal nature of AIDS and condemned sexual promiscuity, are becoming apparent.

In Papua New Guinea, as in South Africa, there is a long tradition of invoking sorcery and witchcraft to explain and to allocate responsibility for misfortune. But a stubborn commitment to tradition alone does not account for the appeal of witchcraft in the face of new disease epidemics. In both cases, the host populations were perfectly willing to use new explanatory models for misfortune (ranging from germs to ghosts, cargo, and political conspiracies) and to experiment with a wide array of new treatments (using whatever biomedicine had to offer). In the context of epidemics, accusations of sorcery and witchcraft reconfigured culpability by shifting blame away from the sufferers. Previous ideas of witchcraft as 'projection' offer a useful starting point toward conceptualizing this capacity. This concept refers to processes whereby subjects disavow and disconnect from feelings or wishes that they cannot tolerate within themselves—in this case, guilt—and relocate these onto others—in this case, the sorcerer or witch (Kluckhohn 1944). This process is both interpersonal and relational (Lambek 2002). It is precisely in the politics of relatedness that witchcraft accusations 'cut' social networks and impose boundaries in an attempt to forge new connections of solidarity, such as those between household members, cognates, and siblings.

Acknowledgments

I acknowledge the help of my fieldwork assistants, Eliazaar Mohlala and Eric Thobela. I also wish to thank Fraser McNeill, Jonathan Stadler, and the anonymous reviewers for their comments and critical feedback.

Isak Niehaus teaches anthropology at Brunel University in London. He received his PhD from the University of the Witwatersrand in South Africa in 1997 and has conducted extensive research in South African rural areas. His most recent monograph is *Witchcraft and a Life in the New South Africa* (2013).

Notes

1. Impalahoek was formerly located in the Lebowa Bantustan and currently has a population in excess of 20,000 Northern Sotho- and Tsonga (Shangaan)-speaking residents.
2. My aim is not to establish a universal explanatory framework. It is simply to explore the co-presence of certain phenomena. Lambek and Strathern (1998: 25–28) contend that engagement in new contexts, conversations, and exchanges helps us to broaden our horizons and to refine our language.
3. Arens (1979) argues that the theory about cannibalism relies upon verbal testimony, including folk tales. According to Steadman and Merbs (1982), the portal of entry

might well have been through mucus membranes of the skin, for example, by rubbing the eyes and nose with unwashed hands.

4. In 1997, Gajdusek was convicted of child molestation, following the adoption of more than a dozen boys from Papua New Guinea (Anderson 2008: 220–225).

5. President Mbeki's government opposed calls by physicians to provide azidothymidine (AZT) and nevirapine (NVP) to women in the last stages of pregnancy to reduce the chances of mother-child transmission of HIV. President Mbeki even became receptive to arguments by dissident scientists who denied the existence of HIV. In 2003, the South African Constitutional Court compelled his government to make NVP available in all sectors of the health-care system to satisfy citizens' 'right to life' (Fassin 2007: 41–49).

6. McPherson et al. (2008) monitored 1,353 patients who received HAART at the Rixile clinic between October 2005 and September 2007. Their median CD4 count was 64. After two years, 84 percent (1,131) of the patients were retained on treatment, 9 percent (124) had died, 5 percent (63) had been transferred out, and 3 percent (35) could not be traced.

References

Anderson, Warwick. 2000. "The Possession of Kuru: Medical Science and Biocolonial Exchange." *Comparative Studies in Society and History* 42, no. 4: 713–744.

Anderson, Warwick. 2008. *The Collectors of Lost Souls: Turning Kuru Scientists into Whitemen*. Baltimore: Johns Hopkins University Press.

Andersson, Jens. 2002. "Sorcery in the Era of 'Henry IV': Kinship, Mobility and Morality in Buhera District, Zimbabwe." *Journal of the Royal Anthropological Institute* 8, no. 3: 425–499.

Arens, William. 1979. *The Man-Eating Myth: Anthropology and Anthropophagy*. New York: Oxford University Press.

Ashforth, Adam. 2002. "An Epidemic of Witchcraft? The Implications of AIDS for the Post-apartheid State." *African Studies* 61, no. 1: 121–145.

Beasley, Annette N. 2006. "The Promised Medicine: Fore Reflections on the Scientific Investigation of Kuru." *Oceania* 76, no. 2: 186–202.

Beasley, Annette N. 2009. "Frontier Journeys: Fore Experiences on the Kuru Patrols." *Oceania* 79, no. 1: 34–52.

Bennett, J. H., F. A. Rhodes, and H. N. Robson. 1958. "Observations on Kuru: A Possible Genetic Basis." *Australian Annuals of Medicine* 7: 269–278.

Berndt, Ronald. 1954. "Reaction to Contact in the Eastern Highlands of New Guinea." *Oceania* 24, no. 3: 190–228.

Cannon, Walter B. 1942. "Voodoo Death." *American Anthropologist* 44, no. 1: 169–181.

Delius, Peter, and Clive Glaser. 2005. "Sex, Disease and Stigma in South Africa: Historical Perspectives." *African Journal of AIDS Research* 4, no. 1: 29–36.

Durham, Deborah, and Frederick Klaits. 2002. "Funerals and the Public Space of Sentiment in Botswana." *Journal of Southern African Studies* 28, no. 4: 777–795.

Epstein, Helen. 2007. *The Invisible Cure: Africa, the West, and the Fight against AIDS*. London: Penguin.

Farmer, Paul. 1992. *AIDS and Accusation: Haiti and the Geography of Blame*. Berkeley: University of California Press.

Fassin, Didier. 2007. *When Bodies Remember: Experiences and Politics of AIDS in South Africa*. Trans. Amy Jacobs and Gabrielle Varro. Berkeley: University of California Press.

Ferguson, James. 2006. *Global Shadows: Africa in the Neoliberal Order*. Durham, NC: Duke University Press.

Herring, D. Ann, and Alan C. Swedlund, eds. 2010. *Plagues and Epidemics: Infected Spaces Past and Present*. Oxford: Berg Publishers.

Hunter, Mark. 2005. "Cultural Politics and Masculinities: Multiple-Partners in Historical Perspective in KwaZulu-Natal." Pp. 139–160 in *Men Behaving Differently: South African Men Since 1994*, ed. Graeme Reid and Liz Walker. Cape Town: Double Storey Books.

Iliffe, John. 2006. *The African AIDS Epidemic: A History*. Athens: Ohio University Press.

Jonsen, Albert, and Jeff Stryker, eds. 1993. *The Social Impact of AIDS in the United States*. Washington, DC: National Academy Press.

Kluckhohn, Clyde. 1944. *Navaho Witchcraft*. Boston: Beacon Press.

Kuhn, Thomas. 1962. *The Structure of Scientific Revolutions*. Chicago: University of Chicago Press.

Lambek, Michael. 2002. "Fantasy in Practice: Projection and Introjection, or the Witch and the Spirit-Medium." Pp. 198–214 in *Beyond Rationalism: Rethinking Magic, Witchcraft and Sorcery*, ed. Bruce Kapferer. New York: Berghahn Books.

Lambek, Michael, and Andrew Strathern. 1998. "Introduction: Embodying Sociality: Africanist-Melanesianist Comparisons." Pp. 1–28 in *Bodies and Persons: Comparative Perspectives from Africa and Melanesia*, ed. Michael Lambek and Andrew Strathern. Cambridge: Cambridge University Press.

Lindenbaum, Shirley. 1979. *Kuru Sorcery: Disease and Danger in the New Guinea Highlands*. Palo Alto, CA: Mayfield.

Lindenbaum, Shirley. 2001. "Kuru, Prions, and Human Affairs: Thinking about Epidemics." *Annual Review of Anthropology* 30: 363–385.

Lindenbaum, Shirley. 2010. "Explaining Kuru: Three Ways of Thinking about an Epidemic." Pp. 323–344 in Herring and Swedlund 2010.

MacPherson, Peter, Mosa Moshabela, Neil Martinson, and Paul Pronyk. 2009. "Mortality and Loss to Follow-Up among HAART Initiators in Rural South Africa." *Transactions of the Royal Society of Tropical Medicine and Hygiene* 103, no. 6: 588–593.

McNeill, Fraser G. 2009. "'Condoms Cause AIDS': Poison, Prevention and Denial in Venda, South Africa." *African Affairs* 108, no. 432: 353–370.

McNeill, Fraser G., and Isak Niehaus. 2010. *Magic? AIDS Review 2009*. Pretoria: Centre for the Study of AIDS, University of Pretoria.

Mfecane, Sakhumsi. 2010. "Exploring Masculinities in the Context of ARV Use: A Study of Men Living with HIV in a South African Village." PhD diss., University of the Witwatersrand.

Myhre, Knut Christian. 2009. "Disease and Disruption: Chagga Witchcraft and Relational Fragility." Pp. 118–140 in *Dealing with Uncertainty in Contemporary African Lives*, ed. Liv Haram and C. Bawa Yamba. Stockholm: Nordiska Afrikainstitutet.

Niehaus, Isak. 2007. "Death before Dying: Understanding AIDS Stigma in the South African Lowveld." *Journal of Southern African Studies* 33, no. 4: 845–860.

Niehaus, Isak. 2013. *Witchcraft and a Life in the New South Africa*. New York: Cambridge University Press.

Niehaus, Isak, with Gunvor Jonsson. 2005. "Dr. Wouter Basson, Americans, and Wild Beasts: Men's Conspiracy Theories of HIV/AIDS in the South African Lowveld." *Medical Anthropology* 24, no. 2: 179–208.

Obeyesekere, Gananath. 2005. *Cannibal Talk: The Man-Eating Myth and Human Sacrifice in the South Seas*. Berkeley: University of California Press.

Posel, Deborah. 2005. "Sex, Death and the Fate of the Nation: Reflections on the Politicization of Sexuality in Post-Apartheid South Africa." *Africa* 75, no. 2: 125–153.

Probst, Peter. 1999. "*Mchape* '95, or, the Sudden Fame of Billy Goodson Chisupe: Healing, Social Memory and the Enigma of the Public Sphere in Post-Banda Malawi." *Africa* 69, no. 1: 108–138.

Pronyk, Paul. 2001. "Assessing Health Seeking Behaviour among Tuberculosis Patients in Rural South Africa." *International Journal of Tuberculosis and Lung Disease* 5, no. 7: 619–627.

Rosenberg, Charles E. 1992. *Explaining Epidemics and Other Studies in the History of Medicine.* Cambridge: Cambridge University Press.

Schoepf, Brooke. 2001. "International AIDS Research in Anthropology: Taking a Critical Perspective on the Crisis." *Annual Review of Anthropology* 30: 335–361.

Stadler, Jonathan. 2003. "The Young, the Rich, and the Beautiful: Secrecy, Suspicion and Discourses of AIDS in the South African Lowveld." *African Journal of AIDS Research* 2, no. 2: 127–139.

Steadman, Lyle, and Charles Merbs. 1982. "Kuru and Cannibalism?" *American Anthropologist* 84, no. 3: 611–627.

Strathern, Marilyn. 1996. "Cutting the Network." *Journal of the Royal Anthropological Institute* 2, no. 3: 517–535.

Thornton, Robert J. 2009. "Sexual Networks and Social Capital: Multiple and Concurrent Sexual Partnerships as a Rational Response to Unstable Social Networks." *African Journal of AIDS Research* 8, no. 4: 413–421.

Wahlström, Åsa. 2002. "The Old Digging Graves for the Young: The Cultural Construction of AIDS among Youth in the South African Lowveld." BSc diss., Brunel University.

Weiss, Brad. 1993. "'Buying Her Grave': Money, Movement and AIDS in North-West Tanzania." *Africa* 63, no. 1: 19–35.

Yamba, C. Bawa. 1997. "Cosmologies in Turmoil: Witchfinding and AIDS in Chiawa, Zambia." *Africa* 67, no. 2: 200–223.

Chapter 2

LAW, OPACITY, AND INFORMATION IN URBAN GAMBIA

Niklas Hultin

The Gambia's National Printing and Stationery Corporation, or NPSC, is located in a large white-walled compound alongside the highway connecting Banjul, the capital, to the bustling intersection known as Westfield, from where one can easily reach the tourist area along the Atlantic coast, the ramshackle conurbation centered on Serrekunda, The Gambia's largest city, or continue inland. From Westfield to the NPSC is a short walk of approximately 20 minutes that takes one past assorted restaurants, a bottling plant and other light industries, a municipal courthouse, and several underused office buildings. Aside from groups of school children, few people were walking on this road the first time that I did so in 2004—a walk that I have repeated with some regularity in 2007, 2009, and 2010.

Over the years that I have visited the NPSC, the compound itself has not changed noticeably. While there is a large iron gate on the highway, to enter the compound one must walk maybe 50 meters down a dirt road to a second gate, where a guard sits in a small booth. When I first visited in 2004, the guard disinterestedly asked me a few questions—to which I answered that I was there to purchase a copy of the Gambian constitution—before letting me into the compound. Past the guard's booth was a large grassy courtyard ringed by small white houses and unidentifiable pieces of broken-down machinery. In the center of the courtyard was a large gnarled tree. There were no placards on the buildings and no signs of activity. After a few moments, the guard, presumably noticing my hesitation, stuck his head out of the booth and pointed at a small house in a corner of the courtyard. Following his directions, I walked up to the house and knocked on the green door. A muffled male voice told me to come in, and I entered a small office, almost tripping over the desk just inside the door. Stacks of official documents in green folders were on the desk and in the bookshelves surrounding it. Assorted notices and posters, faded to the point of illegibility, were on the walls. Behind the desk was a middle-aged man who, seemingly surprised to have a visitor, raised an eyebrow and asked how he could be of help.

I explained that I wanted to purchase a copy of the constitution. The man shook his head and informed me that the constitution was out of print. When I asked when it would be in print again, he shrugged and said that he did not know. I then asked if I could purchase the acts of the National Assembly—The Gambia's legislature—and he responded in the affirmative, asking which acts I wanted. I asked if he had a government gazette or directory of recently passed acts. Again, the response was no.[1] Ransacking my mind for what recent legal developments I had read about in newspapers, I asked for a copy of the Anti-Terrorist Act, the National Media Commission Act, and the Copyright Act. The man stood up from behind his desk, told me to come along, and led me into a different building, where he asked me to wait in a dimly lit and empty hallway before he disappeared into what I gathered was some kind of storeroom. I passed a few minutes peering at what I assumed was a printing machine through a small dusty window in a different door. The man re-emerged with a stack of booklets and explained to me that he had collected a few other acts and bills that he thought might be of interest. I decided to purchase all of them for the price he gave me: 25 dalasis per document (at the time, around 80 US cents). When I grabbed the stack and flipped through the booklets, I noticed that in some cases I had purchased an act and in other cases the corresponding bill. I was now the owner of the Biodiversity Act but not the Biodiversity Bill and the National Centre for Arts and Culture Bill but not its corresponding Act. Based on previous readings of the minutes of the National Assembly, I was aware that the differences between the two are often slight, but I nonetheless asked for the missing documents. The man shrugged his shoulders and explained that they were not available.

It is tempting to dismiss this fieldwork story as just that—a mundane version of the kinds of stories that used to dot anthropological accounts but are increasingly out of fashion (Marcus 2006). When viewed in the politico-legal context of The Gambia, however, this episode takes on greater analytical significance. At the time, the Gambian government was—as it still is—roundly critiqued by domestic civil society groups and international human rights groups for unaccountable security forces and a hostile attitude toward the media (Hughes 2000; Hultin 2007; Saine 2002). In addition, there were persistent rumors of multiple constitutions existing in The Gambia. According to these rumors, shared with me by journalists and lawyers, the government had secretly reprinted the constitution with a pink cover instead of the previous off-white cover and, in the process, had made a few strategic insertions and deletions pertaining to the qualifications and appointment of judicial personnel to the effect of eroding the already questionable independence of the judiciary. In one of the few public discussions of this situation, Halifa Sallah, then the minority leader of The Gambia's legislature and a prominent opposition politician, argued in a newspaper editorial that a Constitution (Validation) Act should be swiftly drafted and passed in order to determine which constitution was authentic. The present state of constitutional doubt, he argued, threatened the "bedrock of the constitutional order" and derailment of the rule of law with "ambiguities, uncertainties, inconsistencies, and impunity" (Sallah 2004: 1–2).

The rumors of multiple constitutions, coupled with my failure to obtain one, underline the indeterminacy of law—its vagueness, ambiguity, and remoteness—in The Gambia.[2] Sallah's letter proposes a remedy: the passing of a new law by the National Assembly. This approach seems somewhat counterintuitive in its assumption that the weaknesses of the law can be fixed by more law. This is the situation with which this chapter will grapple: on the one hand, the law is an ambiguous and indeterminate thing in The Gambia, as it is elsewhere in Africa; on the other hand, a conventional response to this ambiguity is an appeal for more law. My focus is not on the capriciousness and violence of law in contemporary Africa—a vein of inquiry that has been fruitfully mined by the Comaroffs (2006b), Mbembe (2005), and others—but on the relationship between information about the law and the envisioning of a particular social order. Taking a cue from Marilyn Strathern's (2004: 30) suggestion that "a way towards thinking about the nature of [sociality] might be to think about the kinds of communities created in the wake of knowledge as it travels in its diverse directions," the chapter examines how legal information and its circulation and non-circulation give rise to different modalities of relation, inclusion, and exclusion. Rather than analyzing the contents of laws, it examines the transmission of legal information. I will argue that focusing on this transmission process—its interruptions and incompletions—creates political community in contemporary Africa.

This argument will unfold in three steps. In the first section that follows, I will discuss the role of information—or, to be precise, arguments about information—in contemporary Gambian politics. In doing so, I will examine the notion of opacity as a novel and apt way of describing this role. In the second section, I will discuss opacity in view of the approach to knowledge suggested by Strathern and others and will propose that these discussions should be understood as being about relations and belonging. In other words, I will suggest that incidents such as my inability to purchase a copy of the Gambian constitution suggest that the law is opaque and that this opacity is a particular kind of relation characterized by partial exclusion and interruption. In the third section, I will discuss how urban Gambians seek to remedy opacity, which will allow me to elaborate an understanding of how law is perceived in urban African—an approach that is distinct from the anthropological focus on disorder and dramatic ruptures of sovereignty (see, e.g., Comaroff and Comaroff 2006b; Das and Poole 2004).

In making this argument, I am drawing on ethnographic fieldwork in The Gambia that consists of multiple periods, ranging in duration from a year to two weeks and extending from 2003 through 2010. This research has focused on the politics of human rights in The Gambia and the use of international knowledge practices by what might be loosely thought of as the urban middle class, although the participants in this study are more heterogeneous than the class label suggests. These Gambians—lawyers, civil servants, NGO workers, journalists, teachers, and the like—are ethnically and religiously diverse and do not necessarily fall neatly on either side of the line dividing the Gambian government from its critics. Indeed, one of the defining characteristics of this group is its commitment to a particular form of political rationality rather than a particular politics (cf. Werbner 2004 on 'reasonable radicals'). Aside from socio-economic similarities, they are tied together by extended kinship ties and a common associational life. Much of the specific material that I draw upon concerning freedom of speech and information policy is discussed at greater length in an earlier article (Hultin 2007). I also rely heavily on the research experience as such. In part, this is due to necessity: in the absence of elaborate rituals of information sharing, everyday encounters with information is seldom remarked upon. It is also an attempt, following the lead of Tony Crook's (2007) interweaving of anthropological and ethnographic knowledge practices, to abridge and shorten the distance between how knowledge is made (and thought of as having been made) in the different contexts.

Information and Its Interruptions

As noted at the beginning of this chapter, the state of the Gambian constitution in 2004 was uncertain, partly due to its material inaccessibility and partly due to the weak rule of law in the country. Much of this uncertainty was driven by a dispute between the government and the press over the establishment of a regulatory body, the National Media Commission (NMC). Members of the press accused the government of being draconian and seeking to suppress freedom of speech through onerous registration requirements and heavy fines levied for non-compliance, while the government, for its part, suggested that the private press was irresponsible, spreading lies and misinformation and thereby undermining stability.

Members of the private press framed this dispute as one of the right to free expression, but also as one of access to information. The then chairman of the Gambia Press Union (GPU), Demba Jawo, put it thus: "Access to information is our [journalists in the private press] main problem. Hardly anybody in government is willing to talk to the private journalists … You get a lead about a particular story, and then you try to get someone in government actually to confirm or deny it, and nobody is willing to talk to you."[3] Similarly, Deyda Hydara, the editor of the leading newspaper *The Point* before his assassination by unknown assailants toward the end of 2004, told me in an interview that the flow of information is based on the "whims of the permanent secretary ... They [the bureaucrats] would rather tell you to wait for the press release."[4] The difficulty of obtaining information applied to the NMC as well. Jawo told me that at one point he spent the better part of a day walking around Banjul, trying to find the office of the newly established NMC. When he finally found it, it was just an empty, unfurnished room.

Such concerns over access to information about laws—and the palpable frustration with these difficulties—extended to areas beyond the NMC. At around the same time, the National Assembly also passed a new Copyright Act. Soon after its passage, I ran into Jawo on the road leading from the University of The Gambia, where he had consulted with some of the faculty on the NMC matter. We were making small talk when one of us brought up the Copyright Act. Jawo explained that while the GPU was generally in favor of the idea behind the act, it was leery of anything promoted by the government that might be used to regulate the press. He quickly added, however, that the Copyright Act had "not yet been distributed," and until it was widely available, he really did not know what to say about it.

While media professionals' livelihood largely depends on access to information, other Gambians similarly commented on the difficulty of gaining access to legal information due to the infrastructural deficiencies of the Gambian government, including, for instance, the absence of a reliable law-reporting service. Thus, at the end of an interview, a prominent women's rights activist wistfully remarked to me that "it is hard to get information [in The Gambia] ... One has to run around."[5] In other cases, the challenge of obtaining legal information stemmed from the non-existence of a relevant law in The Gambia and the ad hoc use of external standards. For example, during a conversation with a representative of the Medical Research Council (MRC), a British research and public health organization based outside Banjul, I asked about confidentiality and data protection in the MRC's work. The representative told me that the Gambian government had yet to adopt a regulatory framework for human subjects' protection and that, in the interim, the MRC simply applied the United Kingdom's Data Protection Act as a guideline.[6]

The general tenor of these retellings of Gambians' encounters (or non-encounters) with legal information is a peculiar one. People frequently invoke legal information yet express despair at its absence. It is, however, an absence that is never an absolute negation but rather a sort of temporary abeyance. These statements pose an analytical challenge because while they concern things that are not known, they do not concern things that are secret—either in the sense of classified state secrets, or in the sense of guarded, dangerous knowledge. The latter kind of information—that is, secret knowledge—is ingrained in West African ethnography. Cohen's (1976) classic study of political associations in Freetown, for example, makes the Simmelian point that secrecy leads to an intensification of group identity (see Simmel 1906). The connection between secrets and different forms of propertized knowledge and their aesthetic representation has been explored by other scholars of the region (e.g., Bledsoe and Robey 1986; Gable 1997; Murphy 1998; Nooter 1993; Piot 1993). Still others have examined rumors about secret events and actors (witches, criminals, fraudsters, and other illicit elements of society) as a particularly potent form of information sharing that conveys criticism of corruption, political malfeasance, and excessive accumulation (see, e.g., Apter 1999; Geschiere 1997; West and Sanders 2003).

The considerable merits of the above literature notwithstanding, it is not entirely applicable to the current topic for several reasons. The first is the relative absence, in this literature, of the formal state bureaucracy in any shape other than as a target of criticism and skepticism. Secrecy and information as concepts whose trajectories are to be analyzed seem limited to 'traditional' social institutions and practices.[7] This is despite the fact that African states, like states elsewhere, are massive producers of information and that a dominant form of political organizing is implicitly framed as exercises in information sharing that may, in the end, be utterly disconnected from local grievances and concerns (see, e.g., the discussion on civic education workshops in Malawi and Zambia in Englund 2006).

Secondly, the kinds of information flows—or interruptions of information flows, whether deliberate or not—that I have described have very little in common with the secrecy-as-property mode of analysis, according to which knowledge is a controlled substance that sustains a social structure. To be sure, one can interpret the above accordingly, transposing, to use Murphy's (1980) example of Kpelle society, the Gambian government to the role of Kpelle elders and the journalists and other Gambians to the role of Kpelle youth, in which case information sharing simply becomes another facet of a patron-client relationship. Such a transposition, however, assigns to the Gambian cases under consideration a degree of social integration, linearity, and uniformity that is too high. Instead, the relationship between the information that is imperfectly shared and the Gambian journalists and others (including this author) who wish to obtain information can better be described as one of opacity. I am using the term 'opacity' here in a rather specific sense to mean not only non-transparency but also, borrowing from computer science, incompleteness in the sense that the end-user or client can access only part of an operation.

Opacity thus evokes not a complete lack of knowledge and visibility but rather an uncertainty about the parameters within which one operates. In other words, when we speak of the opacity of information, the referent is not primarily secrecy; instead, it is incompleteness and unpredictability as a mode of apprehending the law. Opacity is not the opposite of transparency but the opposite of liquidity as defined by Carruthers and Stinchcombe (1999). In their discussion of financial markets, they argue that liquidity "mean[s] that standardized products can be bought and sold continuously at a price that everyone in the market can know" (ibid.: 353). When such information is not known, for whatever reason, I suggest that we speak of opacity. This further allows for a non-deliberate motive for the lack of sharing. Whereas secret information is secret for a reason (i.e., somebody has classified it as such), opaque information is 'agnostic' on this point. As a consequence, opacity, as used herein, avoids the uncritical assumption of a linear model of information sharing (although opacity does not preclude it) that is assumed in much of the discussion on transparency in politics (Fenster 2006).

To think of legal information in The Gambia as opaque has two broader implications. The first involves the social significance of sharing information. The second concerns how the same actors that identify opacity seek to remedy it. These matters will be discussed in the following two sections.

Sharing (Melanesian) Information

Take two instances where information, over time, has become less opaque. The first concerns the legal framework governing firearms in The Gambia. The relevant legislation is the colonial-era Arms and Ammunition Act of 1923 (subsequently amended several times). Over the course of a few years and multiple visits to The Gambia, I have determined that this act is not widely available, despite gun violence and the control of arms being topics of frequent public discussion. It cannot be purchased from the government printers, nor is it, as far as I have been able to determine, available in the National Archives, the National Library, the University of The Gambia Library, or similar organizations. I was able to obtain a copy only when a senior lawyer in private practice went out of his way to arrange a photocopy for me. Similarly, when I sought to acquire a copy of a landmark small arms control case, concerning five Senegalese nationals who had been intercepted by the Gambian authorities when they allegedly attempted to smuggle AK-47s and similar military-grade weaponry into the country, the records clerk at the municipal courthouse in Kanifing did not give me a copy until after I had convinced her that I in fact knew the magistrate who had presided over the case—a connection that should be immaterial, given that, in principle, legal cases are available to the public in The Gambia. In both situations, I relied, quite literally, on the kindness of strangers to provide information that should be generally available but—due to the logistics of printing (more than any deliberate move) in the first situation, and an unduly restrictive practice (not official policy) in the second situation—is not easily obtainable.

The second instance concerns the launch, in 2003, of an e-government program in The Gambia, a venture that appears to have fizzled out since then. With the support of the African Information Society Initiative (AISI), a program of the United Nations Economic Commission for Africa, the Gambian government was to establish a series of websites that would contain information about public issues and relevant statistics (AISI 2003). Given that this development took place at the same that I was conducting research on the media and the aforementioned NMC, I decided to pursue more information. By calling a phone number listed on a press release, I was able to secure a meeting with the civil servant in the Ministry (then the Department of State) of Finance and Economic Affairs who was in charge of the program. The meeting was short. Whereas I had expected a somewhat structured interview lasting about 30 minutes or so, the civil servant quickly explained—after an exchange of business cards—that

I should just read the official files, since they contained "everything one would need to know."[8] When I asked him where I could obtain the documents, he suggested that I get them from him. He asked if I happened to have a USB flash drive, and when I answered yes, he took it, transferred the documents to it, and handed it back to me. Our meeting was then over.

In these instances, transactions took place, and information was shared. In the terminology proposed earlier, the opacity of information was temporarily suspended or cleared away. When I first published an analysis of my meeting with the e-government civil servant (see Hultin 2007), I adopted an approach heavily indebted to the work of Andrew Barry (2001) and others who focus on how information connotes a moral imperative that is wielded by governments. Accordingly, I emphasized the idea of an informed, moral subject rather than the fact that a transaction had taken place and that it had done so in a context of opacity. To paraphrase Strathern's aforementioned suggestion, I ignored the relation that had been created through the travel of the information that was the subject of the transaction. Admittedly, this formulation sounds a bit hazy, so a brief detour into the work of Strathern and her colleagues is necessary.

In *Kinship, Law and the Unexpected*, Strathern (2005) develops the connection between sociality and information in a context that is altogether different from that of urban Gambia. She describes the Euro-American kinship system (as manifested in US legal cases) as a "kinship system that has a propensity to base relatedness on what can be *known* about people's connections to one another" (ibid.: 72). This is in contrast to the kind of relatedness made possible by genetic knowledge, knowledge that 'concretizes' relationships in a manner that displaces other 'concretivities' (e.g., those stemming from affinity or proximity). This in turn, Strathern writes, brings about a "fractal vision [that] assumes a family within which, as repositories of information, persons are replicas of one another" (ibid.: 73). The implications here are both that there are multiple ways of relating (i.e., that a relationship is not culturally transparent) and that a relationship need not be between two individuated beings but can instead be between genetic as well as generic types (e.g., 'uncle'). Later in the same text, she draws on the Melanesian material when noting that rituals and other public activities are focused on "making relations visible, presenting them as objects of people's attention" (ibid.: 121). From this point of view, an event such as a ritual is something of an aperture that forces a focus on one particular relationship and lets other relationships momentarily fade away. The central theme of Strathern's work here is to foreground the making and unmaking of relations, or, rather, how we come to see different kinds of relations. Her comment that "[i]f property relations are part of the way in which people in modern industrial economies (Euro-American, that is) connect to the world, then they must both shape and take the shape of the way the world is perceived" (ibid.: 152) is thus applicable to relations *tout court* and not just ones of property.

There are echoes here of Strathern's and others' writings on gifts and gift-giving as apertures through which the constitution of subjects (human and non-human, individual and collective) can be glimpsed. A useful summary of this line of analysis is offered by James Carrier's (1998: 86) discussion of Melanesian property, "wherein an object is embedded in and reflects durable relationships between those people implicated in its past." In this view, it is through acts of sharing and transmission that the poles of transmission (the sender and the receiver) are made.

This line of argument has been further developed by Crook (2007) in his study of the Bolivip culture in Papua New Guinea. In brief, Crook argues that the sharing of information (knowledge, in his terms) is a way of 'exchanging skin' so that knowledge "ventures forth in the form of a person: in the way in which it influences and becomes part of other people ... we might even conclude that, as a detachable analogue, 'knowledge' is itself a person" (ibid.: 29). Such exchanges are not spurious events, however, but the outcome of a great deal of care and empathy (ibid.: 108–109). This leads Crook to an analysis that is motivated by a "commitment to the relational composition of knowledge, and the capacity of artefacts to carry social relations, thereby animating relations of their own making" (ibid.: 219).

This Melanesianist approach to information, espoused by Strathern and Crook, differs from two other prominent anthropological understandings of information. First, it departs from the transactionalism of Fredrik Barth (1975: 217), who suggested that "the value of information seemed to be regarded as inversely proportional to how many share it." The Melanesianist approach divorces value from information or, rather, divorces information *and* value from the straightjacket of inverse proportionality. Information can be widely shared and valuable at the same time; indeed, it can (but does not have to) be valuable precisely because it is widely shared. Of course, the social meaning of information does not inhere in its transaction, nor is the existence of a strong relationship of information sharing synonymous with a strong social relationship (cf. Crook 2007: 10). Thus, in an odd kind of way, Strathern (and Crook) socializes information by de-socializing it.

Second, the Melanesianist approach avoids defining information only as a function of its semantic content in relation to context. Gregory Bateson (1972: 315) famously defined a 'bit' of information as "difference which makes a difference." For something to be labeled as information, it must be new and effect some kind of change. The flipside of information, to Bateson, is redundancy, which is brought on by repetition—that which is not different. Bateson's take on information is situational, and he illustrates this by considering three people: A, B, and an observer. A and B each have a message pad, and the purpose of their communicating is to fully replicate the message on A's pad to B's pad. From the observer's viewpoint, assuming he or she has seen A's pad, this transaction is redundant as it does not create any new information (ibid.: 412–413). Bateson's work here emphasizes semantics at the expense of pragmatics. Strathern and Crook, by contrast, emphasize the pragmatic effects of information sharing, or how the possession and sharing of information constitutes relations.

This discussion, not to mention the exchange of skin in Bolivip, seems to be a far cry from the exchange of a flash drive in The Gambia, and the argument that I am advancing is not intended as a West African analogue to Crook's argument. For one thing, my concern herein is not to demonstrate the existence of a particular Gambian ontology of information. Nonetheless, I suggest that three propositions can be extracted from the Melanesian literature that can help put the two incidents with which this section began into a different light: first, information sharing is itself a relation; second, this relation is forward-looking, not necessarily as a relationship but in the sense of a new incorporation of that information into the being of the parties to the sharing; and, third, where such sharing is expected but does not take place, the result is not so much exclusion from a secret society or the like but rather a denial of recognition, a steadfast disinterest in the other and a lack of care. This disinterest cuts both ways in the sense that where there is an assumption of sharing and when such is interrupted in an illegitimate fashion, sociality might be breached or recalibrated as a highly unequal form of sociality that denies the validity of the would-be recipient's concerns.

From this point of view, the e-government and firearms law transactions above take on a new significance, as does the opacity of information discussed in the previous section. The fact that the various actors shared information does not necessarily suggest my inclusion in some kind of in-group (as much of the secrecy literature might suggest). While I can only speculate about the sharer's motivation, and if some rather macabre imagery is excused, it is tempting to think of this as an act of enveloping me in the same skin (as Crook might put it), and vice versa. Even if the material (to the extent that electronic files are material) flow was one way, the exchange was itself an instantiation, however fleeting, of sociality, a registration of a temporary partnership, a commensuration of putting two persons into the same frame, a means of making them interested in each other as persons interested in whatever it was to be exchanged, a form of equivalency. And as there is an element of presumed reiteration in the exchange, it is immaterial whether or not the civil servant shared the information with me alone or with half of The Gambia.

There is an important political valence to this point. As Annelise Riles (2001) has shown with reference to Fijian women's rights NGOs, concretizations of information-sharing practices—in the form of networks, action platforms, and the like—are powerful, if mundane, substitutes for action that enable connections to a larger community of like-minded individuals. Here, attention to information sharing is, firstly, proceduralism as a form of political imagination (cf. Englund 2006). Secondly, concretized information sharing is a kind of enlargement or replication of the self and, as such, offers a way to reiterate one's concerns as concerns of a wider community. If this insight is extrapolated to the Gambian context, it seems plausible to interpret the kinds of information sharing that I have discussed above as a method of forming extensible relations *through*, not just to, the recipient. For example, when the senior attorney made sure that I received a photocopy of the Arms and Ammunition Act, the point was not that he gave it to me as a particular person (that would seem presumptuous); rather, the point was that, in sharing it, he invited himself and our relation to be part of a larger network of interested parties (which in theory could be a limitless group).

To put this differently, my Melanesianst-influenced reading of the information transactions with which this section began suggests that information sharing (both sending and receiving) is a way to extend oneself into the world. When such information sharing does not take place—when information is opaque—the absence of sharing signifies disinterest and condemnation, leaving the presumptive recipient or sender of information relationally adrift. This disinterest is in itself a relation, of course, but it is one that is doggedly unequal. We can see this inequality and separation in the statements by Hydara and Jawo—the two journalists interviewed above. Their frustration did not spring from governmental secrecy as such but from the feeling that the government unjustly excluded the private press from the body politic, which of course runs counter to their axiomatic self-understanding of the press as a conveyor of information. It is thus important to note that opacity here sits at the juncture between information sharing as an individual transaction (I share information with you) and a perceived societal state of affairs.[9] Since the information sought—that which is opaque—is about society (i.e., a set of prescriptions or laws), information and opacity are in their own ways 'motile' (Hetherington and Lee 2000) in that they allow for a scaling or transposing of the pragmatic understanding of information to social criticism and back again.

Herein, then, lies the frustration of opacity: it is not that the non-circulation of information is viewed as legitimate (as is the case, in relative terms, for the Kpelle) but that the opacity of information comes off as unjust, irrespective of the source of the opacity (political decisions, material wants, etc.). This is an injustice, however, that can be overcome by its very source.

Fixing Opacity

A recurring theme in all of the above examples is a normative attachment to information's travels. Opacity is diagnosed as a problem, and non-sharing is viewed as illegitimate—as a 'bug' in society rather than a societal feature. The fix is not avoidance of law but more law or, to stretch the computer analogy a bit further, better code.[10] This is, after all, the impetus behind Sallah's suggestion that the National Assembly pass a Constitutional (Validation) Act: problems pertaining to legal information are fixed with more law (or legal information). A similar point was made by a friend of mine during a conversation about a series of Gambian banking scandals. My friend explained that he was very skeptical of the banks and admitted to having a bank account only for "business reasons."[11] When I asked why he was unhappy with the banks, he explained that the lack of credible legal system and regulatory oversight was part of the problem, and that practices such as publishing the name of defaulters in the newspaper was, in his view, a form of defamation. (The use of the legal term is significant for this argument; the fact that this interpretation is not correct is not.) The remedy, he suggested, was not to stop using commercial banking or to promote alternative processes (e.g., Islamic banking) that are ostensibly more consistent with Gambian practices, but simply to increase and improve existing regulations.

Opacity is a bug to be fixed via the better application of code, that is, a steadier, more predictable flow of information. This view of legal information in The Gambia invites repair and emendation, as opposed to avoidance and dismissal, as ways of apprehending the law. This in turn suggests a reading of law that is different from that which can be found in much recent writing on law in Africa, according to which the dominant mode of engagement is either avoidance of formal state processes in favor of local, non-state ones, or a critique of formal legal processes (state and international) rooted in a vernacular idiom and mode of resistance to law. A comparison with the Comaroffs' (2006b) recent work on law in the post-colony illustrates what I have in mind here. They draw attention to the capricious intercourse between a 'culture of legality', the pluralization of zones of sovereignty, and the experience of a lack of legality in post-colonial Africa. They note how 'the law' is circumscribed, punctured, and caricatured by practices of illegality.

Without disputing that this description of law is appropriate for some Africans (including Gambians), it nonetheless downplays the aspirational quality of law present in Sallah's article and my friend's comment on banking. The Comaroffs' formulation emphasizes a state of affairs and the way people interact with that state, but not how people envision it changing (or changing on them). Here, the dominant mode of critique is one of circumvention and personal success (however defined) that has been achieved despite a flawed legality. What is missing is not only the possibility of wishing for a 'perfect' legality, but also an appreciation that such legality may in fact not be that remote or implausible to begin with. It speaks to the possibility and desirability of regulation and formality in the midst of what might otherwise be seen as capriciousness and opacity.

The problem with the law in The Gambia, from this point of view, is not an ontic mismatch between different culturally determined if-then relationships, as Geertz (1983) referred to legal rules,[12] nor is it simply that there is an ineffectual rule of law hovering above or to the side of social life that is instrumentally invoked or avoided, as the Comaroffs' (2006b) emphasis on 'lawfare' would have it. What I would like to think that this chapter contributes is the introduction of another variable in the discussion of African legal anthropology: the extent to which any single constituent element of a plurality is itself variable along an axis of efficiency or quality. While I grant that there is a plurality of legal orders in The Gambia and elsewhere, I am not sure that it is sufficient simply to note that there is a culturally based disconnect between the formal, state legal system and the mores and norms of a majority of Gambians. What this perspective leaves out is that for some Gambians the disconnect is between an ideal view of what state legal practice ought to be like and the actual legality. This is a disconnect, or mismatch, that is defined by the opacity of the law and by the uncertainty of information and its unpredictable and incomplete sharing.

Conclusion

I began this chapter by sharing information about my failed acquisition of a copy of the Gambian constitution in 2004. The aim was to initiate a thinking through of the relationship between the African state, its legal system, and the circulation of information between Gambians and between Gambians and myself. In the process, I have presented a three-fold argument. First, I have proposed that the malaise of the rule of law in The Gambia (and elsewhere in Africa) can be seen as one of opacity, as a form of non-sharing that is distinct from secrecy and not simply the inversion of transparency. Secondly, drawing on the Melanesianist anthropology of Strathern, Crook, and Riles, I have suggested that opacity leads to a particular form of interruption or forestalling of relatedness and sociality, while information sharing suggests a relatedness with the world. Such interruptions, I have further suggested, are profound. Finally, I have suggested that one way for Gambians to address opacity is to bear down on the law, to aspire to more information sharing with greater predictability. I have advanced this approach to law and information in order to formulate a way to think about law in contemporary Africa that is different from the prevailing trend of disorder and sovereignty.

Of course, this argument is subject to limitations, and the aim is not to displace other understandings of law in Africa but to complement them. By the same token, the departure from the secrecy literature is not intended as a break with it. This is all the more important because the kind of information practices I have discussed herein are of a very limited sort: they uniformly concern the law and public policy, and they take place among a comparatively small group of urban, professional Gambians. In no way do these practices displace traditional norms of secrecy, for instance.

Nonetheless, attending to the opacity of legal information in The Gambia, no matter how parochial a concern it may be, forms a different approach to the study of African law. It underscores the importance of everyday complaints about mundane things while keeping the challenges of structural reform in Africa in sight. Here, the 'running around', to which the gender activist alluded, not only invokes individual frustration, but also points to the uncertainty of everyday life in The Gambia and the work required to maintain an investment in the law.

Acknowledgments

Research in The Gambia was supported by grants from the National Science Foundation's Law and Social Science Program (Award ID 038305) and Swarthmore College. I am grateful to Harri Englund, Knut Christian Myhre, and the anonymous reviewers for their suggestions, which have helped to improve and clarify earlier versions of this chapter. Any errors of fact or analysis are my own.

Niklas Hultin is the Assistant Director of the Global Affairs Program at George Mason University, where he is also a faculty member. He has conducted research in The Gambia, Nigeria, and Senegal with support from, among others, the US National Science Foundation and the Isaac Newton Trust at the University of Cambridge. His research has appeared in journals such as *American Ethnologist*, *African Security*, and *PoLAR: Political and Legal Anthropology Review*.

Notes

1. When I returned to the NPSC in 2010, such a list did in fact exist.
2. Senghore's (2010) slightly more positive review of the Gambian legal system focuses on the relative independence of the Gambian judiciary from the Gambian executive. However, it does not address the manifestation of law in everyday life.
3. Demba Jawo, personal communication, Banjul, The Gambia, 15 March 2004.
4. Deyda Hydara, personal communication, Banjul, The Gambia, 12 July 2004.
5. Isatou Touray, personal communication, Kanifing, The Gambia, 28 June 2004
6. Alex da Costa, personal communication, Fajara, The Gambia, 14 April 2004.
7. Notable exceptions include Hasty's (2005) ethnography of journalists in Ghana, the Comaroffs' (2006a) discussion of the circulation of crime statistics in the South African public sphere, and Bastian's (2003) passing discussion of the release (or lack thereof) of government reports.
8. Modou Drammeh (pseudonym), personal communication, Banjul, The Gambia, 2004.
9. I thank one of the anonymous reviewers for pointing this out.
10. Cf. "code is law" in Lawrence Lessig (2006: 1–8).
11. Madi Touray, personal communication, Serrekunda, The Gambia, 2007.
12. On this point with regard to The Gambia, see Davidheiser and Hultin (2012).

References

AISI (African Information Society Initiative). 2003. "Strategy Paper on E-Government Programme for The Gambia." United Nations Economic Commission for Africa, Addis Ababa.

Apter, Andrew. 1999. "IBB = 419: Nigerian Democracy and the Politics of Illusion." Pp. 267–307 in *Civil Society and the Political Imagination in Africa: Critical Perspectives*, ed. John L. Comaroff and Jean Comaroff. Chicago: University of Chicago Press.

Barry, Andrew. 2001. *Political Machines: Governing a Technological Society*. London: Athlone Press.

Barth, Fredrik. 1975. *Ritual and Knowledge among the Baktaman of New Guinea*. Oslo: Universitetsforlaget.

Bastian, Misty L. 2003. "'Diabolic Realities': Narratives of Conspiracy, Transparency, and 'Ritual Murder' in the Nigerian Popular Print and Electronic Media." Pp. 65–91 in West and Sanders 2003.

Bateson, Gregory. 1972. *Steps to an Ecology of Mind: Collected Essays in Anthropology, Psychiatry, Evolution, and Epistemology*. San Francisco: Chandler Publishing.

Bledsoe, Caroline H., and Kenneth M. Robey. 1986. "Arabic Literacy and Secrecy among the Mende of Sierra Leone." *Man* (n.s.) 21, no. 2: 202–226.

Carrier, James G. 1998. "Property and Social Relations in Melanesian Anthropology." Pp. 85–103 in *Property Relations: Renewing the Anthropological Tradition*, ed. C. M. Hann. New York: Cambridge University Press.

Carruthers, Bruce G., and Arthur L. Stinchcombe. 1999. "The Social Structure of Liquidity: Flexibility, Markets, and States." *Theory and Society* 28, no. 3: 353–382.

Cohen, Abner. 1976. *Two-Dimensional Man: An Essay on the Anthropology of Power and Symbolism in Complex Societies*. Berkeley: University of California Press.

Comaroff, Jean, and John L. Comaroff. 2006a. *An Excursion into the Criminal Anthropology of the Brave Neo South Africa*. Berlin: LIT Verlag.

Comaroff, John L., and Jean Comaroff. 2006b. "Law and Disorder in the Postcolony: An Introduction." Pp. 1–56 in *Law and Disorder in the Postcolony*, ed. Jean Comaroff and John L. Comaroff. Chicago: University of Chicago Press.

Crook, Tony. 2007. *Anthropological Knowledge, Secrecy and Bolivip, Papua New Guinea: Exchanging Skin*. Oxford: Oxford University Press.

Das, Veena, and Deborah Poole, eds. 2004. *Anthropology in the Margins of the State*. Santa Fe, NM: School for Advanced Research Press.

Davidheiser, Mark, and Niklas Hultin. 2012. "Policing the Post-Colony: Legal Pluralism, Security and Social Control in The Gambia." Pp. 123–241 in *Policing in Africa*, ed. David J. Francis. New York: Palgrave Macmillan.

Englund, Harri. 2006. *Prisoners of Freedom: Human Rights and the African Poor*. Berkeley: University of California Press.

Fenster, Mark. 2006. "The Opacity of Transparency." *Iowa Law Review* 91: 885–949.

Gable, Eric. 1997. "A Secret Shared: Fieldwork and the Sinister in a West African Village." *Cultural Anthropology* 12, no. 2: 213–233.

Geertz, Clifford. 1983. "Local Knowledge: Fact and Law in Comparative Perspective." Pp. 167–234 in *Local Knowledge: Further Essays in Interpretive Anthropology*. New York: Basic Books.

Geschiere, Peter. 1997. *The Modernity of Witchcraft: Politics and the Occult in Postcolonial Africa*. Trans. Peter Geschiere and Janet Roitman. Charlottesville: University Press of Virginia.

Hasty, Jennifer E. 2005. *The Press and Political Culture in Ghana*. Bloomington: Indiana University Press.

Hetherington, Kevin, and Nick Lee. 2000. "Social Order and the Blank Figure." *Environment and Planning D: Society and Space* 18, no. 2: 169–184.

Hughes, Arnold. 2000. "'Democratisation' under the Military in The Gambia: 1994–2000." *Commonwealth & Comparative Politics* 38, no. 3: 35–52.

Hultin, Niklas. 2007. "'Pure Fabrication': Information Policy, Media Rights, and the Postcolonial Public." *PoLAR: Political and Legal Anthropology Review* 30, no. 1: 1–21.

Lessig, Lawrence. 2006. *Code: Version 2.0*. New York: Basic Books.

Marcus, George E. 2006. "Where Have All the Tales of Fieldwork Gone?" *Ethnos* 71, no. 1: 113–122.

Mbembe, Achille. 2005. "Sovereignty as a Form of Expenditure." Pp. 148–166 in *Sovereign Bodies: Citizens, Migrants, and States in the Postcolonial World*, ed. Thomas B. Hansen and Finn Stepputat. Princeton, NJ: Princeton University Press.

Murphy, William P. 1980. "Secret Knowledge as Property and Power in Kpelle Society: Elders versus Youth." *Africa: Journal of the International African Institute* 50, no. 2: 193–207.

Murphy, William P. 1998. "The Sublime Dance of Mende Politics: An African Aesthetic of Charismatic Power." *American Ethnologist* 25, no. 4: 563–582.

Nooter, Mary H. 1993. "Secrecy: African Art That Conceals and Reveals." *African Arts* 26, no. 1: 54–69, 102.

Piot, Charles D. 1993. "Secrecy, Ambiguity, and the Everyday in Kabre Culture." *American Anthropologist* 95, no. 2: 353–370.

Riles, Annelise. 2001. *The Network Inside Out*. Ann Arbor: University of Michigan Press.

Saine, Abdoulaye. 2002. "Post-Coup Politics in The Gambia." *Journal of Democracy* 13, no. 4: 167–172.

Sallah, Halifa. 2004. "Halifa's Letter to the Bar: On the Need for a Constitution (Validation) Act—Which Constitution Is the Constitution?" *Foroyaa*, 24–26 May.

Senghore, A. A. 2010. "The Judiciary in Governance in The Gambia: The Quest for Autonomy under the Second Republic." *Journal of Third World Studies* 27, no. 2: 215–248.

Simmel, Georg. 1906. "The Sociology of Secrecy and of Secret Societies." *American Journal of Sociology* 11, no. 4: 441–498.

Strathern, Marilyn. 2004. *Commons and Borderlands: Working Papers on Interdisciplinarity, Accountability and the Flow of Knowledge.* Oxford: Sean Kingston Publishing.

Strathern, Marilyn. 2005. *Kinship, Law and the Unexpected: Relatives Are Always a Surprise.* New York: Cambridge University Press.

Werbner, Richard. 2004. *Reasonable Radicals and Citizenship in Botswana: The Public Anthropology of Kalanga Elites.* Bloomington: Indiana University Press.

West, Harry G., and Todd Sanders, eds. 2003. *Transparency and Conspiracy: Ethnographies of Suspicion in the New World Order.* Durham, NC: Duke University Press.

Chapter 3

FROM CUTTING TO FADING
A Relational Perspective on Marriage Exchange and Sociality in Rural Gambia

Tone Sommerfelt

Among rural Wolof speakers in the Niumi districts north of the Gambia River, a large proportion of marriages are unions between close relatives. In the village where I lived during fieldwork in 2003, about two-thirds of marital relationships were unions between different versions of cousins or between relatives across generational divides.[1] Criss-crossing ties of kinship within and between villages, as well as repeated unions between homesteads and families, extend affinal networks widely. These networks are distinguishable by divisions of hereditary occupational specialization, referred to as 'caste' in much regional ethnography (cf. Conrad and Frank 1995). By and large endogamous, networks occasionally interconnect when marriage takes place across caste distinctions.[2] Within these broad and open social grids, however, affinal connections can be traced nearly indefinitely.

Notes for this chapter begin on page 72.

When new marriages come about, networks of affinity become visible, and they are constituted and reconfigured by a myriad of exchanges. Foodstuffs, livestock, household utensils, furniture, cotton cloth, jewelry and clothing, and a range of other objects are given, received, and redistributed. Money also circulates at various stages. A striking feature of these exchanges is the degree to which many of the transfers are multiply authored and in turn redistributed in small portions within the extensive networks. It seems that individual shares do not increase considerably with higher payments; rather, the larger the wealth to distribute, the greater the number of people who are drawn into the circulation of valuables. Another characteristic is that the number of different prestations is vast, in spite of the fact that money has replaced many prestations that were once given in kind (cf. Diop 1985: 91ff.). Money as a generalized medium has not collapsed the many small and 'detailed' transactions into larger categories.

The many transfers involved in marriage exchange among rural Wolof, I argue, make and remake affinity and materialize persons as well as productive and reproductive relationships within and beyond homesteads. In this chapter, I seek to rethink marriage exchange in Africanist anthropology by exploring how the procurement and redistribution of bridal trousseaus put limits on potentially endless networks. The emphasis on the limiting of affinity is inspired by Strathern's (1996) notion of the 'cutting' of networks, where 'network' is understood in terms of webs of relationships among homogeneous or heterogeneous elements—persons, things, knowledge, places, events, and so forth. In line with Strathern's concept of cutting, I aim to show that the redistribution of bridal trousseaus to a wide range of relatives attributes particular shapes to otherwise undifferentiated networks. At the same time, the circulation of items establishes gradual distinctions of social proximity, rather than unconditional boundaries around units of definite exclusion and inclusion. Accordingly, I suggest that the limiting of networks is best understood in terms of 'fading' rather than cutting: affinal networks obtain their particular shapes when some affiliations grow fainter and others stronger in a manner that rearranges the contours of networks in gradual stages.

I focus on two aspects of the stoppage of flow through fading. First, I explore the way in which the circulation of trousseau valuables limits interpersonal networks. This concept of network resonates with Wolof vernaculars of relatedness, or, literally, of 'people who share [something]' (*mbokka*) and 'in-laws' (*goro*). It is akin to the notion of network in conventional social network theory (e.g., Barnes 1954), with the qualification that interpersonal connectivity here entails that persons are seen as manifestations of relationships and not as resources held exterior to them. In this context, I explore how money calls people into existence; how the materiality of money enlists particular forms of sociality; and how the redistribution of trousseau items establishes distinctions of social proximity. Second, I draw attention to fading in the sense of the situational singling out of aspects of relationships, entailing the weakening of some features and the strengthening of others, in a way that renders relationships recognizable as persons and objects. Focusing on the manner in which money objectifies various relationships, I map out how the redistribution of the trousseau ensures the transformation of the young bride's connections, situates her as an in-law in the homestead, and defines the women of her husband's household in new ways. This transformation makes the bride capable of acting with respect to others (Strathern 1993: 49) and re-creates the nature of others' connectedness to her.[3] In this process, relationships are not cut but rather become recognizable in new ways: certain aspects are allowed to grow stronger while others fade into the background. Since people are connected by a multitude of relationships, this process is essential to establishing close kin as affines.

Trousseau, Marriage, and the Patterning of Relationships in West Africanist Literature

Restrictions on affinal relationships in the Senegambia area have largely been portrayed within the framework of hereditary professional specialization, or so-called caste (see, e.g., Diop 1981; Dupire 1985; Irvine 1973). In more general terms, categorical affiliation to caste groups and identity based on this have been pervasive issues in West Africanist literature. Studies of the Wolof are no exception, and much attention has been devoted to associated ideologies of descent, genealogy, and qualities or rights ascribed at birth (Diop 1981, 1985; Irvine 1978; B. Wright 1989). In the context of marriage, the persistence of endogamy with respect to hereditary occupational groups has directed attention to impediments to marriage based on categorical 'membership' in lineage, that is, to a property that a person either has or does not have.

The focus on impediments to marriage is also due to earlier theoretical currents, in particular, the structuralist emphasis on marriage prohibitions.[4] Descent and alliance perspectives have colored the ethnographic literature on marriage payments, too. Most descriptions concentrate entirely on prestations by the groom and his kin to the bride's group, many of which are referred to as 'bride wealth' (Gamble 1957: 66–67) and interpreted as a purchase of rights, made by the husband's patrilineage, to the woman's offspring (Ames 1953: 57).[5] With reference to Senegal, Diop (1985: 92, 106n5) focuses on the replacement of the earlier 'bride wealth' (can), paid by the groom's group to the bride's family, with a personal payment made by the groom to the 'bride' (alal), as prescribed in the Koran. Diop argues that marriage payments have become driven by personal benefit at the expense of the common good of a large family. He accredits this more general societal change to increased monetization and to an effect of Islam (ibid.: 142ff.), while ascribing it to the Wolof in general.[6]

The analytic bias toward payments and expenses on the part of the groom and his family tallies poorly with the plethora of prestations that circulates in rural Niumi. As I will show, these transfers can only with difficulty be described in terms of gifts and return gifts between distinct 'groups'. The issue of the trousseau is, to my knowledge, mentioned only in passing in older ethnographies of rural Wolof. These texts refer to the bride's 'luggage', an understanding influenced by the literal meaning of the Wolof concept for trousseau—bagaas— a derivative of the French term bagage. In this manner, older texts describe the trousseau as articles brought for the bride's use in order to enable her to start up a cooking unit of her own (Ames 1953: 58; Gamble 1957: 67). These objects' subsequent destiny is not explored further, and one is left with the impression that they remain with the bride. Contrary to this, during my fieldwork it became evident that the largest parts of trousseaus were redistributed among a great number of the groom's kin and acquaintances. This redistribution took place in an elaborate event on the day of the ceremony, called *céyt*, during which the bride transfers her residence to her husband's homestead.[7] Among Niumi Wolof, the part of the trousseau set aside for the bride usually includes a mortar and pestle, customary gifts from her father, a large cooking pot from her mother, as well as a clay water container, one or two enamel bowls of each size, an incense burner, and some other equipment for her room. If she is from a well-off family, she may keep more items, usually bowls, which are displayed on the cupboard in her room in the marital homestead. The size of trousseaus seems to increase, as opposed to the compulsory payment of *can* to the bride (cf. Diop 1985: 113). Subsuming these developments under commercialism alone covers up the complexity of the processes that take place, a point stressed in the extensive literature on changes in marriage payments (e.g., Grosz-Ngaté 1988; Hutchinson 1996; Lambert 1999; Masquelier 2004).

Recent works on West Africa connect bridal trousseaus to debates on consumption, power, and gender, with a focus on women's autonomy in particular (Cooper 1997; Cunningham 2009; Grosz-Ngaté 1988; Lambert 1999; Masquelier 2004).[8] Cunningham (2009: 284–285) discusses the replacement of calabash containers with imported enamels in Mali marriage payments, a change that resulted from broader regional developments toward increasingly moneyed economies in the 1950s and 1960s.[9] Cunningham argues that these trousseaus, and specifically the enamel bowls that brides bring with them, offer an opportunity for young wives to show strength in the 'patriarchal structures' that they enter into upon marriage. The replacement of calabash containers with enamel serving vessels has not inhibited women from using trousseau items to display and further build up their social network (ibid.: 284ff.). Although enamels are a sign of economic wealth, they too are re-gifted and thus "blur distinctions between the different forms of capital ... enamels materialize social capital similar to that contained in the calabashes they have replaced. Yet, as a store of wealth, enamels also display the economic power of the bride and her social group" (ibid.: 288).

Anthropological research in West Africa no longer characterizes social organization according to an unequivocal lineage principle, but belonging continues to be conceptualized in terms of categorical identities that derive from membership in groups rather than in relational terms associated with proximity and degrees of similarity and difference. Thus, marriage payments—whether understood in terms of the transfer of rights in a patrilineal or semi-complex structure, or as a means for individuals to evade or manipulate relations of dominance within patrilineal or patriarchal structures—assume bounded units as givens. In spite of a shift of focus from groups to individuals, position and possession remain the analytical departure points, and individuals' agency is assumed as being theoretically prior to the relations in which it operates (cf. Piot 1999: 10–11; Strathern 1988: 50). In contrast to Diop's (1985) argument concerning Senegalese Wolof, Cunningham (2009) avoids rendering change as a one-dimensional development when he asserts that the replacement of locally produced valuables with imported goods in trousseaus does not entail an absolute transition in women's sources of selfhood from social network and group solidarity to the pursuit and display of economic wealth. However, the conceptualization of social network as 'capital' (ibid.) entails that relationships are seen as resources exterior to the persons (and things) that constitute them. This perspective fails to consider how, and the full extent to which, material flow is central to the constitution of persons and to the patterning of relationships.

Exchange and Marriage Prestations in Niumi Crossroads

The Upper and Lower Niumi districts on the north bank of the Gambia River cover the westernmost part of the narrow strip of land that makes up Gambia's northern riverbank. Squeezed between the river in the south, the Senegalese border to the north, and the Atlantic Ocean to the west, Niumi is criss-crossed by roads and paths that connect the many villages scattered over the rural area. Roads leading inland from the coast link the border area and the ferry crossing to Banjul, Gambia's capital.

In inland Niumi, the most important economic activity is agriculture. Millet is cultivated for consumption, but the main crop, groundnut, is grown for sale and provides the chief source of income. The main staple is imported rice, which makes people sorely dependent on a cash income. Cash also enables people to participate in the area's vivid trade in imported goods, commodities that trickle down from the commercial areas along the river and border area to the smaller market places.[10] Wolof speakers in this area also keep cattle and other livestock. Some Fulbe stay in the outer fringes of villages and assist in the herding of cattle, for payment or in exchange for dairy produce.

Imported goods and cash make up the main part of the material transfers that take place in connection with the entry into marriage. The transfer from the groom that is defined as compulsory is the *can*. It is paid in cash to the bride on the day of the 'tying' (*takka*) of marriage, or a part is paid on this day and the rest postponed until the relocalization of the bride. Typically quite low,[11] the *can* is a matter of family tradition (*aada*), which the trousseau is not. Moreover, amounts of *can* do not seem to be subject to significant increase (cf. Diop 1985: 113). In contrast, other prestations (*maye*) to the bride and her kin are subject to increase, most notably a 'gift to the girl' (*may si ndaw*, also known as 'first gift', *may gu jëkka*), which, at the time of my fieldwork, was a gift of money and jewelry and often a radio with a cassette player.[12] The prestation known as 'outfit for the tying of marriage' (*kompaleeti takka*) consists of two full outfits, and a series of gifts given after the tying of marriage is known by the generic term 'gift for the wife' (*maye jabar*). 'Gifts for the wife' include money, a bed, a cupboard, and a suitcase that contains a number of items—usually seven complete outfits, three wrappers made from woven cloth, two pairs of shoes, jewelry, soap, make-up, and bead chains—many of which are redistributed among the bride's peers. These prestations, too, are the result of the pooling of resources in the groom's network.

Trousseaus are displayed on the day of a bride's transfer to her husband's homestead. The transfer ceremony (*céyt*) may be organized to occur on the same day as the formal tying (*takka*) of marriage, which takes place in the village mosque. Ordinarily, though, some time passes—from a few months up to a year—between the tying of marriage and the bride's transfer. In her husband's home, the wife moves into a room that has been prepared for her, and her co-wives live alongside her in separate rooms. Homesteads house brothers with their respective wives and children, as well as family members from several generations, fostered children, guests, and contract farmers.

During my fieldwork, wedding trousseaus consisted of plastic buckets, pans and kettles, enamel serving vessels of various sizes, and cotton fabric of different qualities, manufactured mostly in Asia or the Netherlands. Pieces of locally woven cotton cloth were also included, and sometimes prayer mats. Occasionally, cash was brought as part of a trousseau, but this was uncommon and amounts were low.

Procuring *Bagaas*: How Money Makes People Appear

In Niumi, the procurement of a trousseau is not a result of the bride's and her mother's efforts in isolation. Instead, a bride's trousseau consists of contributions from a wide range of people, who come forward because they received a share of an earlier prestation known as the *danta*. The *danta* is an amount of money given by the groom to the bride's parents, prior to the formal tying of marriage. *Danta* (bundle) is an approximate quantitative measure of kola nuts, and people in Niumi explained to me that kola nuts have been replaced by cash.

In order to obtain money for *danta*, the groom is assisted by his relatives, and thus the prestation has many sources. In turn, the *danta* handed over by the groom to the bride's mother (*danta ndey*) and to her father (*danta baay*) is split and redistributed in small amounts to a wide network of the bride's relatives. Thus, the mother gives her 'bundle' to her male and female kin on her mother's and father's sides and to fellow *kumpin* women, that is, the women with whom she cooperates over savings and mutual assistance. She also distributes her *danta* to neighbors and friends. The father's bundle, similarly, is distributed on his side to relatives of his mother and father and, in particular, full siblings, half-siblings, and cousins. Friends and neighbors of the father also receive parts of his *danta*. Considering that most spouses are close relatives, persons may receive a part of both parents' *danta*.

Where I lived, the amount given to each parent as *danta* ranged from 200 dalasis up to 700 dalasis. When redistributed, these figures were split into amounts of 1, 2, and, in some cases, 5 dalasis. Siblings and cousins of the parents usually receive the highest amounts, as do persons who have a particularly close relationship with the bride, for instance, those who took care of her during her upbringing.

The presentation of *danta* communicates that a marriage is about to take place. Money's divisibility allows for extensive involvement. Considering the small shares into which the *danta* bundle is divided, the message reverberates in wide circles. Importantly, those receiving parts of *danta* in turn contribute in cash or kind to the bride's family's expenses and, in particular, to the bridal trousseau (*bagaas*). The effects of this prestation and circulation of *danta* are several. The amount of money given as *danta* by the groom and his relatives enables and elicits the involvement of a network on the bride's end. In turn, the more people who are involved on the bride's side—depending on both the size of the amount originally given by the groom and the size of the individual shares redistributed—the larger the number of people who are brought forth to contribute to the *bagaas*. The more numerous the shares of *danta* distributed, the more extensive the network mobilized and the larger the input to the *bagaas*. What is more, the size of the amount received as an individual share of *danta* establishes the expectation of a material response. The highest amount of *danta* (which still is a very modest figure of 5 dalasis) elicits a more valuable response. During my fieldwork, the ordinary matching of a 5 dalasi *danta* was an enamel bowl (which would cost from 35 to 50 dalasis upward) plus two meters of cotton cloth (costing 30 dalasis upward). Thus, there is an obligation to engage back. Yet the response cannot be understood in terms of strict equivalence: people give according to 'strength' (*doole*) and adjust their input according to their capacity.[13]

Occasionally, the bride's mother uses parts of the *danta* directly to purchase items for her daughter's *bagaas*. In addition, the bride may spend a part of the 'first gift' or 'gift to the girl' (*maye si ndaw*) for the same purpose. Finally, either on his own initiative or in response to his mother-in-law's request, the groom may forward a sum of money 'in preparation' (*waajtaay*) for the bride's transfer. This sum should be used to buy household equipment for her new home: bowls, cooking pots, iron, pans, buckets, and so forth. Thus, this prestation too returns to the husband's homestead in the *céyt* ceremony. The *waajtaay* money is handed over to the mother of the bride, who is responsible for the purchase of the items. Not all men forward *waajtaay*, and many women claimed to be embarrassed to ask for such an advance.

Items bought 'in preparation' are the part of the *bagaas* that a bride keeps and brings into marriage. *Waajtaay* items are thus not redistributed on the day of the *céyt*. Considering that it is paid for by the husband, this part of the *bagaas* should not be regarded as part of the trousseau in a conventional sense. The greatest proportion of objects that the bride keeps may in fact have been given by her husband but passed through her mother's hands as the prestation of *waajtaay*.[14] As will become evident, the trousseau mobilized by the bride's network through the process of *danta*, in contrast, eventually becomes subject to circulation rather than possession.

The procurement of a trousseau through the groom's presentation of *danta* to his prospective parents-in-law and its subsequent division reveal how money

visualizes persons' relational make-up: *danta* materializes both the relationships that produced it (between the groom and his relatives and between the
groom and the bride's parents) and the relationships that it brings forth when
redistributed (between the bride and her close and distant connections). In
the redistribution, the form that the flow of small shares of *danta* takes is not
that of lineage relationships, but rather extensive relationships that involve
maternal and paternal kin, neighbors, and acquaintances. What is more, the
redistribution of shares of *danta* elicits responses from the recipients in the
form of contributions to the trousseau (*bagaas*). *Danta* thus gives recognizable
form to the relationships that it eventually brings about, as it carries in it the
prospective trousseau that travels with the bride to the husband's homestead
in order to be redistributed in the groom's wide network.

Redistributing *Bagaas*: Proximity, Distance, and the Shape of Flow

In the following, I consider a redistributive event that took place in the largest
homestead of the Manneh family in a village in the district of Lower Niumi.[15]
The groom, Bakar Manneh, who is one of the younger brothers of the head of
the Manneh homestead, was marrying his first wife, Sohna Saine. The bride is a
close relative of the wife, Ndey Saine, of one of Bakar's older brothers. Marrying a
Saine is a 'path' (*yoon*) followed by the Manneh family and others in the village.

The *bagaas* was brought by car from the bride's village to the Manneh homestead. Shortly after the bride's arrival, people accompanying her carried the
many items from the sandy path outside the homestead and stacked them in the
center of the small courtyard. As the *bagaas* slowly built up under the courtyard
tree, hosts and visitors gathered to have a look. The redistribution of *bagaas* was
scheduled to take place late in the afternoon once the couple had gone through
ritual sequences, prayers had been said, speeches of advice had been given,
and lunch had been served. The bride, Sohna, had returned from a neighboring
homestead and, upon her arrival, had been unveiled from the white cloth that
had covered her during the trip from her village of origin. Now she was dressed
in a new outfit, with her hair plaited and styled according to the latest fashion.

The *bagaas* in this case was large: it consisted of a total of 199 items and a
small amount of money (25 dalasis). The 199 items included 41 plastic buckets, 52 large plastic pans (used for washing clothes) and 2 small ones, 18 large
enamel bowls (used for ceremonies and in big households), 7 medium-sized
enamel bowls (used for lunch), 15 small enamel bowls (used when sauce and
rice are cooked separately), 27 pieces of six-meter fabric (*kompaleet*, used to
make so-called complete outfits), 12 pieces of woven cloth (*sér njaago*), 16
pieces of two-meter cotton fabric (*malaan*), 4 sheets, 4 mats, and 1 kettle.

The redistribution was handled by Ndey Saine, the groom's sister-in-law and
a close relative of the bride: Ndey Saine is Sohna's mother's sister, as well as a
cross-cousin of Sohna's father (see fig. 1). As in other ceremonies, the physical redistribution took place in a public manner, with people crowding around
the *bagaas*. Items were handed to their new owners by a griot woman, who

FIGURE 1 Relationship between Sohna and Ndey Saine

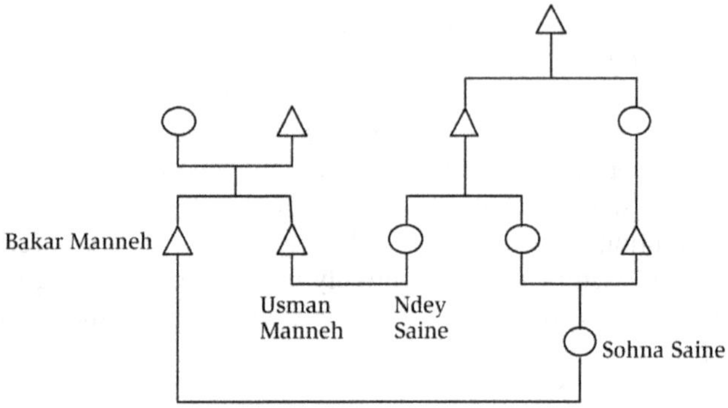

announced the names of the recipients and what they had received. Praises were sung for many of the recipients by other griots as shares of *bagaas* were handed out. Ndey Saine, sitting in the middle of the pile, tried to speed up the process, as did close family members who commented loudly on the tempo of the affair and that darkness and the rain of the wet season threatened. The event was intense, hot, and noisy.

The general form of redistribution is the scattering of small parts in wide circles. The largest portions are named and handed over first, before the remaining and absolutely greatest parts of the trousseau are distributed one item at a time. As noted, shares are kept relatively low, and many persons receive something. In the case of Sohna Saine and Bakar Manneh's wedding, the 199 trousseau items were redistributed in 109 shares, some of which were in turn intended to be divided further. The first two portions of the trousseau were set aside for the groom's late parents—a big enamel bowl and 6 meters of cotton fabric for the father, and a large and a small enamel bowl, a piece of woven cloth, and a small plastic bucket for the mother. These items were later to be divided among their living siblings. A big enamel bowl, woven cloth, and a small plastic bucket were given to each of two sisters of the groom's mother.

Following these four prestations, the distribution turned to the groom's generation, in particular to the sisters and cousins of the groom. Sisters and female parallel cousins of the groom, or 'female husbands' (*njëkke*), get shares among the first recipients, but not all receive equal shares. A patrilateral parallel cousin of Bakar Manneh, appointed 'first female husband' (*premieer njëkke*), received one of the biggest shares: six plastic pans, two pieces of woven cloth, one 6-meter and two 2-meter pieces of cotton cloth, three enamel bowls of different sizes, one small plastic bucket, and a 25 dalasi note. The 'second female husband', a matrilateral parallel cousin of the groom, received one enamel bowl, two plastic pans, two pieces of woven cloth, and one small plastic bucket. The reasoning for these shares centered on a comparison with other 'female husbands', who are genealogically more 'close' (*jege*). Whereas sisters of Bakar who share one or both parents with him are already close, the two others are more 'distant' (*sori*) by virtue of being cousins, and they are brought closer to the couple by being named publically as first and second female husband and by receiving substantial parts of *bagaas*.

The distribution continued to move back and forth between generations with shares given to both men and women, especially to the siblings of the groom and their respective spouses and the siblings of the groom's late parents. The groom was also provided with a piece of the trousseau (a piece of 6-meter cotton cloth), as were some of his close friends with whom he had gone through circumcision. Other people with whom residents of the Manneh homestead socialize (myself included)—for instance, 'guests' (*gan*) to the village who regard the Manneh as their 'host' or 'patron' (*njaatige*), and other people who had contributed to the ceremony by bringing cash or foodstuffs—also received shares. The last piece of the trousseau was given to an elderly Fulani woman who was the mother of the shepherd of the Manneh homestead.

As noted earlier, a majority of marriages are unions between spouses who are closely related. In the case of spouses related as cousins, marriage forms are far more varied than portraits of ideal cross-cousin marriage may indicate, as both patrilateral and matrilateral parallel-cousin marriages take place (Sommerfelt 2010). There are also ties of kinship between women married into homesteads. Moreover, relationships described as constituted by the 'sharing' (*bokka*) of 'blood' (*deret*), 'milk' (*meen*, as associated with maternal relatedness and ties of the breast), 'homestead' (*kër*), or 'village origin' (*dëkka*), by previous marriage in 'affinal' (*goro*) ties, or by other affiliations can be traced almost indefinitely.

The redistribution of trousseaus and other marital prestations activate and display these extensive networks. At the same time, the number of items to be redistributed establishes limits on the potentially endless connections. Consequently, the first question one often gets when returning from a *céyt* ceremony is: "Did they distribute anything to you [*ebbineñ la*]?" Whether or not a person receives a gift tells a story about the biography of specific relationships, as well as a person's relational future and history. Thus, some of the groom's and his parents' siblings and second, third, and fourth cousins receive trousseau items, but many cousins do not. Also, the size of the shares of the trousseau that they receive varies. As in the case of the 'female husbands', differences in the size of portions are discussed in terms of social proximity, with recipients being described as more or less 'close' (*jege*) or 'distant' (*sori*). A greater share of the trousseau redefines relationships as being closer than they were earlier.

The fading of relationships, which comes about when persons are left out of the redistribution of *bagaas*, may reflect processes of emotional and social distancing that cannot easily be turned around. It may also reduce the chances of inclusion in future ceremonial occasions, which are the main arena for young men and women to meet potential spouses. Being left out of the circulation of the trousseau is occasionally also interpreted as a corrective to shallow engagement or stinginess, which encourages a response. Contributing with time and prestations in subsequent ceremonies, especially in the naming ceremonies of children of the married couple, is a way to remedy the process. Another act of counterbalance is to include estranged relatives in the circulation of *danta* in connection with new marriages.

Moreover, as in the case of the *danta*, describing recipients of *bagaas* in terms of their membership in a categorically defined group does not do justice to the form that redistribution takes. Instead, recipients become fewer or receive smaller shares of the trousseau with increasing social distance, or some persons are brought closer by receiving more substantial parts. The result is that the contours of interpersonal networks are drawn in gradual stages.

Materializing Female In-Laws: The Fading In and Fading Out of Affiliations

Through the redistribution of *bagaas*—with items being held up and the names of receivers called out—the bride comes into being as a wife. Her future relational make-up is materialized and made public knowledge. As part of the constitution of wifehood, trousseau items visualize the bride's relationships to other women in the homestead. One set of relationships displayed and reworked are those between wives of brothers. Such classificatory co-wives are referred to by the same term as a direct co-wife, *wujj*, which also means 'rival'. Alternatively, the classificatory co-wife is specified as *wujj peccargo* (i.e., 'wife of a husband's brother'; in the plural, 'women married to brothers'). Relationships between wives of brothers are given careful attention. They are regarded as important for homestead sociality, and even more critical than relationships between direct co-wives (of the same man). The prime mover in rivalry and conflict between classificatory co-wives is said to be 'envy' (*añaan*) over differences in wealth between brothers and in the distribution of wealth to brothers' respective sets of wives in the everyday circulation of food, clothes, and so forth. Many women describe relationships between wives of brothers as more conflict-ridden than relationships between wives of the same man: "Your husband's brother's wife is more stingy [or evil] than your co-wife." In order to elucidate this, they refer to the lack of regulations of classificatory co-wife interactions and the lack of Koranic prescription. *Wujj peccargo* relationships may destroy entire homesteads, as men who take sides with their wives antagonize their brothers. In a way, the nature of a woman's connections to her husband's brothers' wives is a main source of her *joie de vivre*: if amicable, she will have company and few worries; if hostile or distrustful, she risks becoming lonely and unhappy, or even unsafe.

In *céyt* ceremonies, the bride's *wujj peccargo* are named, and their relationship of cooperation in household chores is initiated and 'made to feel nice' (*neexal*) by the giving of trousseau items. In the Manneh-Saine case, 19 *wujj peccargo* received one piece each. The first 13 received a plastic pan, the subsequent 4 were given a big enamel bowl, and the last 2 a small plastic bucket. The difference in monetary value of each item was not given much attention. The point was rather that there are a certain number of items and that wives of the eldest brother are to receive their shares first, following their husbands' birth order. Prior to this distribution, another *wujj peccargo* had received a bigger part of the trousseau. She received a large portion because she was the last to have married into the homestead. In this capacity, she was appointed 'the one who cooks breakfast' for the bride (*togga ndékki*). The 'cooking of breakfast' was until recently a morning meal, but it is presently a gift made up of soft drinks, tea, tinned milk, sugar, and some snacks that is presented to the bride on the day of her arrival. This gift of *togga ndékki* triggers a response during the distribution of the trousseau. In the Manneh-Saine case, the co-wife presenting *togga ndékki* received two plastic pans, one piece of woven cloth, 6 meters of cotton fabric, and one medium-sized enamel bowl.

The redistribution of the trousseau enables the recipients to engage with the bride in productive work in the homestead. Thus, enamel bowls allow both the bride and the recipients to engage in preparing and storing food. Enamel bowls are used not simply for the daily meals within the homestead, but also for sending food to other homesteads, particularly on ceremonial occasions. These containers thus materialize relationships between the bride and her in-laws that engender yet new relationships through the exchange of food between the bride's cooking unit and other cooking units within and outside of the homestead. Similarly, buckets for fetching water, plastic pans for washing clothes and utensils, and pieces of 'cotton fabric' (*malaan*) for carrying children (and for dressing up) make productive and reproductive work possible, facilitating the bride's capacity as a wife, in-law, and mother. Finally, prayer mats and plastic kettles used for ablutions help people do what they can to be good Muslims.

Considering that marriage to Saine women is a path that has been followed earlier by Manneh men, Sohna is already related to other women in the Manneh homestead. One of the wives of the groom's brothers is related to Sohna as an aunt (with intervening links), another as a classificatory grandmother. During the disbursement of trousseau items, by broadcasting to everyone present that these women are henceforth 'rivals' (*wujj peccargo*) to Sohna, and by equipping them with utensils for productive work, the emphasis of these relationships is reworked from an affiliation of 'blood' (*deret*) or 'friendship' (*xarit*) to one of affinity. Previous relational qualities of Sohna to women in her new homestead become faded; instead, attention is drawn to the practical cooperation of female co-affines in relationships that are, at the same time, potentially hostile and competitive. This does not imply that other affiliations between the bride and her classificatory co-wives are permanently ruptured. In times of trouble, parties are constantly reminded of their close relationship in other than 'rival' terms. Yet the distribution of trousseau items accentuates relationships. It highlights and prepares for new realities, in this case by bringing to the fore the cooperative element between female in-laws, condensed in enamels and plastic items.

The presentation of a larger portion of the trousseau to the classificatory co-wife who was the last to have married into the homestead established Sohna not only as a wife among wives in the homestead, but also as a junior wife among the female co-affines. The classificatory co-wife's initial and generous gift of 'breakfast' (*togga ndékki*) to Sohna separated them in terms of seniority, illustrating that the more senior position demands respect from, but also cares for, the junior. By reciprocating with a portion of her trousseau, Sohna acknowledged her juniority. The newly established proximity of the two women—now positioned as classificatory co-wives and potential competitors in relation to the circulation of resources from brothers—is hence made gradual by distinction of seniority in exchange. In this way, gifts "detach people from people" (Strathern 1988: 191), thus increasing social distance.

Proximity among Classificatory Equivalents: Particulars of the Separation of Kin from Affines

Whereas the presentation of the trousseau to many women in the Manneh homestead thus transformed the emphasis in their relation to Sohna from kinship to co-wifehood, the composition and form of the announcement of one particular piece of the trousseau, that of Ndey Saine, established Ndey as different from the other classificatory co-wives. Considering that Sohna and Ndey are married to brothers, they become classificatory co-wives or 'rivals' (*wujj peccargo*). Yet Ndey Saine is already a close relative and friend of the bride, related to her by several paths. Ndey Saine is Sohna's mother's sister and thus her classificatory mother. In addition, Ndey is a cross-cousin of Sohna's father (see fig. 1).

Noteworthy, though, was that Ndey was given nothing from the prestations assigned to the *wujj peccargo*, nor was anything put aside for her. Instead, Ndey received a part later in the distribution, and the size of her share differed from that of the other wives of the groom's brothers: it was bigger, but still considered modest. Ndey was presented with one medium-sized bowl and two plastic pans, a share of the trousseau that was more equivalent with the shares received by sisters of the groom's late mother. By receiving her share of the trousseau in this manner, Ndey Saine's relationship to Sohna was reworked into one between a mother and a daughter-in-law. This was made public when the prestation was announced as being given to 'mother Ndey' (*yaa* Ndey). By the same token, Ndey was described as a 'female father', that is, a father's sister (*bàjen*), during the redistribution. This concept is intended to convey respect, yet it is an ordinary term that is also used to refer to a mother-in-law, the latter practice connected with the common pattern of cross-cousin marriage.[16]

The presentation of a share of the trousseau to Ndey separates the two closely related women and transforms them from kin to affines. Yet the classificatory co-wife aspect of Sohna and Ndey's relationship is situationally faded out through the particular composition of Ndey's share of the trousseau. In practical terms, Ndey Saine was to become Sohna's closest in-law—more of a mother-in-law for Sohna than a co-wife, as Sohna was to take over Ndey's duty of cooking the three daily meals. This, in turn, is related to the fact that Bakar and Sohna did not establish their own household within the new compound but instead joined the cooking unit of Ndey and Usman, Bakar's brother. In this manner,

Bakar was to be 'carried on the back' (*boot*) of his elder brother until he was able to support his wife and eventual children by his own means.[17] The close relationship between Bakar and Usman also encourages the different conceptualization of the relationship between their wives, as compared to the wives of other brothers: not only do Usman and Bakar share the same mother and father, but their household merger also defines them as particularly close.

Notably, in cases when a groom has married wives before, the presentation of shares of the trousseau to direct co-wives differs from the shares presented to classificatory co-wives. For one thing, the presentation is not made part of the public redistributive event. Instead, shares for direct co-wives are put on display in their rooms for people to admire in peace and quiet. Also, shares of the trousseau given to direct co-wives include more items and more valuable items. The reason for this difference is invariably that the relationship between direct co-wives is 'too close' (*jegena torop*) to address in public. The husband's marriage to an additional wife is seen as an emotionally challenging and potentially painful event, and particular care is taken. The distribution of different shares of the trousseau thus contributes to establishing fine-tuned distinctions of proximity between women who formally are ascribed classificatory equivalence as in-laws, co-wives, or rivals.

Conclusion: From Cutting to Fading

Material flows in the procurement and distribution of trousseaus illustrate the complexity of exchange. Different prestations interconnect in the sense that, rather than making up a 'list' of independent transfers, they appear as a sequence in which small prestations trigger new prestations in continuous back-and-forth flows of pooling and distribution. Thus, having been converted from *danta* money, the trousseau that travels with the bride to her husband's homestead makes visible the bride's many connections. Further redistributed at the groom's end, the presentation of trousseau items reworks relationships from kinship to affinity. *Danta* money and trousseau items thus have circulatory power (Strathern 1996: 526). They point to the relationships that are condensed in them and also open up a future perspective—the relationships that they can bring about (Strathern 1988; Weiner 1980).

The flow of trousseau items does not, however, follow linear or lateral biases, nor does it create clear boundaries around categorically defined groups, memberships, and identities. Instead, the contours of networks are rearranged in gradual stages, establishing distinctions of social proximity. By the same token, the manner in which trousseau items transforms relationships does not entail the movement of people between categorically defined positions. Rather, the redistribution of the trousseau establishes relationships as more or less close, drawing the bride's attention to crucial aspects of homestead sociality associated with these graduated social distinctions. In order to bring these points to the fore, I have argued that the importance of Strathern's (1996) focus on the limiting of networks gains impetus in this African setting, but through the fading of relationships rather than cutting. Fading captures the processual character of gradual distancing from open-ended social forms, whereas cutting brings to issue separation and disconnection from closed entities. Agreeing with Strathern's point that "the concept of boundary is one of the least subtle in the social science repertoire" (ibid.: 520), I hope to have shown that processes involved in marriage exchange in West Africa offer an opportunity to rethink the way in which boundaries are drawn.

Acknowledgments

This chapter is based on my PhD work, generously funded by the University of Oslo, the Nordic Africa Institute, the Institute for Comparative Research in Human Culture, and a fellowship provided by Høyesterettsadvokat Per Ryghs Legat (Supreme Court Advocate Per Rygh's Trust Fund). Many thanks are due to my supervisors Knut Christian Myhre, the late Aud Talle, and Marit Melhuus of the Department of Social Anthropology at the University of Oslo. I wish to express thanks to Gro Ween, Heidi E. Fjeld, and the two anonymous reviewers for their valuable comments. I am grateful to the organizers of the workshop 'Afrinesia' held in Uppsala in March 2010, where an early draft of this chapter was presented, and to all participants for their feedback. The largest debt of gratitude is to the people in Niumi, The Gambia.

Tone Sommerfelt received her PhD in Social Anthropology from the University of Oslo in 2013. Based on fieldwork conducted in The Gambia (1995–1996 and 2003), her PhD thesis is a study of contemporary marriage patterns in rural Niumi and focuses on issues pertaining to affinity, relatedness, rivalry, and domestic conflict. Her research interests also include the anthropology of Islam, morality, mobility, and development discourses on childhood and child labor. Since 2013 she has conducted fieldwork in Mali and Haiti and is currently a researcher at the Oslo-based Fafo Research Foundation.

Notes

1. I conducted fieldwork in The Gambia for 12 months in 1995–1996 and 9 months in 2003. The major part of the material discussed here derives from my PhD fieldwork in 2003, when I lived in a rural village in the district of Lower Niumi. In a survey that I conducted of 151 marriages in homesteads in this Niumi village, marriages to relatives included unions between first and second cousins; between spouses related as uncles or aunts and nieces or nephews (directly or as more distant co-laterals); and between classificatory grandparents and grandchildren.
2. A main distinction runs between freemen (*géer* in Wolof), including 'nobles', on the one hand, and professional freemen (*ñeeño*), on the other. The *ñeeño* include

leatherworkers, smiths, Lawbe woodworkers, and griots. People who are considered descendants of slaves (*jaam*) form an additional category. The distinction between freemen (*géer* and *ñeeño*) and *jaam* was made part of the organization of political orders rather than caste (cf. Diop 1981), but at the present the *jaam* category is conceptualized within the same social framework as *géer* and *ñeeño*. See also Irvine (1973) and B. Wright (1989).

3. This transformative process also connects with marriage and sociality in more general terms. Marrying close but not too close—a vernacular Wolof emphasis, viewed as characteristic of semi-complex marriage systems more broadly (cf. Gottlieb 1992: 73)—means that (previously) tied affinity is de-affinalized and re-affinalized when new unions come about.

4. See, for example, Diop (1985) with respect to the Wolof, and Héritier-Augé and Copet-Rougier (1990) on other West African societies.

5. Diop (1985: 91–96) confusingly uses the French term *dot*, corresponding to the English 'dowry', to refer to these same transfers.

6. Buggenhagen (2004) explores the increasing monetary value of marriage expenses among Wolof speakers in Dakar, but focuses on the ways in which remittances from the Murid trade diaspora affect marriage exchange in Murid families. The ethnographic setting is characterized by households in which male elders have lost control over production to young (merchant) men (ibid.: 44ff.), which is different from the rural realities discussed here (cf. Perry 2009).

7. This pattern of redistribution is cause for some uneasiness over the translation of *bagaas* into 'trousseau', considering meanings of the bride's (or couple's) possessions that the latter term easily evokes. Yet I retain it in order to connect with regional literature. The concept of dowry would definitely be an unhappy choice as it does not capture linkages to earlier prestations by the groom, nor does it convey the fact that the largest part is redistributed in wide circles once it arrives in the groom's homestead. It also infers a more compulsory element than is involved in this case. Note that the redistributive events I describe from Niumi differ from recently married women's personal re-gifting of one-by-one trousseau items in the years following their marriage, as is described in other parts of West Africa (see, e.g., Cunningham 2009: 285).

8. In areas where young women are responsible for procuring their own trousseaus, a rise in the cost of trousseaus has been connected to the migration of these women and their participation in the labor market, as housemaids in particular. See, for example, de Haan et al. (2002: 47ff.), Hashim and Thorsen (2011: passim), and Lambert (1999: passim).

9. On these developments, see also Cooper (1997) and Hutchinson (1996).

10. One of the pillars of the Gambian economy is the re-export trade, in which goods produced abroad are imported and re-exported to merchants in countries such as Senegal, Mali, Guinea-Bissau, and Mauretania. Gambian traders make a profit from this trade as import duties in the neighboring countries have been raised in order to stimulate manufacture (D. Wright 2004: 221–223, 248). Many imported commodities also go into retail trade in The Gambia. Much economic activity revolves around the transport of people and goods involved in the re-export and retail trade.

11. Amounts paid in *can* range from 4 dalasis and 25 bututs, which is less than a US quarter (25 cents), to 600 dalasis or approximately 21 US dollars. The average 2003 exchange rate was 28.324972 dalasis per US dollar.

12. Buggenhagen (2004: 38–39) discusses inflation in the 'first gift' (*may gu jëkka*) in the Senegalese Murid trade diaspora, as well as changing uses of the term 'first gift'

itself among young women residing in Dakar. She shows how international trades-men, who live part of the year abroad, send a continuous flow of gifts to women and their families residing in Dakar in order to secure marriage preparation processes.

13. However, it should be underlined that this response is more than a vague expecta-tion of assistance, as is the case for brides' and mothers' procurement of wedding trousseaus in other parts of West Africa (see, e.g., Cunningham 2009: 281).

14. It should be recalled, though, that the bride also keeps certain gifts given to her by her parents.

15. Family and personal names have been changed.

16. According to Wolof kinship terminology, the relationship between Ndey Saine and Sohna through Sohna's father does not readily allow for the use of any specific terms. Usually, the term 'father's sister' (*bàjen*) to denote a cousin of the father is restricted to the father's parallel cousins, not cross-cousins, as is the case here. Peo-ple's references to Ndey Saine as Sohna's *bàjen* in the wedding ceremony conveyed that Ndey is one generation above Sohna. The term also depicted the relationship as one of respect.

17. The concept of *boot* (to carry, tie, or support) is also used to describe women's tying of babies to their backs. For young men who have recently taken their first wife, support from an elder brother given in this manner is considered a transitory phase. Typically, the two married couples do not match in economic strength. In this case, Bakar is supported by his brother, receiving food and other benefits in the new compound. He assists Usman in his fields, and Sohna performs many of the domestic tasks. The couples' relationship is viewed in terms of cooperation and regarded as mutually beneficial.

References

Ames, David W. 1953. "Plural Marriage among the Wolof in The Gambia, with a Con-sideration of Marital Adjustment and Patterned Ways of Resolving Tensions." PhD diss., Northwestern University.

Barnes, John A. 1954. "Class and Committees in a Norwegian Island Parish." *Human Relations* 7, no. 1: 39–58.

Buggenhagen, Beth A. 2004. "Domestic Object(ion)s: The Senegalese Murid Trade Diaspora and the Politics of Marriage Payments, Love, and State Privatization." Pp. 21–53 in *Producing African Futures: Ritual and Reproduction in a Neoliberal Age*, ed. Brad Weiss. Leiden: Brill.

Conrad, David C., and Barbara E. Frank, eds. 1995. *Status and Identity in West Africa: Nyamakalaw of Mande*. Bloomington: Indiana University Press.

Cooper, Barbara M. 1997. *Marriage in Maradi: Gender and Culture in a Hausa Society in Niger, 1900–1989*. Portsmouth, NH: Heinemann.

Cunningham, Jerimy J. 2009. "Pots and Political Economy: Enamel-Wealth, Gender, and Patriarchy in Mali." *Journal of the Royal Anthropological Institute* (n.s.) 15, no. 2: 276–294.

de Haan, Arjan, Karen Brock, and Ngolo Coulibaly. 2002. "Migration, Livelihoods and Institutions: Contrasting Patterns of Migration in Mali." Pp. 37–58 in *Labour Mobil-ity and Rural Society*, ed. Arjan de Haan and Ben Rogaly. London: Frank Cass.

Diop, Abdoulaye-Bara. 1981. *La société wolof. Tradition et changement: Les systèmes d'inégalité et de domination*. Paris: Karthala.

Diop, Abdoulaye-Bara. 1985. *La famille wolof*. Paris: Karthala.

Dupire, Marguerite. 1985. "A Nomadic Caste: The Fulani Woodcarvers. Historical Background and Evolution." *Anthropos* 80: 85–100.

Gamble, David P. 1957. *The Wolof of Senegambia: Together with Notes on the Lebu and the Serer*. London: International African Institute.

Gottlieb, Alma. 1992. *Under the Kapok Tree: Identity and Difference in Beng Thought*. Chicago: University of Chicago Press.

Grosz-Ngaté, Maria. 1988. "Monetization of Bridewealth and the Abandonment of 'Kin Roads' to Marriage in Sana, Mali." *American Ethnologist* 15, no. 3: 501–514.

Hashim, Iman, and Dorte Thorsen. 2011. *Child Migration in Africa*. London: Zed Books.

Héritier-Augé, Françoise, and Elisabeth Copet-Rougier, eds. 1990. *Les complexités de l'alliance*. Vol. 1: *Les systèmes semi-complexes*. Paris: Éditions des Archives Contemporaines.

Hutchinson, Sharon E. 1996. *Nuer Dilemmas: Coping with Money, War, and the State*. Berkeley: University of California Press.

Irvine, Judith T. 1973. "Caste and Communication in a Wolof Village." PhD diss., University of Pennsylvania.

Irvine, Judith T. 1978. "When Is Genealogy History? Wolof Genealogies in Comparative Perspective." *American Ethnologist* 5, no. 4: 651–674.

Lambert, Michael C. 1999. "Have Jola Women Found a Way to Resist Patriarchy with Commodities? (Senegal, West Africa)." *PoLAR* 22, no. 1: 85–93.

Masquelier, Adeline. 2004. "How Is a Girl to Marry without a Bed? Weddings, Wealth and Women's Value in an Islamic Town of Niger." Pp. 220–253 in *Situating Globality: African Agency in the Appropriation of Global Culture*, ed. Wim van Binsbergen and Rijk van Dijk. Leiden: Brill.

Perry, Donna L. 2009. "Fathers, Sons, and the State: Discipline and Punishment in a Wolof Hinterland." *Cultural Anthropology* 24, no. 1: 33–67.

Piot, Charles. 1999. *Remotely Global: Village Modernity in West Africa*. Chicago: University of Chicago Press.

Sommerfelt, Tone. 2010. "Forbindelser gjennom bryst: Om melk, sosial tilknytning og passende ekteskapspartnere blant wolof-talende folk i Vest-Afrika." *Norsk Antropologisk Tidsskrift* 21, no. 1: 32–45.

Strathern, Marilyn. 1988. *The Gender of the Gift: Problems with Women and Problems with Society in Melanesia*. Berkeley: University of California Press.

Strathern, Marilyn. 1993. "Making Incomplete." Pp. 41–51 in *Carved Flesh/Cast Selves: Gendered Symbols and Social Practices*, ed. Vigdis Broch-Due, Ingrid Rudie, and Tone Bleie. Oxford: Berg.

Strathern, Marilyn. 1996. "Cutting the Network." *Journal of the Royal Anthropological Institute* (n.s.) 2, no. 3: 517–535.

Weiner, Annette B. 1980. "Reproduction: A Replacement for Reciprocity." *American Ethnologist* 7, no. 1: 71–85.

Wright, Bonnie L. 1989. "The Power of Articulation." Pp. 39–57 in *Creativity of Power: Cosmology and Action in African Societies*, ed. W. Arens and Ivan Karp. Washington, DC: Smithsonian Institution Press.

Wright, Donald R. 2004. *The World and a Very Small Place in Africa: A History of Globalization in Niumi, The Gambia*. 2nd ed. Armonk, NY: M.E. Sharpe.

Chapter 4

GATHERING UP MUTUAL HELP
Work, Personhood, and Relational Freedoms in
Tanzania and Melanesia

Daivi Rodima-Taylor

Diverse informal associations have become ubiquitous in African societies in recent decades. Mutual help and cooperative work groups, savings and credit associations, informal neighborhood councils, and natural resource user groups offer their members vital options to deal with growing instabilities. Often building on traditional forms of association, they help to circulate new types of resources and create novel freedoms and constraints. The multiplication of the local associational environment raises questions about the nature of the emerging public spaces in Africa and the kinds of freedoms and modes of sociality they facilitate. The focus of this chapter is on women's mutual help groups among the Kuria people of northwest Tanzania. The social legitimacy of the groups is heightened by their reliance on traditional mechanisms of affiliation and sharing, but they also provide fluid sites for renegotiating identities and combining diverse

Notes for this chapter begin on page 92.

resources and institutional templates. Participation in work groups is often framed by the sentiments of collectivism and sharing, but the groups can contribute to individual accumulation and social differentiation. The chapter investigates the socialities and freedoms that are reproduced in the women's collectivities and the nature of the public spaces that are coming into being. To understand the true nature of the 'sovereignty' of contemporary Kuria businesswomen, attention is paid to particular collectivities and relationships that are responsible for producing the rights and freedoms that constitute this independence.

Although voluntary associations in both their older and more modern forms abound in African communities, their impact on public spaces is far from evident. Multiple institutional models and knowledge practices contribute to the rise of composite sites of authority and association that merge in a 'twilight zone' between the public and private, formal and informal (Lund 2006). Intensifying global flows of capital and information are transforming local conceptualizations of property and person, accelerating mixed proprietorial forms and commoditized notions of personhood (Maurer and Schwab 2006). Public participation in Africa has often been conceptualized by means of abstract human rights, predicated on the autonomy of individuals and communities. However, Englund (2004: 3) calls for more attention to the various "intermediate solidarities" that complicate the individual-society dichotomy in Africa and the need to investigate the "historically specific reasons for modes of belonging and identification." Arguing for a more relational perspective on freedoms, Englund (2006: 10) points out that the definition of "human rights as freedoms" has frequently led to empty, technical conceptualizations of empowerment and participation that are separated from local reproduction of persons and their associational environment.

The Western-centric idea of society as consisting of autonomous individuals separate from the social order assumes a parallel analytical separation between social action and legal norms.[1] This fails to do justice to the relational and positional nature of rights and obligations in many non-Western societies. Several classic studies of African property rights and disputes have demonstrated the material and affective grounding of rights and obligations. Among the Lozi of Southern Africa, the rights that may have seemed to be attributes of unchanging status depended on a series of informal conveyances that affected one's personhood and social reputation (Gluckman 1965). Material transfers served to bring about relationships of obligation where they did not exist before (ibid.: 29). It is therefore one's material connectedness with other people (and its associated expectations and obligations) that gives rise to the concept of rights, rather than moral or jural absolutes. As Shipton (2003: 66) puts it: "Rights are realized only in practice, and with the inclusion and support of other people." Strathern (1992) calls for exploring the indigenous models of relationships that mediate exchange, rather than viewing it as a mechanism of social integration. Drawing attention to the mutual constitution of both objects and persons through exchange can illuminate a profoundly relational nature of value and self-interest. It can also problematize social relations by highlighting conflicts of interest that encourage alternatives.

This chapter suggests that in studying people's material and social connectedness in the current era of proliferating informality, Africanist anthropology stands to benefit from an engagement with certain Melanesian perspectives on relationality. The question of a temporally situated understanding of sociality has been raised in several recent studies on the broader global changes that have affected personhood in both of these geographical areas. Central in this discourse is the concept of the 'partible person' or 'dividual' who is a product of his or her relationships with others, composed of the detached parts of other persons by means of transactions and exchanges (Mosko 2010; Strathern 1988). While it captures culturally relevant dynamics of relationality, the concept can also lead to an essentializing distinction between assumed Western and non-Western or modern and pre-modern modes of personhood (see also LiPuma 1998: 75; Smith 2012: 54). This can result in a presumed replacement of the relationally oriented sociality with individualistic orientation in the conditions of modernity. A focus on the materialities and temporalities involved in interactions with novel exogenous actors and frameworks calls attention to ongoing processes of change, highlighting the diachronic potentialities inherent in the relationality (Mosko 2010) and offering alternatives to evolutionary approaches to personhood and sociality.[2]

The growing complexity of connections and associational pathways also affects the conceptualization of obligations and claims. In modern conditions, 'reciprocal' networks and the claims that they entail have become potentially limitless. The expanding flows of money and technology obscure old categorical divisions and raise new concerns about controlling the movement. As Latour (1993) has noted, the resulting effort toward purification to counteract the growing diffuseness fuels the rise of hidden hybridities and a further expansion of networks. The containment of claims and flows of materiality has become an issue that is central to social relationships and the tools for their study (Strathern 1996). There is an increasing focus on a 'symmetrical anthropology' that brings together human and non-human, technological and social, modern and pre-modern in the same order of analysis (Latour 2005; Riles 2000; Strathern 1996). The treatment of such social contexts often borrows from a sociological approach that "hybridizes its tools of social analysis" (Strathern 1996: 520)— that is, the notion of heterogeneous networks. Whereas conventional networks are based on chains of belonging and cooperation, heterogeneous networks also incorporate material and ideational elements that allow the social analyst to note the points in the web of actors where important connections are revealed and value conversions occur. As an analytical tool, this approach allows us to observe modern and pre-modern, old and new elements through the ways in which they interact and the social effects that they produce.

Paying attention to the processes of containing relationality or 'cutting the network' enables one to study the types of ownership claims or value conversions that can effect the 'gathering up' of flows and the emergence of new relationships. Strathern (1996: 521–522) comments on the ways that networks are operationalized by people pursuing their interests: setting a limit to the expansion renders the network expressible. In a relational setting, that point of summation occurs when the relationships and transactions that constitute a person are laid out and made visible.

This chapter studies new ways of containing relationality that occur among Kuria women entrepreneurs with the integration of novel resources and normative templates into the local economy. Emerging Kuria same-sex institutions—such as women's work and contribution groups, as well as modified woman-to-woman marriages—are examples of such settings where a person is defined in terms of obligations and the claims of others, and where different material items are used to build attachments and social ties. Attention to curtailing these networks enables a better understanding of the processes of negotiating obligations and constructing new relational 'freedoms' that these institutions allow. Situating contemporary women's collective institutions in a historical perspective, the chapter explores Kuria women's creative ways of cutting the flows of relationships and obligations, allowing for considerable independence in the patriarchal system. The focus is on the materially grounded strategies available to women for cutting relationships wrought with conflicts or excessive demands. It is argued that the processes of gathering up material and relationship flows and the value conversions involved in these can also illuminate the tensions between public and domestic sociality, situating the evolving alternative modes of collectivity in a broader context of kinship and personhood.

The Mediating Passageways for Extending the Kuria Person: Historical Perspectives and Recent Transformations

An understanding of Kuria relationality demands a look into the ways that Kuria personhood is constructed through collective activities and materialities of exchange. I suggest that the culturally accepted patterns of 'building a person' in Kuria society affect the forms of collective work and illuminate the dynamics of modern-day mutual help groups. Work activities have been central to personhood in many African cultures. Comaroff and Comaroff (1999) argue that the social production of personhood among the Tswana of South Africa was grounded in the concept of labor. It embraced all activities that "yielded value in the form of persons, things, and relations" (ibid.: 12). Work did not exist as an abstract or alienable quality but was instead "the positive, relational aspect of human social activity; of the making of self and others in the course of everyday life" (ibid.). As an integral aspect of Tswana personhood, work activities entailed building a person through an ongoing succession of actions and exchanges. Personhood was not an ascribed state but rather "a mode of becoming" (ibid.: 4), a complex process that involved agency but was also embedded in relationality. Managing alliances as well as oppositions was an important part of that process (ibid.). Similarly, among Kuria, both warfare and material production provided important settings for extending the person.

Public collective activities and their domestic bearing affect the connections and separations that define social persons. Munn (1983, 1992) has viewed the exchange transactions of kula valuables in Melanesia as intimately connected to building one's social and political influence. Arguing for the connectedness of the individual and larger social levels of these processes, Munn describes the kula exchange as constructing a particular cultural form of spacetime while simultaneously serving as a medium for an actor to control and manipulate that larger structural level. The Gawan person does this by exercising acts of influence and persuasion to control the movement of kula shells in the inter-island chain of circulation, in this way building up one's 'fame'. Munn (1983: 284–288) maintains that having one's name associated with a valued shell shows the effectiveness of one's own agency, with the result that one becomes the focus of others' attempts to influence their actions. By engaging others and extending one's agency, a person also contributes to the larger socio-temporal synthesis of the system of action, generating continuities between the past, the future, and the ongoing present (ibid.: 280).

The intimate connection between politics and constituting persons through exchange calls for a more relational view of political processes and authority, highlighting the politically motivated nature of claim-making. The importance of relationality is also reflected in the construction of political sociality and the practices of 'making' a person among the Kuria of Tanzania. Kuria are semi-pastoralists who occupy the hilly grasslands on the shores of Lake Victoria in northwest Tanzania. According to Ruel (1959, 1962), Kuria clans traditionally had a 'loose' community structure, with public order shaped through informal discussions and public opinion. The clan as a 'moral community' was conditioned by communal rites as well as the 'secret council of elders' (*inchama*). Besides clan and descent segments, various cross-cutting categories—such as generation classes, age grades, and circumcision sets—added to the fluidity of allegiances. They increased contacts between individuals from different localities and age groups, enforcing a cultural idiom of 'extending oneself' that is also expressed in Kuria rituals and cosmology. The concept of personal effectiveness in a historical context of diffuse solidarities was largely a function of Kuria relationships with others.

The cultural principle of extending one's influence over the outside environment as a lifelong process of becoming was symbolically reflected in many facets of Kuria social organization, spatial symbolics, and rituals (Ruel 1997, 2000). The Kuria concept of the person focuses on linkages and interdependence expressed through a central theme of a 'passageway' (*omooyo*) that leads to an 'opening' (*ogotora*). Translated as 'throat' or 'windpipe', through which life-sustaining substances can pass, *omooyo* is a vessel of flow and movement, underlining 'openness' as a condition of life and continuity (Ruel 1997). That dialectical relationship between an orderly inside and an unpredictable outside, indispensable for a person's growth, could be interpreted as a metaphor of the interaction between the Kuria person and the wider social environment, with its diffuse and circumstantial solidarities. In my experience, the concept of *omooyo* was used in everyday conversations to convey the ideas of life force, desire, or motivation. Frequently, the term was used to indicate the 'spiritual strength' that was required for an action, such as working together in a cooperative group.

Omooyo therefore denotes the dimension of a radical relationality in Kuria social experience. Mediation is an important element in the operation of this transactional pathway. Traditionally, most Kuria rituals were mediated by 'ritual elders' (*abagaaka abasubi*) who directed the outside sources of 'fecundity' to contribute to personal and social growth. Engaging both material and social dimensions was vital for a proper securing of growth (Ruel 1985). Through channeling the outside flows and shaping proper distinctions, *omooyo* constituted a conceptual template for mediating socially relevant conversions and recombinations. A Kuria person appeared to be perpetually engaging in different claim-making activities, looking for new exchange partners and modes of extending debt. These have included cattle transactions as well as various labor exchanges. Cattle raiding contributed to the social prestige of a person, which was boosted by recounting one's 'feats' at public gatherings in the form of self-praise songs. Disputes involving cattle frequently escalated into violent incidents between different community groups, with violence seen as an integral part of Kuria personhood.

Mutual help mobilization was another transactional area that enabled a Kuria person to extend his or her influence and expand the mutability of exchange items. Historically, it had created a field of social ties that bonded together people from different territorial settlements, kin groups, and age sets. Collective work was tied to 'making' a person and to the renewal of the social order at large. In the past, collective work was mobilized less regularly and took place mostly within larger social networks based on kinship or age organization. In contrast, present-day Kuria work groups are more permanent, with clearly defined structures and by-laws. Their evolvement has been affected by the wider political-economic context of the country. The history of mutual help in Tanzania reveals that the concepts of 'sharing' and 'working together' have been used to legitimize coercive state reforms, but they have also facilitated the emergence of novel peer work groups. President Julius Nyerere's ideology of *Ujamaa* or Tanzanian socialism was inspired by an idealized vision of a 'traditional' village commune. However, the centrally administered communal production schemes failed to work in most areas. Launched in 1973, forced resettlement efforts, including Operation Mara, destroyed Kuria traditional hilltop settlements. Paradoxically, perhaps, the period of '*Ujamaa* villagization' also witnessed an unprecedented rise in economic associations between people not related by kin, especially among women and youth. Further impetus for the informal sector was provided by escalating economic instabilities and by the decline of the formal sector, which was associated with the oil crisis of the 1970s and with the African debt crisis and the subsequent structural adjustment reforms of the 1980s (Bryceson 2010). This led to a proliferation in mutual aid societies, such as rotating savings and credit schemes, burial societies, street-catering enterprises, retail shops, and various informal associations for traders and market-women (Mbilinyi 1999; Swantz and Tripp 1996).

Informal associations were also flourishing among Kuria people at the time of my field study.[3] Recent social and environmental impacts included a massive socialist villagization resettlement, growing instabilities in resource access due to periodic droughts and floods, economic out-migration to the Serengeti lowlands and the neighboring Mwanza Region, and increasingly violent cattle rustling. As the local economy became more commercialized, work groups gained in significance because of their ability to mediate socially relevant flows and conversions. Novel opportunities for advancement were created using the old idiom of 'working together'. Cash transactions and transfers mixed with flows of other types of resources, resulting in innovative conversions and the blurring of conceptual boundaries (Rodima 2007). The work groups are currently active in agriculture (labor rotations on members' fields and often group farming) and non-agricultural activities (carpentry, brick making, tailoring, handicrafts, retail stalls, and market trade). Frequently incorporating various savings-credit arrangements, the groups may manage a common fund. Another important function of the group is 'selling' work days to outsiders, whereby the group receives cash payments to do work for wealthier members of the community.

During my fieldwork, the groups demonstrated flexibility with regard to their functions and a potential for creative recombinations. Almost every work group practiced more than one economic activity, mixing farming with off-farm projects and group-managed enterprises with individual businesses. Some work groups formed alliances for specific activities, facilitating connections between organizational and spatial scales. Kuria mutual help groups enabled their members to turn routine labor contributions and occasional cash income into more durable sources of wealth and assistance, including group funds, communal field or business enterprises, or large loans through rotating credit arrangements. The activities of the groups with their novel vocabularies and organizational templates served to conventionalize new types of value conversions in the commercializing local economy. The mixing of different templates and norms frequently led to a tension between the indirect and consensus-oriented authority patterns borrowed from Kuria clan organization, on the one hand, and the more recent central authority-oriented elements, on the other.[4] By-laws and other formalized features were subject to contestation and contextual interpretation, further highlighting the fragmented and partial nature of formalization in the work groups.

Work, Gender, and Sociality: Multiplying Obligations to Curtail Claims

In relational contexts, the changing construction of gender mutuality can profoundly affect collective solidarities. Strathern (1988: 74–75) suggests that the tendency in the Western cultural discourse to represent the public-domestic divide through male-female polarization has its underlying assumptions about power and control: women are associated with the domestic realm and are seen as less likely than men to participate in organized collectivities. However, in several recent contexts of changing Melanesian subsistence economies (in Hagen, Vanuatu, and Daulo), women appear to be intensely involved with broader social orientations and novel collective endeavors (ibid.: 76–86). But this does not imply that the new gendered activities have reordered the social domains or increased women's participation in local politics, according to Strathern. Instead of assuming women's empowerment or gender-based polarization as a concomitant of 'modern' changes, it is important to investigate the nature of emerging socialities and their relation to shifts in collective activities.

The Kuria house property complex, with its intriguingly complex gender dynamics, has played a significant role in defining the emerging collectivities. Relationships in these complexes were shaped by the materiality of culturally significant flows of exchange, most notably cattle and labor transfers. The role of bride-wealth cattle as a means of transferring a woman's fertility and labor power was expressed in the cultural principle that 'cattle, not seeds, count' (see also Bernhardsdotter 2001). This provided women with an effective array of materially grounded strategies for cutting relationships wrought with conflict or excessive demands.

Despite widespread polygyny and levirate (whereby a man marries his brother's widow), both men and women in the Kuria household had access to a range of options and resources. The 'extended family household' (*umugi*) that is formed after a man's marriage consists of the 'matrifocal houses' (*inyuumba*) of his wives and daughters-in-law, through which descent and property inheritance are traced. Bride-wealth cattle attached the labor power of daughters-in-law to the houses of their mothers-in-law, enabling the latter to rise in wealth and prestige. This also made it possible for an older woman to 'branch off' from her husband's *umugi* in case of conflicts and effectively set up her own house and lineage with her sons and daughters-in-law (see Bernhardsdotter 2001: 70).

More recently, other options to cut the limiting relationship flows have emerged along the lines of the same cultural principle. One such arrangement is Kuria 'woman-to-woman marriage' (*omokamoona*), which provides the means for a woman who does not have a son to continue her house by attaching daughters-in-law through bride-wealth cattle. The institution of *omokamoona* is quite recent, dating from the beginning of the twentieth century (Rwezaura 1985). Its relevance has grown with the increasing spread of the money economy, with women using cash to purchase cattle and set up their own 'extended families'. It can also serve as a means for divorced or separated women to set up a business enterprise. Although it affords women more economic initiative, contemporary woman-to-woman marriage remains dependent on socially recognized ties and connections. As Rwezaura claims: "[I]n the course of seeking economic autonomy outside the traditional sphere, these women needed the assistance of a number of people to whom they were attached by a recognized kinship bond" (ibid.: 158). It is therefore important to consider the whole field of relevant connections that frame these kin and associational ties in their contemporary forms. Material transfers involving cattle, labor, and crops served as important mechanisms for defining these connections by regulating relationship flows; thus, changes in these processes are central to shaping associational transformations.

Both Kuria women's and men's collective activities have undergone profound changes over the past century. With the decline of traditional hilltop settlements, men's collective activities have become increasingly neighborhood-based as opposed to the broader kin and descent orientation of the past (Ruel 1959). Cattle raiding has been transformed from a community-based institution into a violent and commercial activity (Fleisher 2000). New collective activities have emerged: besides work groups, many men participate in informal 'neighborhood councils' (*litongo*) with their armed vigilante units. Traditional cross-cutting ties still continue to affect same-sex collective action. Groups of youth formed on the basis of circumcision sets frequently participate in cattle rustling and in marauding activities (see also Fleisher 2000; Ruel 2000).

Cattle continue to be recognized as one of the most important kinds of 'wealth' (*oboome*), which is seen as arising from social and material 'fecundity' (*oboronge*). But the ability of cattle to define social bonds and mobilize collective action has changed. While the bride-wealth payment was traditionally completed in installments over the years, a growing preference for a lump sum has emerged in recent decades: "Cattle, which in pre-colonial times were circulating only among elders in a closed system of marital exchanges, could now be purchased by men who had acquired money through a variety of non-traditional economic activities" (Rwezaura 1985: 59). The escalating cattle rustling of the 1980s and 1990s caused a further decline in cattle stocks and bride-wealth rates (see Heald 2005; Kjerland 1995). Although the ownership of cattle may have lost some of its functions as a means of alliance building between social units, it continues to define culturally relevant connections in their reconstituted forms.

Women's collective endeavors have also changed. Women's work groups are a relatively recent phenomenon among Kuria. With the movement of men from cattle rearing to agriculture and their monopoly of local cash crops, women have been pushed into cultivating less profitable crops and have had their workloads increased as well (see Bakema-Boon 1993). Kuria women are the principal agricultural producers, particularly in polygynous settings. The harvest from extended family fields customarily functioned as a shared subsistence reserve and was stored in the homestead's 'granary' (*emonko*). In recent decades, *emonko* production has expanded, accompanied by its individual use by male household heads. The proceeds have been used to obtain cattle and new wives and to fund men's business projects.[5] Changes in the *emonko* savings mechanism have also affected women's collective labor mobilization. *Emonko* production was traditionally dependent on women's work teams that were convened around the maternal houses and consisted of kin and friends (Tobisson 1986: 185). By the time of my fieldwork, the role of these larger ad hoc work teams had diminished in favor of smaller, individually centered mutual labor arrangements that afforded women more flexibility.

Certain parallels to changes in gender-based collective activities can be drawn with a Melanesian case. The decline of traditional collective activities of the Kuria men, such as cattle raiding and inter-clan warfare, can be compared to the abatement of men's cults and the subsequent emergence of smaller-scale business activities among the Daulo of the Eastern Highlands of Papua New Guinea. Strathern (1988: 83) describes how the Daulo women had "taken up the ritual slack" that resulted from the cessation of the men's collective activities and had "created new rituals of regeneration" through their own collective commercial enterprises. These were novel 'savings associations' (*wok meri*) that developed partly as a countermeasure to men's monopoly over resources. The concept of 'nurture' was central to the groups, which remained dependent on interpersonal kinship ties and were modeled on particular kinship relations among the women (ibid.: 84). Despite the public nature of these collectivities, Strathern questions the extent to which they contributed to the creation of a new 'political sociality'. There was no evidence that these activities had "shifted the basic structure of control over household resources" (ibid.: 87) or moved local political action from the male to the female domain. However, the embeddedness of women in domestic sociality and kinship-oriented activities did not mean that they were any less integrated into Daulo society than men.

Belonging to a work group enhanced a Kuria woman's public visibility, but its impacts on her standing as a social person were more complex. The groups could serve as steppingstones toward greater economic security. Participating in several groups at the same time was considered advantageous economically and socially, yet it could also lead to fragmentation and conflicting tasks and liabilities. One's participation in a work group affected one's standing in different networks of obligations. The novel ways that group activities contained and redirected relationship flows offered new opportunities but also presented difficulties in handling the complexities, as revealed in the following case study.

Rhobi was a member of a large 'savings-credit group' (*ikomiti*). She also participated in a smaller 'rotating work contribution group' (*ekesangero*) that was composed of the members of the *ikomiti*. Recently, she became engaged in the sale of *dagaa* (local sardines) and thus had to take long trips to the coastal markets of Lake Victoria in order to bring the fish to highland Tarime. As the new schedule conflicted with her weekly farm work obligations to her *ekesangero*, Rhobi's repeated absences were brought up at an *ikomiti* meeting. She tried to argue that her *ekesangero* relations did not have a direct bearing on her *ikomiti* activities, pointing out that she had also asked her daughter-in-law to work for her occasionally. She even offered to part with the *ekesangero* because of her demanding new schedule. The *ikomiti* secretary argued that since the women of the *ekesangero* had met through their mutual participation in the *ikomiti*, the larger group was partly responsible for their activities. It was decided that Rhobi could not leave the *ekesangero* and must remain in the *ikomiti*, and she ultimately consented to paying her fines.

Rhobi's obligations to one group had a significant effect on her duties to another, and group members refused to recognize the two memberships as separate, highlighting the mutual dependency of these arrangements. Realizing that her identity as a businesswoman active in *dagaa* trade would not have been possible without her *ikomiti* membership, which in turn depended on her participation in the *ekesangero*, Rhobi chose to make alternative arrangements to manage the obligations involved in all three. In the act of paying the fine, she laid out the claims of different groups, individuals, and activities: by making these constitutive relationships visible, she gathered them up to start a new and transformed cycle. This act of cutting revealed the complexity of intersecting group boundaries and relational networks that characterizes contemporary mutual help obligations. In the past, 'festive work parties' or 'beer parties' (*igikinga, irisaga*) that were convened occasionally for labor-intensive tasks served as a venue that made visible which relationships and debts one chose to reciprocate and which social alliances one chose to confirm. With the decline of festive work and the rise of regularly convening reciprocating work groups, the boundaries involved in various networks and groups had become more pronounced. The greater involvement of new types of materiality (e.g., money) and organizational norms (e.g., group by-laws and fines) added to the complexity.

Recent transformations in the socio-temporal field of Kuria labor exchanges are most vividly reflected in the duration and speed of transactions. Munn (1983, 1992) has characterized modalities such as duration, directionality, and succession of exchange transactions as defining the field of kula spacetime, with delayed and long-term versus binary and speedily reciprocated transfers enabling different modes of control for the actors involved. These modalities also bring to light changes in Kuria labor mobilization. Due to the spreading money economy, festive contributions had become increasingly expensive and reciprocation uncertain. The shortening of the duration of the debt repayment cycle reflected the changed capacities of the actors to influence the social field. These changes have also affected the symbolic dimensions of cooperation. According to Munn (1983), one's control over motion in the kula network finds a symbolic expression in a person's social 'fame' as well as in the individually constructed paths of transfer partners. One's fame therefore reflects a "capacity to synthesize kula spacetime through creating a potentiality for future acquisitions" (ibid.: 287) and consists of ongoing "influence-building acts of individuals" (ibid.: 279) to control the movement of the items transacted. The symbols of that influence can be seen as "icons of the acts which produce them" (ibid.: 277). The history of Kuria cooperative labor reflects the processes by which people assert control over the movements of labor contributions. As reciprocating work groups rapidly became icons of emerging patterns for constructing sociality and personhood in local communities during the process of commercialization, they also gained the power to legitimize new categories of actors and modes of action.

Participating in the web of cooperative work was therefore also an important means of building one's personhood, as it provided the opportunity to concentrate upon oneself the socially recognized symbols of personal effectiveness and control. The seemingly 'independent' Kuria businesswomen juggled multiple obligations to various work groups and different kin segments. Most of the local market-women belonged to at least one rotating cash contribution group, and many were members of several. Small daily contributions were part of their morning routine, as they helped each other finance the day's purchases. Many of the already established businesswomen had belonged to a women's contribution group in the past, at least initially, as it was not considered appropriate for a poor woman to be involved in public activities on her own. After they had gained the ability to collaborate with a wider array of exchange partners, several women became involved in informal lending services to their fellow villagers, further expanding their networks of influence. A person's membership in mutual assistance networks enhanced her effectiveness in claim-making and extending debt. In transactions that involved women who belonged to mutual assistance groups, the exchange partners interacted with more specialized sets of constitutive relationships than when dealing with women as members of their kin units. Through group participation, some women from polygynous family settings established themselves, in the absence of their husbands, as heads of their households, managing and supporting their co-wives. Women also occupied other social spaces previously considered 'male' spheres, such as becoming business owners or obtaining the labor power of their daughters-in-law via woman-to-woman marriage.

According to Strathern (1988), Daulo women's *wok meri* (savings groups) did not result in the creation of new spaces of wider political relevance. In contrast, Kuria women's social prestige and relational options were enhanced when they participated in these associations. Through woman-to-woman marriage, or by supporting and mobilizing their co-wives in polygynous marriages, women claimed social roles previously reserved for men only. Work group participation enabled these women to be recognized publicly as entrepreneurs. Many organizational elements of the women's groups originated in clan-based secret councils that have traditionally been an important domain of men's collective action.

Throughout history, creative ways of curtailing the flows of relationships and the obligations involved in these relationships have allowed Kuria women considerable independence in the strictly regimented patriarchal system. These include various practices of breaking off from the extended family household to set up a separate lineage by reliance on the labor of a woman's daughters-in-law, as well as contemporary work and savings associations. More recently, the associational environment has been characterized by a growing lateral expansion of the ties of quasi-kinship (including various innovative polygynous, leviratic, and woman-to-woman marriage arrangements), expressed in an assemblage of contextually emerging connections.

The kind of relationality facilitated by Kuria women's groups enabled them more transformative recombinations of social ties and material resources, with more profound consequences to certain kin ties than in the Daulo case. The Kuria notion of relational growth with its material grounding has some differences from the Melanesian 'composite person' as defined through his or her constitutive relationships. The Kuria person's *omooyo* (passageway), identified with a windpipe through which vital substances flow, was metonymical and body-centered in character. As a vessel for containing material and relationship flows, it was dependent on external mediation. Various types of mediators—expert elders, ritual arrangements, novel institutions, diverse ownership claims, value conversions—became vital in allowing a person to define his or her connections with the outside. *Omooyo* could therefore become a mechanism for creating new freedoms, in accordance with the demands of the changing environment. In the Papua New Guinea Highlands, men's and women's collective activities did not necessarily result in new political spaces or greater gender separation. In local men's cults that make efforts to set up boundaries to facilitate a single-sex collectivity, concerns about the other gender were ever-present through ritual references and artifacts. As that collective association was defined through a reference to "kinship and cross-sex interdependencies," the resulting sociality could be called "collective domesticity" (Strathern 1988: 120–121). Concern with the opposite gender is also present in Kuria same-sex activities, but they are structured somewhat differently. In contrast to Melanesian forms of relational personhood that are elicited through compositions of gendered elements, men's and women's collective activities among the Kuria are facilitated through a cultural focus on the mediating aspects of relationship flows.

Functioning like a vessel for facilitating new connections, the Kuria version of relationality may also contribute to more profound transformations in kin ties and socialities. Kuria mutual help transactions make visible both past and existing relationships, but more importantly they reveal emerging points for new connections. These contain important potentials for transformation that the actors can draw upon in their quest to extend their influence over the environment. The act of cutting the network can therefore be viewed through the lens of creative action—as a focal point in forging new connectivities and the actors' evaluations of these acts. Munn has shown how Gawan attempts to control the spacetime depend on the creation of alliances through diverse obligations that result in the construction of 'levels of value' of varying complexity. The focus is on the acts of practice that are involved in extending the obligations and on people's representations of these acts as an investment of time and effort (see also Graeber 2001: 43–46).

The dynamics of Kuria alliance creation can thus be seen as critical to the social form of mutual help groups. Kuria patterns of mutual help reveal a profound fluidity of group boundaries, with multiple and frequently changing memberships and alliances. Attention to people's actions and motivations when struggling with these obligations gives us useful insights into the dynamics of gathering up relational and material flows. As structures of action, the diverse patterns that Kuria have historically employed for alliance creation are being reinvented through a wide array of social forms, of which the work groups are one of several. Familial and kinship practices of extending obligations for mediated growth affect also the formation of a novel but increasingly widespread mutual assistance arrangement, that is, Kuria woman-to-woman marriage. Rhobi's attempts to untangle her interweaving obligations to increasingly complex relational networks—rather than the formal elements of the work groups—may therefore be more revealing of the power dynamics contained in the present-day mutual help arrangements.

Autonomy through Relationality

A relational approach to Kuria work groups allows for a more comprehensive perspective on contemporary mutual help than the evolutionary assumptions of a linear movement toward growing individualization and formalization. Some earlier ethnographic reports viewed mutual help institutions as transitional formations on a path to Western-style commercialization and suggested that cooperative work initiatives were declining. Recent studies, however, show that collective work groups, with their intermingling of exchange and festive labor elements and diverse resources, continue to be relevant in the commercializing economies of Africa. The rising costs of festive work parties have led to the emergence of alternative cooperative arrangements that are still in line with local norms and values. My research on Kuria work groups demonstrates a mixing of customary and novel loyalties and normative frameworks, in which kin-based idioms of work mobilization intermingle with newer organizational templates and solidarities. This gives rise to hybrid forms of local cooperation and resource management that combine haphazard elements of formalization with a reliance on traditional structural patterns and idioms. The modern Kuria mutual help arrangements are fostering a growing hybridity between individualism and collectivism, resulting in broader open-ended sharing and balanced exchange. The increasing formalization of the organizational structures of the groups is occurring alongside a multiplication and overlapping of obligations and relational networks, fueling novel transformational possibilities.

It is suggested here that the different types of mutual help groups have acted as a culturally accepted means to mediate with 'the outside', helping to integrate new kinds of resource flows that have emerged with the expanding money economy. The growth of a person in Kuria society was the result of a constant reconfiguring of one's personhood through mediated pathways with the outside in order to access substances vital to that growth. Mediators like *abagaaka abasubi* (ritual elders) fulfilled the role of an *omooyo* (channel) through which contact with the outside was effected, and their mediation authorized changes in the flows of transactions, indicating new directions and legitimizing the crossing of classificatory barriers. The value conversions that they facilitated added novel dimensions to both human and material participants. Guyer (2004) has suggested that conversions in the contexts of historically multiple sources of valuation can constitute changes in circulation pathways that have the potential to transform "the attributes of exchange goods in ways that define the social direction of future transactional possibilities" (ibid.: 30). The conversions taking place in the work groups mediated the building of a Kuria person through that individual's regulated connectedness to people and material resources. The changing collective activities were not centered on facilitating individual accumulation in the context of a growing money economy, but on new modes of building a person in culturally accepted ways.

In the processes of limiting relationality and containing material and relationship flows, these points of value conversions should be seen as instrumental. Strathern (1996: 524) suggests that claims over materiality and property ownership can effectively 'truncate' the chain of claimants in heterogeneous networks. Cooperative work mobilization that had been historically an important mechanism for self-extension of the Kuria person therefore became central in mediating the changing environment. Due to their symbolic power as mediators, work groups gained an important role in regulating the impacts of money and its conversions with labor. The groups became vehicles for lifting their members into a higher socio-economic category, which was particularly important for poor women and youth. Kuria work groups provided a means to forge and negotiate relationships that was suited to the demands of the historical moment of commercialization and novel niches. The growth of the money economy affects the social construction of mutuality, but this occurs along the lines of particular aesthetic forms that define emerging connections and separations in the social contexts of relationality.

Kuria personhood is built through interacting with others in socially meaningful ways, which often entails being interwoven in diverse obligation and debt networks and accumulating potential exchange partners. That is why a person strives to belong to several mutual assistance groups and networks at the same time, even though, like Rhobi, they often face conflicting obligations. In order to gain the status of a businesswoman and be able to enter into transactions with the wider community, one has to reveal one's identity as a successful member of a mutual help group. A person without a work group history lacks relevant constitutive relationships and is not accorded the same social rights as others. The Kuria case demonstrates the constitution of a 'sovereign market-woman' through her membership in various cooperative groups: she becomes socially recognized as being 'independent' only through intensive participation in diverse networks and collectivities. As group members, the women are defined by the ties of obligation contained in that membership. When they are engaged in transactions with outsiders, the material obligations that are extended are still impacted by their group participation. By revealing her constitutive relationships as a work group member, the woman's personhood also becomes defined through her relationship with her new trading partner. Kuria persons are thus multiply authored through their activities of claim-making and extending debt.

Kuria women's collectivities, such as work groups and alternative 'marriage' arrangements, are partly a reflection of the diversifying interactional contexts that have become available due to the changes taking place in Tanzanian society. The expanding networks promise women new opportunities but also present more demands, whose containment becomes a focal issue as women strive to find strategies for managing their obligations to kin and associates. In that process, the mechanisms of 'cutting the network' of these ties and obligations (Strathern 1996) become relevant, often finding expression in the formation of various 'hybrids', that is, mixed categories of resources and identities. These include various combinations of cooperative and individual work mixed with cash payments and monetary loans, as well as 'autonomous' businesswomen who are also cooperative group members. The proliferation of these combinations could be associated with the growing role that money plays in Kuria mutual help and kinship institutions, emphasizing and reinforcing categorical divisions (Latour 2005) and thereby encouraging conversions and innovations. The Kuria case shows that in the process of integrating new resources and norms into the local economy, relationality has remained important, although different ways of containing the relationships and cutting the flows may emerge. The interpretive exercise of looking at women's contemporary work arrangements through a focus on relational flows and their containment can thus offer novel perspectives on the proliferating informality in African communities.

Concluding Remarks

The investigation of Melanesian perspectives on personhood provides fruitful insights into the importance of the concept of relationality and the challenges and opportunities that it presents for analyzing social change in Africa. The issues raised in the Melanesian studies, as well as the conceptual tools utilized, contribute to a dynamic, temporally situated understanding of relationality. This is especially relevant at the present time, when relationally diverse social forms are on the rise. The study also revealed some marked differences in the ways that relational personhood is conceptualized in Tanzania and in Melanesia. In contrast to the Melanesian aesthetic of a person as a composite of gendered components, dependent on the assertive elicitation of his or her constituent parts, Kuria personhood seems predicated on facilitating an assemblage of transitory connections and relations through directing material and relationship flows. Diverse mediators and conversions play a central role in building the Kuria person, enabling a wider range of transformative options and revealing a greater capacity for mixed forms. This may also account for the differences in the effects of women's collective activities with regard to wider public spaces and kin ties among the Kuria and Daulo, as discussed above. The broader social significance of women's associations in the Kuria communities remains to be seen, however. On the other hand, growing tensions between the composite and individual aspects of personhood due to the advancing 'capitalist encompassment' have also been noted in some Melanesian ethnographies (e.g., LiPuma 1998). Further explorations of the differences in the perspectives on relational growth in Africa and Melanesia could provide interesting insights into the increasing tensions in local negotiations of collective and individual values and the effects of these processes on emerging public spaces. The comparative study of relationality in its older and newer social forms would benefit from a more 'symmetrical' engagement of Melanesian and Africanist anthropology.

A relational view of Kuria mutual help offers new perspectives on the existential aspects of freedoms and obligations. In such contexts, freedoms may be embedded in networks of mutual obligations that make visible the broader origins of the motivations and interests involved (see also Englund 1999, 2008). In the case of Kuria market-women, freedoms may reside in the very ambiguity between one's sovereignty and group-belonging: the new attribute of 'independence' is a product of rights and obligations that are relational. The Kuria case illustrates the need to situate the evolvement of alternative modes of collectivity and changes in political and domestic sociality in a broader context of personhood and kinship. It underlines the politically motivated nature of domestic claim-making and the highly relational nature of emerging public spaces. A relational view of the person and her obligations enables us to conceptualize with more clarity the 'composite' character of contemporary political and legal institutions in African communities and to understand more comprehensively the historical continuities in local forms of relatedness.

Acknowledgments

Special thanks to the participants and organizers of the workshop "Explorations of Afrinesia: Experimental Approaches to Legal and Political Anthropology in Africa" (Uppsala University, March 2010) and of the African Studies Association 52nd Annual Meeting session "Obligations in the Era of Rights: Individualism and Collectivism Reconsidered" (New Orleans, November 2009) for providing stimulating venues for intellectual collaboration. I would particularly like to thank Knut Christian Myhre, Harri Englund, and two anonymous reviewers for their comments on earlier drafts of this chapter. The fieldwork was supported by the Wenner-Gren Foundation for Anthropological Research, the Sigma XI Foundation, and Brandeis University.

Daivi Rodima-Taylor is a Senior Academic Researcher at the Center for Finance, Law & Policy and a Lecturer at Boston University's Pardee School for Global Development. She leads CFLP's Financial Inclusion work stream and the BU Remittance Task Force. Her research focuses on financial inclusion and access, fiduciary culture, migration and migrant remittances, digital and mobile finance, land and natural resource tenure, and social and institutional innovation. She has taught sustainable development and anthropology, has contributed to international development work in the fields of financial inclusion, participatory planning, and community governance, and has conducted longitudinal ethnographic research in Africa. A Visiting Researcher at BU's African Studies Center, she has published in academic and policy-oriented journals.

Notes

1. For a critique on this topic, see Strathern (1985).
2. The implications of partible personhood have remained influential in many practices involving religious transformations and conversions (Mosko 2010; Robbins 2004; Werbner 2011). According to Werbner (2011: 199), among many Christian charismatics in African Apostolic churches, alternating or variable personhood prevails in the long term. A person is alternatively a dividual and an individual, resulting in a 'twinning' or 'alternate' personhood.
3. The ethnographic research took place in Mara Region of Tanzania over a period of 32 months in 1999–2002. The main research sites included six villages of Tarime District and three villages of Serengeti District.
4. Green (2010) has suggested that the role of the state has remained paramount in the transition to decentralized modes of governance in post-socialist Tanzania and that civil society organizations continue to be shaped by a long-standing focus in local governance on bureaucratic form and hierarchy. Although the Kuria groups were indigenous in their formation, they, too, possessed a variety of unique elements that referenced the bureaucratic form of different socialist and post-socialist organizational structures.
5. See Tobisson (1986) for an analysis of the commercialization of household reserves.

References

Bakema-Boon, Alida. 1993. "A Gender Analysis of the Kuria Society." Research paper, Institute of Social Studies, Wageningen.

Bernhardsdotter, Ann-Britt. 2001. *The Power of Being: The Study of Poverty, Fertility and Sexuality among the Kuria of Kenya and Tanzania*. Uppsala: Acta Universitatis Uppsaliensis.

Bryceson, Deborah. 2010. *How Africa Works: Occupational Change, Identity and Morality*, ed. Deborah Bryceson. Warwickshire: Practical Action Publishing.

Comaroff, John, and Jean Comaroff. 1999. "On Personhood and Anthropological Perspective from Africa." ABF Working Paper 9903, American Bar Foundation, University of Chicago.

Englund, Harri. 1999. "The Self in Self-Interest: Land, Labor and Temporalities in Malawi's Agricultural Change." *Africa* 69, no. 1: 138–159.

Englund, Harri. 2004. "Introduction: Recognizing Identities, Imagining Alternatives." Pp. 1–29 in *Rights and the Politics of Recognition in Africa*, ed. Harri Englund and Felix Nyamnjoh. London: Zed Books.

Englund, Harri. 2006. *Prisoners of Freedom: Human Rights and the African Poor*. Berkeley: University of California Press.

Englund, Harri. 2008. "Extreme Poverty and Existential Obligations: Beyond Morality in the Anthropology of Africa?" *Social Analysis* 52, no. 3: 33–50.

Fleisher, Michael. 2000. *Kuria Cattle Raiders: Violence and Vigilantism on the Tanzania/Kenya Frontier*. Ann Arbor: University of Michigan Press.

Gluckman, Max. 1965. *The Ideas in Barotse Jurisprudence*. New Haven, CT: Yale University Press.

Graeber, David. 2001. *Toward an Anthropological Theory of Value: The False Coin of Our Own Dreams*. New York: Palgrave.

Green, Maia. 2010. "After *Ujamaa*? Cultures of Governance and the Representation of Power in Tanzania." *Social Analysis* 54, no. 1: 15–34.

Guyer, Jane. 2004. *Marginal Gains: Monetary Transactions in Atlantic Africa*. Chicago: University of Chicago Press.

Heald, Suzette. 2005. "State, Law, and Vigilantism in Northern Tanzania." *African Affairs* 105, no. 419: 265–283.

Kjerland, Kirsten. 1995. *Cattle Breed, Shillings Don't: The Belated Incorporation of the AbaKuria into Modern Kenya*. Bergen: University of Bergen.

Latour, Bruno. 1993. *We Have Never Been Modern*. Trans. Catherine Porter. New York: Harvester Wheatsheaf.

Latour, Bruno. 2005. *Reassembling the Social: An Introduction to Actor-Network Theory*. Oxford: Oxford University Press.

LiPuma, Edward. 1998. "Modernity and Forms of Personhood in Melanesia." Pp. 53–79 in *Bodies and Persons: Comparative Perspectives from Africa and Melanesia*, ed. Michael Lambek and Andrew Strathern. Cambridge: Cambridge University Press.

Lund, Christian. 2006. "Twilight Institutions: Public Authority and Local Politics in Africa." *Development and Change* 37, no. 4: 685–705.

Maurer, Bill, and Gabriele Schwab. 2006. "Introduction: The Political and Psychic Economies of Accelerating Possession." Pp. 1–17 in *Accelerating Possession: Global Futures of Property and Personhood*, ed. Bill Maurer and Gabriele Schwab. New York: Columbia University Press.

Mbilinyi, Marjorie. 1999. *Gender and Microenterprise Development in Tanzania*. Report for the Ministry of Women and Community Development, Dar es Salaam, Tanzania.

Mosko, Mark. 2010. "Partible Penitents: Dividual Personhood and Christian Practice in Melanesia and the West." *Journal of the Royal Anthropological Institute* (n.s.) 16, no. 2: 215–240.

Munn, Nancy. 1983. "Gawan Kula: Spatiotemporal Control and the Symbolism of Influence." Pp. 277–308 in *The Kula: New Perspectives on Massim Exchange*, ed. Jerry Leach and Edmund Leach. Cambridge: Cambridge University Press.

Munn, Nancy. 1992. *The Fame of Gawa: A Symbolic Study of Value Transformation in a Massim Society*. Pb. ed. Durham, NC: Duke University Press.

Riles, Annelise. 2000. *The Network Inside Out*. Ann Arbor: University of Michigan Press.

Robbins, Joel. 2004. *Becoming Sinners: Christianity and Moral Torment in a Papua New Guinean Society*. Berkeley: University of California Press.

Rodima, Daivi. 2007. "'Sharing Work and Sharing Money': Cooperative Work Groups and Personhood among the Kuria of Tanzania." PhD diss., Brandeis University.

Ruel, Malcolm. 1959. "The Social Organization of the Kuria: A Fieldwork Report." Unpublished manuscript, Cambridge University.

Ruel, Malcolm. 1962. "Kuria Generation Classes." *Africa* 32, no. 1: 14–37.

Ruel, Malcolm. 1985. "Securing Growth: The Ritual System of an East African People." Unpublished manuscript, Cambridge University.

Ruel, Malcolm. 1997. *Belief, Ritual and the Securing of Life: Reflective Essays on a Bantu Religion*. Leiden: Brill.

Ruel, Malcolm. 2000. "The Kuria Homestead in Space and Time." *Journal of Religion in Africa* 30, no. 1: 62–85.

Rwezaura, Balthazar. 1985. *Traditional Family Law and Change in Tanzania*. Baden-Baden: Nomos Verlag.

Shipton, Parker. 2003. "Legalism and Loyalism: European, African, and Human 'Rights.'" Pp. 45–79 in *At the Risk of Being Heard: Identity, Indigenous Rights, and Postcolonial States*, ed. Bartholomew Dean and Jerome M. Levi. Ann Arbor: University of Michigan Press.

Smith, Karl. 2012. "From Dividual and Individual Selves to Porous Subjects." *Australian Journal of Anthropology* 23, no. 1: 50–64.

Strathern, Marilyn. 1985. "Discovering 'Social Control.'" *Journal of Law and Society* 12, no. 1: 111–134.

Strathern, Marilyn. 1988. *The Gender of the Gift: Problems with Women and Problems with Society in Melanesia*. Berkeley: University of California Press.

Strathern, Marilyn. 1992. "Qualified Value: The Perspective of Gift Exchange." Pp. 169–191 in *Barter, Exchange, and Value: An Anthropological Approach*, ed. Caroline Humphrey and Stephen Hugh-Jones. Cambridge: Cambridge University Press.

Strathern, Marilyn. 1996. "Cutting the Network." *Journal of the Royal Anthropological Institute* (n.s.) 2, no. 3: 517–535.

Swantz, Marja L., and Aili M. Tripp. 1996. *What Went Right in Tanzania: People's Response to Directed Development*. Tanzania: Das es Salaam University Press.

Tobisson, Eva. 1986. *Family Dynamics among the Kuria: Agro-Pastoralists in Northern Tanzania*. Gothenburg: Acta Universitatis Gothoburgensi.

Werbner, Richard. 2011. "The Charismatic Dividual and the Sacred Self." *Journal of Religion in Africa* 41, no. 2: 180–205.

Chapter 5

RETHINKING ETHNOGRAPHIC COMPARISON
Persons and Networks in Africa and Melanesia

Richard Vokes

In 1962, John Barnes opened his now famous article "African Models in the New Guinea Highlands" with the observation that the "peoples of the New Guinea Highlands first became accessible for study at a time when anthropological discussion was dominated by the analyses of political and kinship systems that had recently been made in Africa. Ethnographers working in New Guinea were able to present interim accounts of the poly-segmentary stateless systems of the Highlands with less effort and greater speed by making use of the advances in understanding already achieved by their colleagues who had studied similar systems in Africa. Yet it has become clear that Highland societies fit awkwardly into African moulds" (1962: 5). In so doing, Barnes hoped to define a new agenda for Melanesianist anthropology, one that acknowledged its Africanist intellectual heritage but also broke with what he saw as

Notes for this chapter begin on page 110.

the theoretical restrictions of African models of descent. However, himself an Africanist who had subsequently moved to the Australian National University, it was not Barnes's intention that this new Melanesian work should develop in isolation. On the contrary, the explicit aim of his own piece was to "suggest topics that should form part of [a] detailed comprehensive comparison" (ibid.).

Yet such a comparison between African and Melanesian ethnography never did materialize. In the years following Barnes's publication, the first currents of what became the textualist critique in anthropology led to a growing suspicion of any comparative project of this sort. As Herzfeld (2001) has observed, during the 1970s the discipline began to fracture along lines that are now familiar. On one side were those anthropologists who would today "generally insist on a literal reading of 'the facts' as a necessary precondition for their analyses" and for whom certain sorts of comparison remained valid; on the other side were those who instead "emphasize the literary production of ethnography, [who] prefer to treat factuality as a peculiar form of representation and to focus on the consequences of reflecting on the role of the analyst in creating or constructing it" (ibid.: 259–260). Not only did the latter group quickly become dominant within anthropology, but, more significantly, they were led by a group of scholars working in Melanesia (Alfred Gell, Marilyn Strathern, Roy Wagner, among others). For these scholars, the interpretivist strategy was taken even further, in that reflexivity was for them not just an artifact of ethnographic writing; it was also (or at least should be) immanent in anthropological research itself, that is, in fieldwork. One result—there were others as well—was that the move toward an ever-more tightly defined regionalism became particularly marked in what later became known as the New Melanesian Ethnography (although most of it was produced in the 1970s and 1980s and is therefore not particularly new any more).[1] In addition, though, Africanist anthropology was also becoming increasingly regionalist in orientation at this time, albeit for quite different reasons (see Fardon 1990). Thus, while a number of projects have continued to take in both Africa and Melanesia as their objects of study—most notably Lambek and Strathern (1998)—these have tended to do so by framing their works less as a comparison and more as a 'dialogue' between now increasingly distinct regional traditions (ibid.: 3).

Yet if this describes a general trend in anthropology over the last three decades or so, a more recent body of writing has begun to propose an entirely new type of comparative project. One key proponent of this new project is Herzfeld himself, who argues that in order to overcome the rigid division between what he identifies as the 'fact'-based and the interpretative approaches in anthropology, it is necessary to think in terms of a new type of 'reflexive comparison' (2001: 260).[2] In other words, comparison itself may be cast as less problematic, when it too—like ethnography—is explicitly acknowledged to be informed by the theorist's own positioning, to be an outcome of his/her own social imaginaries. According to Herzfeld, this move also confers upon the anthropologist greater freedom to develop more 'creative' types of comparison that are less bound by predefined spatial metaphors, as in former comparisons of 'localities', 'cultural groups', 'national contexts', 'global processes', and so forth (cf. Peacock 2002), or by specified temporal scales.[3]

In this sense, then, the project of comparison may be conceived less as an attempt to document similarities and differences between peoples who inhabit predefined types of spaces, or who share certain sorts of 'traits' (however these are defined), and more as an attempt to imagine one ethnographic context—as may be defined in terms of any number of spatial or socio-temporal scales—through interpretative strategies developed by anthropologists (and others) working in other places and times. This requires the ethnographer to engender something of a 'double fiction', yet it may also generate particularly powerful insights as a result. Moreover, the New Melanesian Ethnography may be a particularly good body of work to use in a project of this sort, given that it is marked by a reflexive orientation from the outset— perhaps more so than other regional ethnographies of its time. As Gell (1999: 33) has observed of Marilyn Strathern's writing, in particular, its orientation even produces a kind of idealism, one which is "deployed as an interpretative heuristic." For Gell, it is essential to grasp that "the 'Melanesia' of Strathern's discourse (or mine) is not a 'real' place ... or more precisely the site of certain problems of expression and understanding, peculiar to the cultural project of anthropology ... 'Melanesia' stands for an intellectual project rather than a geographical entity because the methodological usefulness of Strathern's interpretative technique is not restricted to (geographic) Melanesia, as opposed to Africa, America, Asia or anywhere else ... Perhaps the best way to think about Strathern's Melanesia ... is to think of Melanesia as the anthropological equivalent of Abbot's Flatland: that is, the setting for a sustained thought experiment. As Strathern pointed out to me (pers. comm.) neither realists or idealists can obtain visas for Flatland, yet both may take profitable if imaginary trips there" (ibid.: 34).

The aim of this chapter is to develop a 'double fiction' of exactly the sort that Herzfeld describes, in which concepts of personhood and sociality in one context—in Highland parts of the Great Lakes region of Eastern Africa, where I have been working for 15 years[4]—are examined through interpretative strategies developed in Melanesia, in the period of its 'new' writing between roughly the 1970s and 1980s. In other words, the key purpose is to engage in Strathern's 'thought experiment' by imagining that the peoples of the African Great Lakes are, in effect, part of Melanesia. The argument which emerges is that Melanesianist strategies for interpreting personhood as the product of shared and gendered substances are applicable to this particular African setting, albeit with modifications. Moreover, Melanesian discussions about 'cutting the network' are also helpful in directing analytical attention to certain types of social action here. However, as I will go on to show, the exercise also highlights the limits of Melanesianist interpretative strategies. In particular, it demonstrates that these strategies do not place sufficient emphasis on the role of non-human actors, especially livestock (in this case the bovine body), in shaping personhood.

The Partible Person

Central to Melanesianist interpretation is the notion of the 'partible person', the 'extended person', or just the 'dividual'. Deriving, ultimately, from the South Asian ethnography of McKim Marriott and Ronald Inden, the concept involves a reading of indigenous ontology in which persons are conceived not as individual or unitary entities but instead as "unique composites of diverse, subtle and gross substances derived ultimately from one source ... divisible into separable particles that may be shared or exchanged with others" (Marriott and Inden, cited in Keen 2006: 516). Over the last 20 years, this idea has been employed across an increasingly wide range of ethnographic contexts, including Australia (Keen 2006), West Africa (Piot 1999), South Asia (Busby 1997), and Amazonia (Vilaça 2011). However, it has become particularly associated with Melanesia, especially following Marilyn Strathern's elaboration of the concept in her *magnum opus* on the New Guinea Highlands, *The Gender of the Gift* (1988). Significantly, Strathern argued that in this Melanesian context all of the 'diverse, subtle, and gross' substances that make up the composite self are invariably marked as gendered. Not only are all bodies conceived of in terms of differential male and female 'parts', but, more importantly, the fact that these substances can be exchanged means that these same bodies can also become differently gendered over time. As a result, images of 'cross-sexing', non-gendering, and androgyny become common in Highland areas, especially in ritual performances. In addition, it means that personhood may also be 'extended' beyond the boundaries of a single body to signify those relations of (substantial) exchanges that exist across multiple bodies.

Therefore, my first question here concerns the extent to which this same interpretative heuristic can be used to elaborate notions of personhood in the African Great Lakes region. Certainly, it is notable that a growing body of recent scholarship by medical anthropologists and others working in this region has demonstrated that a category of 'the person' (sing., *omuntu*; in the abstract, *obuntu*) is in fact generally thought of as a composite of diverse elements and, moreover, that these elements are to some degree gendered. Specifically, selves are understood to be an amalgamation of the two fundamental liquid elements of 'blood' (*eshagama*) and 'water' (*amaizi*). As described by Ugandan medical anthropologist Stella Neema (1994), these elements are made manifest and combined during sexual intercourse through the female menstrual blood (*eshagama y'omukazi*, lit., 'blood of a woman') and the male sperm (*amaizi g'omushaija*, lit., 'water of a man'). When conception occurs, the fetus is taken to be a composite of the two substances and is referred to as *eshagama y'omushaija* (lit., 'blood of a man'), which is in a sense a play on words as it is one of the few contexts in which blood is linguistically marked as specifically male. Following conception, the levels of blood and water contained in the unborn child do not remain constant but may instead be altered through the 'addition' of various other sorts of liquids and substances. For example, a woman may attempt to increase the blood of her unborn child by drinking cold milk (*enyanja*) (cf. ibid.: 66) or by consuming white meat, especially chicken (*enkoko*)—both of which are commonly referred to as 'women's foods'.[5] Similarly, a man may attempt to increase the water of his unborn offspring by 'adding' sperm to it during subsequent sexual intercourse with his pregnant partner. For this reason, regular sexual contact is regarded as particularly important during pregnancy, especially for a couple who hope to produce a boy. A pregnant woman may also try to alter the levels of blood or water within her unborn child by ingesting soups made with various types of herbs, some of which are regarded as women's herbs, others as men's (cf. ibid.: 141–146).[6]

It is not only in unborn children that levels of blood and water may be altered in such ways. The possibilities for changes of this nature are perceived to exist across the entire life-course. For example, following a girl's first menstruation, she is encouraged to consume cold milk (again) and a range of other women's foods, especially boiled eggs, in order to 'replace' the blood that she has lost. Young men regularly consume honey—the procurement of which is a strictly male affair—as a means of 'increasing' their water and, by extension, their sexual potency. In the same way, adult men, by consuming banana wine (*tonto*), which is made from a species of banana called *embiire* that is cultivated only by men, may also increase their water, but at the expense of decreasing their blood. Meanwhile, by consuming cooking bananas (*matookye*), the staple throughout much of southwestern Uganda and beyond, which is usually prepared by women, all persons are able to increase their blood. These same sorts of logic appear to hold for other parts of the Great Lakes region as well. For example, Brad Weiss (1996) has argued that with respect to the Bahaya in neighboring northwestern Tanzania, regarding their category of blood in particular, it is essential to grasp that "[w]ithin the body, according to [local] physiological theories, blood is not simply a constant volume that is altered only by traumatic intervention. Rather, the quality, consistency, and volume of blood is in constant flux in an active body. For example, Haya men and women often refer to the ability of certain foods to 'increase the blood' (in Haya, *okukiza obwamba*; in Swahili, *kuongeza damu*) or to 'decrease the blood' (in Haya, *okuiyao*; in Swahili, *kupunguza*). According to informants, meat (especially organ meats), leafy vegetables, and fish are held to increase blood, while bitter foods like black coffee and citrus fruits will decrease blood" (ibid.: 207).[7]

However, even if the person is conceived of as a composite of substances (which are differentially gendered) and the levels of these substances can be altered through patterns of consumption, this does not appear to result in any particular elaboration of a concomitant idea that persons may therefore be internally partitioned. In this sense, then, Kinyankole notions of personhood may more closely resemble those of South Asia, as described by Busby (1997), who similarly finds that "although the person is not rigidly contained and the body is 'permeable', persons in South Asia are not conceived of as internally divided" (Busby, cited in Keen 2006: 516). Therefore, while Banyankole men who drink cold milk, eat boiled eggs, or prepare *matookye* for cooking, or Banyankole women who eat honey or drink *tonto*—all of which are relatively common transgressions—may be acting inappropriately, they are not understood to be in some sense 'altering' their gendered constitutions. Certainly, elaborate notions of gender changing, such as those described by Strathern for New Guinea, are simply not present in this case, either in ritual or in any other context.

On the other hand, notions of 'extended' personhood certainly are elaborated here. In local understandings, both blood and water can be transferred 'out of' the body, either directly or through a number of metonymic substances. Moreover, such transfers do result in the exchange relations (through which they have taken place) becoming, quite literally, incorporated across the multiple bodies involved. I have described how the exchange of a woman's blood and a man's water during sexual intercourse may become incorporated into the body of an unborn child. Similarly, a woman is believed to transfer part of her own blood (in the form of milk) to her suckling infant during breastfeeding, and it is through this transfer that a maternal bond develops. In addition, it was formerly common for two men to exchange blood in order to form reciprocal bond-partnership (*obukago*), which is often glossed as 'blood brotherhood'. As described in 1890 by the first European traveler to the region, H. M. Stanley, and as documented most fully by the administrator-anthropologist Lukyn-Williams (1934), the rite for creating *obukago* involved both men making an incision in their stomachs, from which blood flowed. The blood from the two men was collected, mixed together (with milk and two coffee beans added as well), and then ingested by both parties. Significantly, the relationship that was formed through this exchange cast each man's personhood as now being incorporated into the body of the other participant. As a result, any (physical) threat to a bond-partner's body was regarded as an imperilment to the self as well, while sexual relations with any of his relatives would be viewed as incest.[8]

There are other, more quotidian ways in which an exchange of substance can extend one's personhood. For example, practically every act of eating is understood to involve an exchange of saliva between bodies, given that everyday consumption involves people eating with their fingers from a communal serving bowl. In this way, a durable bond is formed between all those who eat together, whereby the health and vitality of their separate bodies become interconnected. These concepts are especially marked for women, for whom a category of 'cooking partners' (*abateeki*) carries particular social significance, since cooking partners also regularly eat together. So, too, the drinking of banana wine—or its distilled variant, *waragi*—has a similar effect, given that most alcohol is consumed from communal vessels. Drinking practices engender particularly potent forms of shared sociality among men, given that the alcoholic drinks themselves are derived from the male species of banana, *embiire*. As a result, drinking groups tend to produce a wide array of different types of social networks and informal associations among men, many of which endure over time.

If the maintenance of a healthy body requires a good balance of blood and water, and if both of these are primarily circulated through exchanges that occur between bodies, then the processes of biological and social reproduction become, in a sense, homologous with each other. In other words, if, as medical anthropologist Christopher Taylor (1988: 1344) puts it, "people are produced, in part, by consuming the things they receive as gifts from others," then an ongoing set of exchanges of this sort may be seen not just as optional but as imperative. According to Taylor, in neighboring northwestern Rwanda it is for precisely this reason that a particular emphasis is placed "on *liquids* [as] especially privileged vehicles of this symbolism, because these possess the capacity to *flow*"—that is, to move easily both within and between bodies—and "thus to mediate between distinct realms of being" (ibid.: emphases added).[9] Rwandans therefore place particular importance upon the maintenance of appropriate, or correct, levels of these flows, both within and between bodies. One outcome is that bodily ailments are invariably interpreted in terms of flows being either "lacking or blocked within the body, as in the symptoms of dry mouth, impotence, inadequate vaginal secretion during intercourse, amenorrhea, and insufficient lactation. In other instances, liquid substances [are] reported to leave the body in an uncontrollable manner, as in symptoms of diarrhea, projectile vomiting, the vomiting of blood, the urination of blood, and hemorrhagic menstruation" (ibid.: 1343). In addition, affliction might also be caused by the unintended ingestion of inimical fluids, for example, following an act of poisoning (*uburozi*). By the same logic, Taylor also argues that in the pre-colonial Rwandan context, at least, "the unimpeded flow of these liquids also symbolized the ideal of smoothly proceeding social life—continuity in production, exchange, and fertility" (ibid.: 1344), such that social problems were again represented in an "imagery of anomic flow: liquids flowing uncontrollably as in inundation, or liquids prevented from flowing" (ibid.: 1345).

Moreover, in the pre-colonial context, the social order was understood to be homologous with the cosmological realm as well, as a result of which the model of fluid exchange extended to an image of the cosmos. Thus, the Nyaborongo River occupied a particularly "important place in the ritualization of Rwandan mythology ... Rwandan divine kings spent their lives in bellicose or peaceful meanderings defined by the Nyaburongo's course. In their journeys Rwandan kings established capitals, investing the land with *Imaana*, a term which one could think of either as God, as missionaries have done, or, more accurately, as a 'diffuse fecundating fluid' of celestial origin ... The king's bodily fluids were repositories of *Imaana*, as is evident in the numerous instances in ritual where the king, in order to assure the fertility of Rwanda as a whole, was called upon to copulate with one of his wives. The king's saliva was important as well" (ibid.: 1344). It follows that problems of a cosmological nature were also referenced through a language of flow, especially as this related to, for example, an overabundance of rainfall or, conversely, to a lack of rain (i.e., drought). Although Taylor's arguments here refer primarily to pre-colonial Rwanda, he has elsewhere shown how this same ontology of personal, social, and cosmological flows is still present in more recent Rwandan contexts. For example, in his later work *Sacrifice as Terror*, Taylor (1999) demonstrates how these same concepts of fluid flows—and, more importantly, their corollary ideas of 'anomic flows'—played a significant role in shaping both ideas and actions in the period leading up to and during the Rwandan genocide of 1994.

Controlling Flows

Melanesianist interpretativist strategies are therefore useful for analyzing concepts of personhood in the African Great Lakes region. Yet their application also highlights certain key differences. In particular, as opposed to a Melanesian image of 'unit'-based transactions that may produce internal differentiation, here the emphasis is more on continuous flows of vital substances, which, if harnessed correctly, can result in a sort of outward 'swelling' of the composite person. However, in both cases, Strathern's (1996) further ideas about the creative possibilities of 'cutting the network' provide an important extension. According to Strathern, in all contexts in which bodies and substances/objects are mutually constitutive,[10] particular anxiety appears to emerge around how to define appropriate categorical boundaries between the body and the world and between the (extended) person and the wider social realm, and this in turn generates new possibilities for social production. In other words, in contexts in which bodies can, at least potentially, be endlessly transmuted through the incorporation of inanimate substances/objects and in which personhood may therefore become extended across an infinite number of bodies (at least in theory), people appear to develop a particular concern for defining the boundaries of the body and the limits of their extended networks of exchange.[11] This in turn generates practices that aim to *"control the flow"* of substantial exchanges (A. J. Strathern, cited in ibid.: 519; emphasis in original), practices that may themselves then produce new social forms in their own right.

The significance of these ideas for the Great Lakes example relates to the fact that previous studies of personhood and flow in this region have tended to interpret not only blockages of the body but all other types of blockage as well in entirely negative terms. The logic is that because all forms of flow (other than anomic types of flow) are regarded as healthy, it follows that anything that interrupts them must, by definition, be pathological. In recent years, this argument has been further applied to a range of contemporary social problems. For example, in one of the best known applications of his work, Taylor (1990) has applied precisely this logic to explain the low uptake of condoms among sexually active adults in the Rwandese capital of Kigali. More than 59 percent of the women in his study "claimed that they did not like condoms" (ibid.: 1023). Elsewhere in Africa, Suzette Heald (2006: 33–34) has similarly argued that in parts of Botswana "a flow of bloods, between legitimate sexual partners ... is deemed health-giving in itself. A corollary of this is that the condom could be seen as designed not to prevent infection but as an agent in its origin and spread. In stopping such flows, it was interpreted by traditional doctors and the leaders of spirit churches as a vector of ill-health and disease" (see also Heald 2002).

However, in pursuit of a Melanesian interpretative heuristic, attention is also drawn to other examples in which techniques for cutting the network are cast as socially productive rather than pathological. Key here is to recognize that in my own field site in southwestern Uganda, at least, ideas of extended personhood do engender anxieties about conceptual boundaries, and these concerns also generate practices aimed at controlling the (imperative) flows of blood and water and their associated substances. Moreover, such anxieties and practices relate not only to anomic flows. More importantly, in terms of everyday social action, they are also associated with practically all 'proper', or intended, types of flows as well. In fact, these practices become so ubiquitous that attempts to trace and to control the limits of *all* flows may even be seen as one of the primary dynamics of everyday social life in this setting.

Since eating is understood to involve the exchange of saliva between bodies, everyday discourses about, and interactions involving, food are typically marked by attempts to delimit the network of other persons with whom one might appropriately eat. Therefore, as the women of a household and/or their cooking partners prepare the daily meals (lunch, *kyamushana*, and dinner, *kyakiro*), much of their conversation typically revolves around who, for one reason or another, should not be allowed to eat in their homes. Almost daily, one of the women identifies someone who has recently eaten in the home yet should not have done so—and should be barred from doing so again in the future. To cite just a few examples, complaints will often be heard against neighbors' children, who frequently wander into other people's homes and take food, even though it is not proper for them to do so. Moans will often be heard when the discussion turns to former itinerant workers (*bapakasi*; sing., *mupakasi*) who are still taking lunch in a household, even though they are no longer in that home's employ and so are no longer entitled to eat its food. Gripes will often be directed against the friends of *bapakasi*, who frequently use the occasion of casual visits to their associates to eat from other households' communal plates. While the visits themselves are perfectly legitimate, such eating is not permissible, given that it is only the *mupakasi* him/herself, and not the friend as well, who has a direct connection to a household, which enables the sharing of food. These discourses of cutting the network not only are attached to activities associated with food production but also may become manifest during the meal itself. For example, it is considered right and proper that visitors who do not have substantial relations with any member of the home should excuse themselves when food is served. Moreover, action may be taken when this does not occur. The failure of such visitors to leave may result in the decision of the head of the household to delay the serving of a particular meal.

I can recall more than one occasion during my fieldwork on which a prolonged stay by a visitor with whom no one had substantial relations resulted in dinner being delayed until the visitor had left. On at least three separate occasions, these delays even resulted in all members of the household going to bed on empty stomachs, as the food that had been prepared was not served. In addition, I recorded another incident in which a visitor who had no substantial ties to a homestead decided to eat openly from that home's communal bowl, regardless. In this case, the man's actions resulted in the head of that household (*nyin'eka*) becoming highly irate—to such a degree, in fact, that it was only through the intervention of other household members that the incident did not escalate into a full-blown fight.

Similar ideas about delimiting networks of substantial relations also inform discourses about, and practices involving, the exchange of alcohol. For example, following the purchase of any glass (or other vessel) of *tonto* or *waragi*, close attention is always given to the question of who may, and who may not, drink from it. Yet the issue of who *does* have the right to drink rarely needs much elaboration, given that most drinking networks meet on a more or less daily basis anyway. Therefore, much of the actual discourse surrounding the sharing of drinks focuses, again, on delimiting those who instead may *not* partake of the communal cup. A host of transgressions might be invoked against any existing member of a drinking network as a means of excluding him (it is usually a him) from a particular drinking session. In addition, attempts are made to bar those with whom no pre-existing substantial ties exist from taking part in the sessions. In both instances, such accusations and strategies are invariably met with strenuous denials and other forms of resistance, as a result of which drinking sessions often engender heated debate (which may often bring in all of the patrons who are present in a bar). And yet exclusions of this type are regularly enforced. Indeed, much of the drama of everyday drinking practices derives from people being sometimes physically removed from tables, from people 'storming out' of bars, or even from the various parties actually coming to blows. For example, I recorded one incident in which a 'work party' from Bugamba was traveling to a neighboring village to deliver building supplies for a member who was planning to build a house there, drinking from a communal bottle of *waragi* along the way. When one of the party inadvertently handed the bottle to an outsider, other members of the group erupted in anger, with one telling the outsider: "Tindikurigasa machwante gaawe!" (I cannot lick [share] your saliva!).

Notions of cutting the network attach not only to quotidian food and alcohol exchanges; in addition, they can be observed during more formal occasions. For example, anyone who is hosting a 'feast' (*obugyenyi*) that requires the circulation of often vast quantities of food and alcohol—an integral element of any formal function, such as a baptism party, a 'house-breaking' ceremony, a graduation party, a wedding ceremony, and so forth—will invariably employ a team of 'servers' (*abagabuzi*) to oversee the distribution of food and drink to the dozens, sometimes hundreds, of guests who attend. These servers are ostensibly employed for purposes of making sure that all guests receive an equal share. However, in my experience (and I have attended dozens of this sort of function), much of their time is actually spent policing the distributions to make sure that food and drink are given only to those guests with whom the host household has bona fide substantial ties. Rather than serving food, *abagabuzi* therefore spend much of their time taking food away from uninvited guests. Once the event is over, discussions (sometimes lasting for weeks, or even months, afterward) rate the servers' performance and focus on the identification of people who ate and drank in ways that they should not have done.

In all of these examples, the key point is that concerns over how to define the limits of exchange networks, and the practices that these concerns generate, are in fact socially productive. In other words, it is through their daily conversations over who should and who should not eat in their homes that the women of a household and/or their cooking partners form tight-knit gossip networks. These networks may later be mobilized for social action, for example, in order to bring in the millet harvest in late January, an activity that invariably requires communal labor. Similarly, it is through participation in work parties of the type described above that young men's drinking networks develop a sense of communitas or collective belonging—something that, again, may later be mobilized to serve a variety of ends. So, too, by assisting a household head with the 'server' duties (especially when these are undertaken over a period of time), a young man or woman may form a significant bond with the host's household. I have recorded at least two cases in which the household head later paid his former servers' school fees, and another in which the *nyin'eka* involved appointed the young man his permanent 'housekeeper'. In these ways, then, it is through the very acts of cutting that people, in a sense, come to define the relationships that are relevant to them (cf. Strathern 1995; see also Myhre 2007; Stasch 2011).

"But There Are No Cows in New Guinea"

If Melanesianist strategies yield important insights here, their application to the African Great Lakes context also highlights certain limitations.[12] In particular, if the main aim of the New Melanesian Ethnography was to "dissolve the hierarchical relations between symbol (ritual, myth) and social life, bringing together two domains of analysis hitherto treated separately" (Josephides 1991: 145), then—reflecting the wider theoretical concerns of the discipline at that time—this was mostly pursued through an explication of modes of meaning making ('creativity', and the like) and of processes of social action.[13] One consequence, though, is that much of the work tended to place analytical primacy upon human agents, with non-human actors actualized as indexes of this. For example, in de Coppet's (1994) work among the 'Are'are of the Solomon Islands, the significance of pigs stems from the fact that they are receptacles of human substance, especially human breath. Similarly, in *The Gender of the Gift*, Strathern (1988: 148–159) relates the importance of pigs to the fact that they index a range of human activities and values, including women's labor, men's wealth, a kin group's social status, and so forth. Yet if persons really are constituted in and through shared substance, it follows that greater analytical attention might usefully be paid to non-human actors in their own right and to the ways in which these actors are also active agents of personhood.

This move turns out to be particularly important in the Great Lakes setting, where understandings of *obuntu*, or personhood, certainly are actively shaped by a wide range of non-human actors. For example, if water may be altered through the addition of, say, banana wine, then it follows that the plants on which the bananas grow, the land on which they are planted, the prevailing weather conditions, and many other elements besides are all potentially active agents in the processes through which personhood becomes extended across multiple bodies. However, perhaps the most important non-human agent affecting personhood in this context is that of the bovine body. Not only are concepts of, and practices related to, personhood in the Great Lakes region constantly animated in and through the bovine body, but in various ways cattle also become active agents within this wider 'system'. The centrality of cattle here derives from the belief that human selves are an amalgamation of blood and water, and bovine bodies are of course made up of much greater quantities of these very same substances. In addition to the fact that all cattle have more blood and that cows produce more milk, people are keenly aware that cattle, as ruminants, also produce copious amounts of saliva. Moreover, if human selves can be extended through an exchange of blood, milk, meat, and so forth, then the fact that even a single animal may (potentially at least) provide an abundant supply of all of these things makes them more significant still. Such perceptions are doubtless reinforced in and through practices such as 'milch pastoralism' (which historically, at least, was common throughout southwestern Uganda) and butchery.

These perceptions were impressed on me during an episode that occurred early in my first period of doctoral fieldwork. I had learned that a cow was soon to be slaughtered at a neighbor's home in preparation for a wedding feast, and I took this as a good opportunity to explore local perceptions of the bovine body and the practices associated with its slaughter. As I was unable to attend the killing myself, I invited a young man, who was a member of the 'butcher's gang', to take some pictures of the event, using a camera that I had recently given him. Of the resulting photographs, just over half (13 images) focused primarily on the dead animal's blood, which had been collected in two large calabashes during the killing. One of the images contained nothing more than a close-up shot of only the blood itself (i.e., it was an entirely red frame). The 11 remaining photographs focused on the slaughtered meat. In some images, the meat was being held up by the young men of the butcher's gang, it being customary for each member to receive an often sizable payment of meat for his participation. In others, the uncooked beef was simply laid out on banana leaves on the ground. Moreover, when the photographer later explained the images to me, he repeatedly stressed that his choice of shots was intended to show me just how much blood is collected when a cow is slaughtered and just how much meat is generated.

The bovine body is therefore a significant and powerful vehicle for the transmission of vital substances, and this produces a range of outcomes. For example, cattle blood and saliva are considered to be particularly potent within various medicinal interventions, and bull's semen is especially so regarded. More commonly, the bovine body and its constituent elements objectify personhood across the entire life-course. For instance, it was formerly typical for a new bride's natal kin, in a ceremony called *okuramukanya*, to give her a calf as a means for inducing her first pregnancy (cf. Vokes 2009: 54). In general, men regard cows as a key measure of their socio-economic status. Interestingly, it is quite common for them to refer to their herds with the verb 'to be', as in "Nyin'ente zinana" (lit., "I *am* four cows"), instead of the verb 'to have'. Finally, following a person's death, the bovine body is used to render his/her status visible. A deceased's relatives and neighbors will invariably enter into a (some-times protracted) discussion about how much beef should be served at his/her funeral, the logic being that the greater the deceased's social standing, the more meat should be distributed. Typically, this might result in a baby's burial requiring no meat at all, a young woman's funeral requiring 10 kilos (purchased from a local butchery) to be cooked, and a male elder's burial requiring that a bull be slaughtered.[14]

Moreover, because the processes of biological and social reproduction are homologous with each other, it follows that the bovine body also becomes the 'ultimate' vehicle for fluid exchange. Since notions of personhood here envisage a swelling of the composite person, the bovine body has the potential to amplify greatly this sort of 'intensive quantification'.[15] Precisely because cows are made up of so much blood, milk, and meat, their substance can be distributed to a particularly large number of exchange partners. Both the blood and the milk of just a single cow can be distributed across a potentially limitless network of associates (as long as the milching practices are performed correctly), while the meat of a medium-sized cow can feed several hundred people (as long as it is butchered properly). In addition, of course, cattle have the potential to reproduce themselves. This is most explicitly emphasized in a form of cattle exchange that accompanies men's creation of the highly significant reciprocal bond-partnership discussed above. Following the *obukago* ceremony, one of the bond-partners is expected to give his associate a fertile heifer in an act called *okugaba*. Later, the donor receives a reciprocal gift in the form of that same heifer's first calf (*empaano*). In this way, the two men's extended and ongoing bond is itself effectively made manifest through (i.e., it becomes objectively enacted through) the mechanism of bovine reproduction.

Finally, given that the social order is homologous with the cosmological realm as well, it is noteworthy that cattle exchanges (or exchanges of cattle products) are a common element of origin myths across the Great Lakes. For example, the myths of the Bachwezi, which are common to all of the his-torical kingdoms of Western Uganda, describe a series of foundational cattle exchanges. According to one cycle of legends, the heroic Bachwezi once owned all of the cows on earth. However, when one hero, Mugyenyi, lost his favorite cow to fever, he decided that the earth was no place for demi-gods. After a series of machinations, he led his fellow beings and their herds back to the other world. But one of Mugyenyi's nephews, Wamara, took pity on human-kind. He decided to stay behind on earth and to found a new kingdom, called Kitara. This he did by handing out his own cattle (now the last cattle left on earth), giving one to each of the clans of his new realm (Mungonya 1958).[16] Moreover, the association between cattle and events of cosmological signifi-cance is not limited to myth. Even within everyday speech, it is common for the outcome of major events—such as droughts or other natural disasters, but even periods of political turmoil—to be narrated in terms of the impact that they have had on cattle. In Bugamba, the fact that people were forced to "eat their cattle" following a particular drought in 1999 emphasizes just how bad that event was. A series of mudslides in 2003 destroyed part of a school and a church, as well as at least a dozen homes and various other properties, but the fact that two herds of cattle were almost completely wiped out demonstrates the catastrophic effects. In terms of political unrest, people frequently recall that large numbers of cattle were brought to Bugamba during the period of state breakdown in Uganda (especially during the Amin regime, from 1971 to 1979), partly as a result of geographically distant kin trying to "hide" their cattle wealth in Bugamba's high valleys at that time.

Therefore, if the processes of biological, social, and cosmological reproduction are homologous in this particular ethnographic setting, then cattle are the key homologue across all of these different scales. In other words, rather than being simply reflective (or symbolic) of persons, relations, and cosmological events, the bovine body is an integral part of, and is immanent in, key social relations and cosmological events at various points in the life cycle.[17] It also follows that since cattle are a major vehicle for personhood in these ways, particular anxiety also attaches to ideas about, and practices involving, the 'proper' or anomic flow of cattle and of their products.[18] For example, householders who go to great lengths to ensure that all of their food and drink is shared only with appropriate persons must supervise who does, and who does not, consume the household's milk. If the host of a party typically employs servers to limit the distribution of his/her food and alcohol, then these employees will usually take particular care over how they circulate plates of beef. In this way, it is expected that the 'better cuts' will be reserved for those guests with whom the host has more substantive ties. Even more marked are the ways in which people perceive circulations of the animals themselves. Someone who has received an offer of a cow will rarely accept it outright, even when the person who has pledged it does have an animal immediately available. Instead, the completion of the exchange is delayed while the recipient seeks further reassurance that his potential partner will make a reliable and trustworthy associate. I have recorded one case in which a person postponed the completion of a cattle exchange for almost 3 years, although the two men continued to visit each other's homes and to engage in mutual business activities during that period. In addition, the termination of a cattle exchange is regarded as one of the gravest possible violations. So serious is the return of *okugaba*, in fact, that it requires both the giver and receiver of the heifer to undertake a special ritual of purification, called *ok'wita obukago* (lit., 'to kill *obukago*'). In 15 years working in Bugamba, I have known of only one occasion when this ceremony took place. Finally, cattle theft is regarded as one of the most heinous crimes. The only murder that has taken place in the village during the period of my association with it was committed in revenge for such a theft (at least, this is how the motive was generally perceived).

One critical point is that cattle themselves are also active agents within these processes. In other words, personhood is shaped here not only by human intention, but also by the ways in which cows and bulls themselves behave. If a man measures his socio-economic status through cows, his standing may be suddenly impacted by the death of his animals. For example, during one episode, in 2001, several high-status individuals were rapidly reduced in stature due to an outbreak of foot-and-mouth disease. All of these men continued to own large pieces of land and therefore remained well placed economically, but the diminished number of their livestock was interpreted, both by them and by others, as effecting a disastrous reduction in their social standing. Similarly, if the completion of *obukago* requires the return of *empaano*, then the failure of the original cow to reproduce, for whatever reason, effectively stops that relationship from reaching fruition (and I have known of several occasions when this occurred).

The agency of the cow may even be seen as the pivotal element of the infamous Rwandese practice of cattle exchange known as *ubuhake*. Irrespective of *ubuhake*'s relative political and economic importance in Rwanda, an issue that is much debated in the historical and sociological literature on that country,[19] it is clear that where *ubuhake* did occur, the animal's own actions (or lack thereof) were crucial in making the relationship a primarily hierarchical one. Specifically, it was precisely because the animal given in *ubuhake* was always barren, and therefore could not produce, that no equivalent of *empaano* could ever be made. As a result, the giver of an animal in *ubuhake* was always able to extend his own personhood, while the receiver could not. To return to my own data, it is also the case that if particular attention is invariably paid to controlling the flows of cattle and their products, then the animals themselves have the ability to undermine people's best efforts in this regard. It is quite common—in fact, it is the norm—for village courts to hear cases in which animals have strayed from their owners' fields or from communal cattle tracks (*ebihandigazi*) to destroy other people's fields and crops. Such actions on the part of the animal will often force their owners to enter into new, substantial relationships with the injured parties through payments of compensation. In many cases, events of this sort result in cattle owners having to pay a portion of their own produce over time—in one instance, over a period of more than two years.

Conclusion

The aim of this chapter has been to develop a sustained 'thought experiment', one in which I have attempted to interpret my own reflexively constructed ethnography of southwestern Uganda through the lens of an imagined Melanesia. In other words, my intention has been to a engender a 'double fiction' of the type that Herzfeld calls for, whereby my own field site of Bugamba becomes interpretatively located within an entirely different ethnographic realm. The results have drawn attention to how useful the notion of the 'extended person' might be for understanding concepts of the body, as well as ideas about how the body relates to society and to the world, in this particular setting. They have also suggested an explanatory framework for interpreting a wide range of social practices that appear to be oriented toward containing substantial flows. Finally, the exercise has drawn attention to the role of various non-human actors, especially the bovine body, in shaping concepts of, and practices related to, personhood in the Great Lakes context. While the observation that cattle are important in this part of Africa is not new, of course, an (extended) Melanesian analytics has provided an additional set of insights into why they are so important—that is, because they are the ultimate vehicle for fluid exchange and are therefore particularly potent agents of the 'intensive quantification' of the composite person. Moreover, these insights have important implications for current debates on the history and sociology of the Great Lakes region. In these ways, then, the analysis developed here has demonstrated the possibilities of imaginative comparison and the ongoing relevance of comparativism for anthropology.

Acknowledgments

An earlier version of this chapter was presented at the workshop entitled "Afrinesia: Experimental Approaches to Political and Legal Anthropology," which was held at the Nordic Africa Institute in Uppsala, Sweden, in March 2010. I would like to thank the organizers of the workshop and all of the participants for their useful comments and advice. I would also like to thank Knut Christian Myhre and two anonymous reviewers for their later comments. Of course, any mistakes or omissions remain mine alone.

Richard Vokes is a Senior Lecturer in Anthropology and Development Studies at the University of Adelaide, Australia. He has long-standing research interests in the Great Lakes of East Africa, especially in southwestern Uganda, where he has been conducting ethnographic fieldwork since 2000. He is the author of *Ghosts of Kanungu: Fertility, Secrecy and Exchange in the Great Lakes of East Africa* (2009) and the editor of *Photography in Africa: Ethnographic Perspectives* (2012).

Notes

1. The term 'New Melanesian Ethnography' was first used by Josephides (1991). For a critique of its lack of a wider comparative dimension, see Fardon (2001).
2. Herzfeld (2001) proposes that anthropologists should extend their existing notions of reflexivity beyond ethnography itself to the processes of comparison and also 'theory building'. As he sees it, "comparison only works when it is sensitive to its own context of production: it must be reflexively reflexive" (ibid.: 261).
3. Herzfeld's argument on temporal scales has some similarities with the Comaroffs' discussion in "Ethnography on an Awkward Scale" (Comaroff and Comaroff 2003).
4. In the context of this particular creative comparison, I define the Great Lakes primarily in terms of my own field site, the village of Bugamba, in the Rwampara Hills of southwestern Uganda (which I refer to as the 'Kinyankole' context). I have been working in Bugamba since 2000 and have completed over 30 months of fieldwork

in the locale to date. However, my research also takes in other parts of the region, including some that are not, strictly speaking, Highland areas at all.

5. Milk and chicken are by far the most common ingredients in all types of perinatal remedies.

6. Again, many of these herbs also feature prominently in perinatal medicine.

7. Cf. Myhre's (2007) work in Rombo District, in the Kilimanjaro area.

8. In recent years, and especially since the onset of the HIV/AIDS epidemic, it has become far less common for participants to exchange actual blood during the rites of *obukago*. Nevertheless, the logic of these blood exchanges and of the types of sociality that they engender remains deeply ingrained in local understandings, as they do across all parts of the Great Lakes region (see Vokes 2009: 45n18; cf. Neema 1994: 63; Taylor 1988: 1344).

9. In southwestern Uganda, a majority of the exchanges described above are similarly referred to with the verb 'to flow' (*okujwa*).

10. This description may be equally valid for both Highland New Guinea and the 'Western world', Strathern (1996: 519) argues, in an era of new (especially medical) 'technology'.

11. Incidentally, the local actor's position is mirrored by that of the outside analyst, who is faced with a similar set of problems as to how to define the boundaries of his/ her descriptions of these same human to non-human interactions. See especially Strathern's (1996: 519–521) discussion of 'mixed narratives'.

12. The statement above that opens this section was made by one of my respondents, Arnold Kashuja (a pseudonym), when I discussed an earlier draft of this chapter with him.

13. For example, see Josephides (1991: 146–147) for a discussion on Strathern's ideas of social action.

14. In all instances, the requisite meat is provided by both the deceased's relatives and the members of his/her local 'burial society' (*bataka tweziike*).

15. I would like to thank one of the anonymous reviewers for suggesting this phrase.

16. Similarly, the origin myth of Rwanda narrates how the founding king, Kigwa (who had descended from heaven), "sired three sons—Gatwa, Gahutu and Gatutsi. To choose his successor Kigwa decided to entrust each of his sons with a pot of milk to watch over during the night. When dawn came it turned out that Gatwa had drunk the milk; Gahutu had gone to sleep and spilt his milk; only the watchful Gatutsi had stayed up through the night to keep guard over his milk. To Kigwa this was conclusive evidence that Gatutsi should be his successor and be forever free of menial tasks. Gahutu was his serf. As for Gatwa, who showed himself to be utterly unreliable, his station in society was to be that of a pariah" (Lemarchand 1970: 33).

17. However, it must be stressed that this observation is not, in itself, a comment on the relative economic or political importance of cattle in these societies, which is highly changeable over time. This point emerges in relation to several of the examples already described in which it is the *potential* for the cow or the bull to operate in the ways described that is important, even when no actual (physical) animal is involved. In other words, although it was historically common for a new bride to be given a calf by her natal kin, it is today highly unlikely that any but the wealthiest mother would receive such a sizable gift. Instead, it is more likely that the woman, or her husband, will be given some portion of beef. Similarly, when people talk about 'their herds', they frequently include not only animals currently in their possession or over which they may have usufruct rights, but also any animals that they are 'guaranteed' to earn eventually or that may potentially be given to them some day. For example, one of my respondents in Bugamba, Musinguzi

Fred, who is widely regarded as one of the poorest householders in the village, nevertheless claims to be of high social standing based on his worth in cattle. Although he currently owns no cattle at all, he has four daughters and therefore fully expects to receive eventually a sizable number of beasts in bride price. Even if he were to receive a modest two cows at each daughter's wedding, he would end up with eight animals, which certainly would be a sizable herd. Just as commonly, people may also calculate their worth in cattle with reference to any animals that they might expect to receive one day as gifts, for example, in reciprocity for any animals that either they or members of their patrilineal kin may have previously given out as *okugaba*. Finally, while it is very common for people to pledge cattle publically for exchange (barely a function goes by in which a cow is *not* pledged), the vast majority of these pledges never result in an animal actually changing hands. In all of these ways, then, everyday discourse may continue to revolve around cattle, even when relatively few households actually own any (as is the case in Bugamba).

18. This is already present in the Rwandan origin myth (above), one reading of which is that Gatutsi demonstrated an ability to control the flow of cow's milk, while Bahutu caused it to flow in an anomic way. Meanwhile, Gatwa, by ingesting the milk himself, symbolically stopped it from ever flowing at all.

19. For an introduction to these debates, see Pottier (2002: 110–123).

References

Barnes, John A. 1962. "African Models in the New Guinea Highlands." *Man* 62, no. 1: 5–9.

Busby, Cecilia. 1997. "Permeable and Partible Persons: A Comparative Analysis of Gender and Body in South India and Melanesia." *Journal of the Royal Anthropological Institute* 3, no. 2: 261–278.

Comaroff, Jean, and John Comaroff. 2003. "Ethnography on an Awkward Scale." *Ethnography* 4, no. 2: 147–179.

de Coppet, Daniel. 1994. "'Are'are." Pp. 40–65 in Cecile Barraud, Daniel de Coppet, Andre Iteanu, and Raymond Jamous, *Of Relations and the Dead: Four Societies Viewed from the Angle of Their Exchanges*, trans. Stephen J. Suffern. Oxford: Berg.

Fardon, Richard, ed. 1990. *Localizing Strategies: Regional Traditions of Ethnographic Writing*. Washington, DC: Smithsonian Institution Press.

Fardon, Richard. 2001. "Why Melanesia Is the Only Other." *Times Literary Supplement*, 8 June.

Gell, Alfred. 1999. "Strathernograms, or, the Semiotics of Mixed Metaphors." Pp. 29–75 in Alfred Gell, *The Art of Anthropology: Essays and Diagrams*, ed. Eric Hirsch. London: Athlone Press.

Heald, Suzette. 2002. "It's Never as Easy as ABC: Understandings of AIDS in Botswana." *African Journal of AIDS Research* 1, no. 1: 1–10.

Heald, Suzette. 2006. "Abstain or Die: The Development of HIV/AIDS Policy in Botswana." *Journal of Biosocial Science* 38, no. 1: 29–41.

Herzfeld, Michael. 2001. "Performing Comparisons: Ethnography, Globetrotting, and the Spaces of Social Knowledge." *Journal of Anthropological Research* 57, no. 3: 259–276.

Josephides, Lisette. 1991. "Metaphors, Metathemes, and the Construction of Sociality: A Critique of the New Melanesian Ethnography." *Man* (n.s.) 26, no. 1: 145–161.

Keen, Ian. 2006. "Ancestors, Magic, and Exchange in Yolngu Doctrines: Extensions of the Person in Time and Space." *Journal of the Royal Anthropological Institute* 12, no. 3: 515–530.

Lambek, Michael, and Andrew Strathern, eds. 1998. *Bodies and Persons: Comparative Perspectives from Africa and Melanesia.* Cambridge: Cambridge University Press.

Lemarchand, René. 1970. *Rwanda and Burundi.* New York: Praeger.

Lukyn-Williams, F. 1934. "Blood Brotherhood in Ankole (Omukago)." *Uganda Journal* 2, no. 1: 33–41.

Mungonya, Z. C. K. 1958. "The Bacwezi in Ankole." *Uganda Journal* 22, no. 1: 18–21.

Myhre, Knut Christian. 2007. "Family Resemblances, Practical Interrelations and Material Extensions: Understanding Sexual Prohibitions, Production and Consumption in Kilimanjaro." *Africa* 77, no. 3: 307–330.

Neema, Stella B. 1994. *Mothers and Midwives: Maternity Care Options in Ankole, Southwestern Uganda.* Copenhagen: University of Copenhagen.

Peacock, James. 2002. "Action Comparison: Efforts Towards a Global and Comparative Yet Local and Active Anthropology." Pp. 44–69 in *Anthropology, by Comparison*, ed. Andre Gingrich and Richard G. Fox. New York: Routledge.

Piot, Charles. 1999. *Remotely Global: Village Modernity in West Africa.* Chicago: University of Chicago Press.

Pottier, Johan. 2002. *Re-imagining Rwanda: Conflict, Survival and Disinformation in the Late Twentieth Century.* Cambridge: Cambridge University Press.

Stasch, Rupert. 2011. "Word Avoidance as a Relation-Making Act: A Paradigm for Analysis of Name Utterance Taboos." *Anthropological Quarterly* 84, no. 1: 101–120.

Strathern, Marilyn. 1988. *The Gender of the Gift: Problems with Women and Problems with Society in Melanesia.* Berkeley: University of California Press.

Strathern, Marilyn. 1995. *The Relation: Issues in Complexity and Scale.* Prickly Pear Pamphlet No. 6. Cambridge: Prickley Pear Press.

Strathern, Marilyn. 1996. "Cutting the Network." *Journal of the Royal Anthropological Institute* 2, no. 3: 517–535.

Taylor, Christopher C. 1988. "The Concept of Flow in Rwandan Popular Medicine." *Social Science and Medicine* 27, no. 12: 1343–1348.

Taylor, Christopher C. 1990. "Condoms and Cosmology: The 'Fractal' Person and Sexual Risk in Rwanda." *Social Science and Medicine* 31, no. 9: 1023–1028.

Taylor, Christopher C. 1999. *Sacrifice as Terror: The Rwandan Genocide of 1994.* Oxford: Berg.

Vilaça, Aparecida. 2011. "Dividuality in Amazonia: God, the Devil and the constitution of personhood in Wari Christianity." *Journal of the Royal Anthropological Institute* 17, no. 2: 243–262.

Vokes, Richard. 2009. *Ghosts of Kanungu: Fertility, Secrecy and Exchange in the Great Lakes of East Africa.* Woodbridge: James Currey.

Weiss, Brad. 1996. *The Making and Unmaking of the Haya Lived World: Consumption, Commoditization and Everyday Practice.* Durham, NC: Duke University Press.

Chapter 6

MEMBERING AND DISMEMBERING
The Poetry and Relationality of Animal Bodies in Kilimanjaro

Knut Christian Myhre

People see it as a contradiction but for Albert destruction was the completion of the act of creation: like cutting a string to the right length.

— Tim Parks, *Dreams of Rivers and Seas*

The slaughtering of animals has long allured anthropologists working in Africa and is at the core of classic studies of social life south of the Sahara. According to Malcolm Ruel (1990: 324), however, the ethnography of animal killings has been overdetermined by the notion of 'sacrifice', whose apparent unity derives from its Durkheimian conception as a means of communication between the sacred and the profane, as well as from "the evident drama of the taking of life." The result is that diverse phenomena are lumped together without regard for the different dynamics that are at play in various forms of slaughtering.

Notes for this chapter begin on page 129.

To delimit the concept of sacrifice, Ruel explores and proposes 'non-sacrificial ritual killing' as an alternative notion.[1] Such killings, he claims, are central among eastern Bantu speakers and differ from sacrifice in that they are not directed at a deity. They are moreover bloodless killings, often by means of suffocation: it is the life *in* the animal, not the life *of* the animal, that is of concern (Ruel 1990: 332). In such killings, the animal is not a surrogate whose life is taken in substitution for that of a particular person. Rather, the life in the animal is conferred elsewhere by removing its chyme and transferring it to a particular place or person, whose life and well-being are thereby restored or enhanced. The animal's death is thus not the central concern; it is rather a practical and nearly incidental consequence of the manipulation of life.

Ruel's idea regarding the eversion and conveyance of life from the animal allows for a consideration of the significance of slaughtering and especially the division and distribution of meat. In my view, this is another topic that has been obviated by the concept of sacrifice. Evans-Pritchard (1956: 214), for instance, mentions that the meat from collective sacrifices "is divided among relatives, both paternal and maternal, in traditional portions," but he refrains from describing and analyzing these portions and their significance. Instead, he claims: "I want to make it clear indeed that the cutting up of the victim, the preparation of its flesh, and the eating of it are not parts of the sacrifice. To regard the eating of the animal as part of the sacrificial rite would be like regarding a wedding feast as part of the marriage service in our country" (ibid.: 215).

Evans-Pritchard's claim contrasts with the situation among the Chagga-speaking people of Rombo District on the eastern slopes of Mount Kilimanjaro in Tanzania, where particular attention is accorded to the butchering of animals. Chyme plays a role in some slaughterings in this eastern Bantu-speaking area, but it is far from central to all of them. Rather, the chief concern is the division of the animal, and great care is taken to specify how its different parts belong to particular persons for specific reasons that are justified with reference to certain relationships.

In this chapter, I pursue and extend Ruel's idea concerning the eversion and conveyance of life, using insights from Marilyn Strathern's work on the aesthetic elicitation of relationality in order to analyze the mode and significance of butchering in Rombo.[2] The topic of butchering entails that processes of cutting arise from, and are central to, the ethnographic material itself. However, I furthermore argue that the activity of butchering disrupts and directs flows of bodily power, or *horu*, which constitutes persons, animals, and things and which enables and encompasses a particular form of life. To butcher an animal is therefore a process of cutting and connecting that renders social relations in a specific and particular form. Yet the significance of these practices and processes emerges only when the language involved in butchering is taken into account. In other words, persons, things, and relationships are revealed when their accompanying talk is listened to. Processes similar to those that Strathern describes for Melanesia can hence be identified among the people of Rombo, and these can be understood as transfers or conveyances of life, but only when local claims and justifications are taken into consideration. The language use of the people of Rombo is therefore poetic in James Weiner's (2001) sense that it reveals the conditions of life in a particular place at a particular time. Conjoining language to Strathern's concern with persons, things, and actions cuts the expanse of social life in a manner that makes room for language use in a novel way (Myhre 2012). An engagement with the ethnography from Kilimanjaro thus enables an extension and transformation of Strathern's analytics from Melanesia.

Butchering in Rombo

Despite more than a century of missionization and a nearly wholesale conversion to Roman Catholicism, the people of Rombo regularly and enthusiastically slaughter livestock for more or less ceremonial purposes. The reasons for these slaughterings vary, but they are always performed using precisely the same method, which appears to have a certain historical longevity.[3] A small animal, such as a goat or sheep, is usually thrown down and killed by applying pressure to its muzzle with one's bare hands until it suffocates. The dead animal is then raised as if standing on its legs and stabbed in the chest to drain its blood. The first blood that emerges is made to fall on the ground, while the remainder is gathered in a vessel and put aside for human consumption.

A cow or bull, on the other hand, is always killed by slitting its throat and letting some of its blood spray the ground before the rest is collected for later use. Informants say that cattle were previously stunned by a blow to the head with the back of an axe before their nostrils were stuffed with banana shoots and their muzzles tied with a rope.[4] Nowadays, this is not done, although a cow or bull may be stunned before its throat is cut, and its nostrils are sometimes blocked and its muzzle tied while it is bled, which informants say is done as if the animal were being suffocated.

When the animal is dead and bled, it is rolled onto its back and skinned. The eldest man present is called to make the first cut, which leaves a small piece of fur in the shape of a diamond on the animal's breastbone. The skinning is then usually left to some of the younger men present. When the hide is removed, the animal is placed on top of fresh banana leaves (*machawa*), and the dismemberment of the carcass begins. The first section to be removed is called *mrite*, which consists of the subcutaneous fat and tissue on the lower part of the animal's belly. The *mrite* often includes *taramea*, two tendons that extend down the inside of the hind legs. Genitals are part of a male animal's *mrite*, while the udder is part of a female animal's *mrite*. On some occasions, the *mrite* is allocated to *sumbua*, the share of meat claimed by the people who perform the butchering. On others, however, it is included in *molisa*, the claim of the person who fed and cared for the animal.

Following the *mrite*, the right and left forelegs are removed. According to some, the right foreleg is the claim of the person who provided the animal. Others call it *ngari* and include it in the share of the classificatory brothers (*wanandie*) of the person who conducts the slaughtering.[5] The left foreleg, which is not the claim of anyone, is often divided and added to the other shares of meat from the animal carcass. Otherwise, it is kept and eaten by the members of the homestead where the slaughtering takes place, usually the wife and children of the person who provides the animal.

The section called *ikamba* consists of a triangular-shaped piece of the animal's breast and is removed next. The *ikamba* starts at the throat and includes the digestive tract, a part of the breastbone, and the tips of the ribs, extending down to the topmost half of the animal's belly. The *ikamba* is considered one of the best shares of meat and is the claim of the male elders (*wameku*). The diamond-shaped piece of fur that was created when the elder made the first cut is used to identify this share of meat and enables the male elders' claim. The reason for their claim, people say, is that your father lay on his chest when he conceived you, so you owe him this part of the animal.

The removal of the *ikamba* opens the abdominal cavity and reveals the intestines. The *uanga*, or caul, the fatty net-like membrane that surrounds the intestines, is cut out first. Considered a great delicacy, it is given to the eldest woman of the homestead where the slaughtering takes place. This person is usually the wife or the mother of the man who conducts the slaughtering, and informants say that she is presented with the *uanga* in order to show her how well she has cared for the animal. The appearance of the *uanga* is always a matter of great interest and excitement, since its size and heft indicate the animal's health and strength.

Following the *uanga*, the intestines are pulled out and placed on the ground. The *itasura*, which is the omasum or the ruminant animal's third stomach, is cut off and put aside for the person who removed the animal's manure from the livestock pen and placed it in the banana garden as fertilizer. The recipient is nearly always a woman of the homestead where the slaughtering takes place and is most commonly the wife of the person who conducts the slaughtering. However, it may be someone unrelated to the homestead if the animal was involved in a livestock-lending relationship (*ihara*) or if the homestead in question has a laborer employed. The *itasura* is the only part of the intestines that is someone's specific claim, and it is not uncommon to hear a woman joyfully say "Ngalya itasura [I am eating the *itasura*]" when taking manure out of the pen and putting it in the banana garden. The rest of the intestines is divided up and added to the other shares of meat.

The liver is removed after the intestines, and the smaller caudate lobe, called *imanyamadu* (lit., 'to gather grass or leaves'), is sliced off and given to the person who cut the banana leaves on which the butchering takes place. As with the intestines, the remainder of the liver is shared among the other recipients of the meat.

Next, the head of the animal is cut off and put aside for the person who provided the animal, but first most of the neck (*itingo*) is removed. In the case of an *ihora kaa* ceremony,[6] the *itingo* is shared among the butcherer (*moshisha*) and the married daughters of the homestead (*wana wa kaa*), whose task it is to gather the bloodied banana leaves and the chyme and place them as manure in the banana garden after the slaughtering is over. In the case of smaller events, however, the *wana wa kaa* are often not involved, and thus the *itingo* is the sole claim of the butcherer. The justification for both of these claims is that the recipients' necks hurt from the strain of butchering the animal or of cleaning up afterwards.

After the *itingo* follows the *lhoom*, which consists of a section of the backbone with the three topmost ribs on both sides attached. The ribs are joined by the remaining breastbone and shelter the lungs (*mafori*) and heart (*ngoo*) inside. The *lhoom* is the claim of the *washiki* of the person conducting the slaughtering: this includes both his sisters and his father's sisters due to the skewing of generations in the kinship terminology, which is of the Crow-Omaha kind. In relating this claim, informants emphasize how the *washiki* carried you when you were a child, holding their arms up to show how women hold children against their chests.

Next is *mbari sa ngari* or *mbari sa wanandie*, which consists of the contiguous section of the backbone with four ribs attached on both sides.[7] The *mbari* is the claim of the classificatory brothers of the person who conducts the slaughtering. It is justified by saying that these are the people you may rely on in case of trouble. When explaining this, men puff up their chests in a display of bravado to show that the rib cage is related to strength and courage.[8] If the right foreleg is included in the *mbari*, they also raise their right hand, as if throwing a spear, to justify the link between the right arm and bravery.

The *molisa* (shepherd), or *ulisa* (herd), consists of the next part of the backbone, also with four ribs attached on both sides. As the name indicates, this section belongs to the person who fed and cared for the slaughtered animal. These days, this means finding and cutting fodder for the stall-fed livestock, while previously, when grazing land was available, most of the animals were herded, either in the vicinity of the homesteads or by *bomas* (livestock enclosures) in the plains. Informants say that, at an earlier time, the *molisa* was the claim of one or more of the young men working as shepherds. Now, though, the *molisa* is most commonly claimed by the person who conducts the slaughtering and in whose homestead it takes place. However, if the animal was subject to a lending relationship, the *molisa* is claimed by the person who borrowed and fed the animal. Similarly, if the animal was bought for the occasion, it is the due of the person who provided the money. In one sense, the demise of herding and the practice of stall feeding contract the claims to the *molisa*, while the increased market exchange in livestock enables the extension of such claims in a different direction.

The share that follows consists of a large part of the animal's loin and is called *moongo*, which means, among other things, 'back'. The *moongo* contains the remaining ribs, inside of which the kidneys are attached. It also includes the lower part of the animal's belly and therefore emerges as a large, circular piece of meat. The *moongo* is the claim of the parents of the wife of the person who conducts the slaughtering. It is variously justified with reference to how the wife's mother lay on her back when she conceived or gave birth to her daughter, who became the wife of the person who conducts the slaughtering. Sometimes the claim is also justified with reference to the wife's mother having carried her daughter on her back as an infant.

After the *moongo* comes *ksi*, which consists of the remainder of the animal's loin and is the sole claim of the butcherer. This claim is justified with reference to the pain caused in the lower back from bending over and sitting on one's haunches while butchering. Together with the others involved, the butcherer also has a claim to the *sumbua* and the *itingo*, but the *ksi* is solely his reward for undertaking this task.

Only the hindquarters remain after the removal of the *ksi*. The hind legs are separated by cutting out the rump (*kishingiri*) with the tail attached. The *kishingiri* is the claim of the female elders (*washeku*), and people account for this by saying that the female elders have grandchildren resting on their laps. When stating this, they pat the inside of their legs, thus indicating that this area, rather than the back, is the significant part of the *kishingiri*.

At this point, only the hind legs remain, and from the left one, the *uvaha* is chopped off by means of a machete or an axe. is A large chunk of meat, the *uvaha* is the claim of the mother's brother of the person who conducts the slaughtering. It consists of the ilium, the blade-shaped top of the pelvic bone, located above the hip joint. The *uvaha* is taken from the left hind leg because matrilateral relatives are of the left-hand side (*kumoosoni*). No further justification is given for why the mother's brother should receive precisely this part of the animal's left-hand side, but informants point knowingly to their own pelvic bone, when stating that it belongs to the mother's brother, for reasons that I conjecture below.

Dwelling and the Divisions of Meat

Like Evans-Pritchard, Ruel (1990: 330) does not consider how an animal is butchered and its meat shared, but his claim that the Kuria of Tanzania describe chyme as the 'life' or 'well-being' (*obohoro*) of the animal provides a clue to the division and distribution of meat in Rombo. The Kuria notion of *obohoro* is a cognate of the Chagga concept of *horu*, which can be translated as 'power', 'strength', or 'force'. Constitutive of human capability and well-being, *horu* is converted, transmuted, and exchanged between human beings, domesticated animals, and cultivated plants through the complex and composite activity *ikaa*, or 'dwelling' (Myhre 2007: 321). *Ikaa* consists of the interrelated practices of production, reproduction, and consumption that take specific forms in this setting. The term 'dwelling' is adopted from Ingold (2000, 2008) to designate how *ikaa* enfolds these activities, which unfold particular relational fields that constitute and situate specific beings through their practical engagements with the surroundings, thus enabling and encompassing a distinct form of 'life' (*moo*).

In the context of slaughtering, the crucial matter is the manner in which engagement in the various activities that constitute dwelling figures in the statements that justify and motivate the specific claims to the different parts of the slaughtered animal. In the claims to both the *ikamba* and the *moongo* sections, references are made to how the claimants used the corresponding parts of their bodies in reproductive activities that brought the person who conducts the slaughtering and his wife into being. In a related manner, *lhoom* and *kishingiri* are justified with reference to the use of the corresponding body parts by the claimants in caring for and looking after their siblings and grandchildren. In the case of *lhoom*, the *washiki* are said to have used the same part of their bodies in carrying the person responsible for the slaughtering when he was a child. In the case of *kishingiri*, however, a more general reference is made to female elders caring for their grandchildren and allowing them to rest in their laps. Care and protection of a different kind feature in the justification for the *mbari sa ngari* section, whose enacted connection between the chest, or rib cage, and the claimants' strength and bravery relates this part of the body to the notion of *horu*.

In all these cases, the claimants have engaged in practices of reproduction, care, and protection that concern the existence and well-being of the person who conducts the slaughtering and his wife, as well as their children. These specific people have claims to these particular parts of the animal because they used the corresponding parts of their own bodies to contribute to the birth, capability, and well-being of those who slaughter. In a manner similar to Strathern's (1988: 180) account from Melanesia, the persons who slaughter are the reified effects of the activities and relationships that involve the body parts of the recipients that correspond to their shares of the meat.

Productive practices, meanwhile, motivate claims to some of the other parts of the animal. The claims to the *uanga*, *itasura*, and *molisa* are all justified with reference to engagement in activities that contribute to the slaughtered animal's power and well-being. However, in these cases the relationships between the claimants, their activities, and the specific parts of the animal take different forms. The claim to the *uanga* is based on the person's contribution to the animal's *horu*, which is manifest in its large and thick caul. However, it is based not on the claimant's use of the corresponding part of her own body, but rather on her contribution to the part of the animal that she claims. In the case of the *itasura*, on the other hand, the claim is based neither on her use of the same part of her own body, nor on her contribution to the part of the animal. Instead, her claim is based on the removal of a substance—manure—which passes through the part of the animal that she claims. It is only when the right foreleg is included in the *molisa* that the claim is based on the person's use of the corresponding part of his body, either in herding or cutting fodder for the livestock.

Productive practices also subtend the claims to the *itingo*, *imanyamadu*, and *ksi*. However, in these cases the claims are not based on activities that precede the slaughtering, but rest on practices relating to the butchering itself. In the case of *itingo* and *ksi*, the claims and their justifications resemble those that are based on reproduction. It is because they use and strain their necks and lower backs in butchering and cleaning up that these people may claim these shares of the animal. Their expenditure of *horu* enables claims to parts of the animal that correspond to the parts of their own bodies that they used in expending power. The *imanyamadu* does not involve any practical or material link between the claimant and the parts of the animal. Instead, it involves a link to the object that was utilized in the activity on which the claim is based. In combination, however, the various claims and their justifications relate to different aspects and elements of the compound and composite activity of dwelling. It is the engagement in these practices, whose unfolding relationships constitute persons and animals, that subtends the specific claims of particular persons to certain shares of the meat of the slaughtered animal.

Butchering as Elicitation

As mentioned above, the occasion for slaughtering may vary, but the subject of these events is nearly always different from the person who conducts the slaughtering. In Strathern's (1990: 32) terminology, the latter is the "agent or doer" of the slaughtering, but this person is separate from he or she who occasions it. Furthermore, both of these people differ from the multitude of persons who compel the form that the butchering takes. In other words, the cause and the agent of the slaughtering and those who determine the division and distribution of the slaughtered animal are different persons. The last two are those whose engagement in dwelling contributed to the existence, capability, and well-being of someone else. It is their different expenditures of *horu* that enable them to elicit certain parts of the slaughtered animal, which retain relationships to the use of their own bodies or to the bodies to which they contributed. The animal body thus contains multifarious practical, material, and conceptual relationships, which are cut and drawn out as shares of meat by the people who engage in these relationships. Butchering is therefore an act of elicitation, whereby the particular forms of the different shares of meat objectify and evoke specific relationships. In this way, butchering entails and enacts a certain 'aesthetic', which attests to and makes evident the outcome and effect of preceding actions and relationships (Strathern 1988: 181).

The ability to elicit the different parts of the animal pertains to specific subject positions in relation to the person who conducts the slaughtering. Conversely, the person who conducts the slaughtering makes a claim to be a person of a specific kind in relation to each of those who receive the meat. Each claim to meat is based on a particular relationship and is a single reference point, which compels the person to butcher the animal in a specific way. As an agent, he is made to act on the basis of these multiple relationships and is personified as an objectification of them (Strathern 1988: 273). The mode of butchering is thus the effect of a range of relationships that constitute a network of persons in the classic sense (Barnes 1954). Both bestowing and receiving particular parts of the butchered animal consist in dispositions or capacities to act in certain ways that are constitutive of specific subject positions. Through the processes of butchering, people are distinguished and constituted as persons of specific kinds by virtue of the social relationships that are intrinsic to their personhood (Strathern 1988: 191). The act of cutting the animal is thus a way of separating people on the basis of their various engagements in the activity of dwelling.

A focus on subject positions, however, elides the material character of these processes. In Rombo, meat is considered a substance that contains an abundance of *horu*. The shares of meat are thus prestations of *horu* that are elicited on the basis of relationships in which power has been converted and transferred. Butchering cuts the flow of *horu* and "condense[s] claims into socially manipulable objects of consumption" (Strathern 1996: 527). Consequently, the butchered meat does not simply objectify relationships: it replaces the *horu* provided through those relationships. The meat substitutes for a previous act on the part of the recipient (Strathern 1988: 291) and becomes part of his or her capability and well-being, enabling continued engagement in dwelling. The flow of *horu* is thus turned around to facilitate its extension in a specific direction (Strathern 1996: 528). My friend and assistant Herman recognized this when relating how the *uanga* is given to the female elder of the homestead in order to show her how well she cared for the slaughtered animal and to ensure that she continues to look after the livestock in the same way. The shares of meat are not only based on preceding productive and reproductive relationships, but become part of future engagements in dwelling. In this way, the division and distribution of meat is part of the reproduction and regeneration of persons, things, and social relationships (A. Weiner 1980: 71), which in turn enable these claims to meat.

Dwelling is simultaneously the cause and effect of butchering, making past history and future potential central to the prestations and consumption of meat. Thus, younger men with a claim to the *ngari* often talk excitedly about how they will one day claim and eat the *ikamba*. They envisage moving from one share of meat to another, which they justify with reference to their advancing age, the growth of their children, and the imminent arrival of grandchildren. Similarly, the wife of the person who conducts the slaughtering moves from eating the *itasura* when she is younger to consuming the *kishingiri* after the arrival of her grandchildren. Longevity and reproductive accomplishments enable claims to better shares of meat that take different forms. In turn, these meats replenish the *horu* expended through a long life of dwelling to make possible continued engagement in these activities. Male and female elders can therefore be circumscribed as those with a disposition or capacity to elicit and eat *ikamba* and *kishingiri* based on the multiplicity and duration of their relationships engendered through dwelling. People contribute to the constitution of others and, in turn, claim meat that contributes to their own well-being. Animals are thus taken apart in order to propagate dwelling, which makes butchering a destructive act that is constitutive of social relationships and subjectivities. As in the epigraph above, destruction and creation are linked, which in the case of animal killing involves butchering and cutting the animal in the right way.

Butchering as Decomposition

In this light, butchering is an act of 'decomposition', in which an object is taken apart to reveal its constitutive relationships (Strathern 1992: 245). The claims to the *uanga*, *itasura*, and *molisa* are based on practices and relationships that involve parts of the animal's body or the corresponding part of the claimants' bodies. These parts of the animal objectify relationships that unfold in certain activities, which are constitutive of the slaughtered animal. The relationships are made manifest in the division and distribution of the shares of meat, whose forms reveal the character of the relations involved. Each relationship is literally cut from the animal's body, and so, in being butchered, the animal discloses its own constitutive relationships. Or, rather, the animal compels the butcherer to reveal the relationships that brought it into existence and ensured its good health.

However, butchering divulges more than the relational constitution of the animal. The *ikamba, uvaha, lhoom, ngari, moongo,* and *kishingiri* manifest relationships of reproduction, care, and protection that enable and constitute the persons who dwell in the homestead where the slaughtering takes place. The animal body contains both its own constitutive relationships and those that constitute the human inhabitants of the homestead. The relationships that compel the mode of butchering form a network in an expanded sense (Strathern 1996), where humans and animals engage in exchanges, conversions, and transmutations of *horu*. As I describe elsewhere, stall feeding and banana farming entail mutual relationships between crops and livestock on which human consumption and capability depend (Myhre 2007: 318). These relationships are partly constituted through the human expenditure of *horu*, but they also depend on the participation of livestock. This is illustrated by the procedure called 'to taste with the cow' (*ikombia umbe*), which makes milk available for human consumption.

When a calf is born, the cow's milk is at first reserved for its offspring. But if the supply is ample, an increasing share is milked, kept, and curdled. After a month's time, the curdled milk is added to boiled and mashed bananas to make a dish called *kena*, which the most senior man of the homestead feeds to the calf by means of a long-handled wooden spoon. While doing so, he says, "Ngakombera lunu ngashe" (I have occasioned a taste today, calf). After the calf has tasted the *kena,* the man eats from the same spoon before giving some to his eldest son, who stands by his side. The rest of the *kena* is then shared by the remaining members of the homestead and even invited neighbors and relatives, if the milk is plentiful.

Since the calf has already suckled the milk, the statement made must mean that the calf is given a taste of the food that will be prepared by means of the milk its birth occasioned. The calf's taste of the prepared food makes the milk available for human consumption, while informants say that the failure to perform this act may make the cow's milk dry up prematurely. In this light, *ikombia umbe* is a prestation that elicits the animal's response to human engagement. The act is an example of what Latour (2000: 372) calls 'propositions', or "*offers* made by an entity to relate to another under a certain perspective." Propositions are not necessarily statements, but occasions that allow different entities to articulate and be talked about in certain ways.

Milk and *kena* are both considered high in *horu,* so *ikombia umbe* is a prestation of power in one form that enables its extraction in a related form. The milking process intervenes in the flow of milk between the cow and the calf, diverting it for engagement in the human concerns of cooking and consumption. The prestation then redirects the milk toward the calf in the transformed state of *kena* to include the calf in the exchanges and transmutations of *horu* that enable and activate dwelling. *Ikombia umbe* is thus an offer to relate under the perspective of *horu*, whose acceptance initiates a 'becoming with' between the calf and the homestead's inhabitants, which continues and develops through dwelling to make humans and cattle "messmates, companion species, and significant others to one another" (Haraway 2008: 15). The character of this relationship was recognized by Bruno Gutmann (1924: 136), the missionary and early ethnographer of Kilimanjaro, who described how humans and livestock share a 'unity of life' or *Lebenseinheit*. The prestation cuts and combines the connection between the cow and the calf, as well as between livestock and people, to achieve a particular relationship between animals and humans. It is the relationship forged through this prestation, which develops through continued stall feeding, milking, and cohabitation, that eventually enables the animal to disclose the relationships of dwelling through its decomposition and the elicitation of its different parts.

The exchanges and transformations of *horu* entail that humans and animals are hybrid entities that enfold numerous relationships between heterogeneous elements. In the act of butchering, these relationships are cut from the animal's body as shares of meat, whose forms condense specific gatherings of persons, practices, and objects. As these shares are dispersed among different people, humans and animals are unfolded as networks and rendered as the effects of manifold relationships, whose character and efficacy are evinced in the different forms of the meat. Butchering thus cuts and contains the flow of *horu* to differentiate relationships and situate the various activities of dwelling on a singular scale (Strathern 1996: 526). *Horu* involves a flow of similarity that is cut to differentiate relations and create a network of distinctions (cf. Wagner 1977). Butchering summates these relationships in the animal's body and momentarily cuts and condenses the networks of dwelling (Strathern 1996: 523). Looking at an animal, one can therefore see "a throng of persons, relationships and events" (Strathern 1999: 150).

It follows from this that the singular animal does not substitute for the individual person, in the manner implied by the notion of sacrifice. Rather, the various parts of the animal manifest different relationships that involve a multitude of persons, each of whom has a claim to its meat. No person possesses an exclusive claim to the animal; instead, different persons have diverse interests in the same animal based on multifarious relationships. The case of Rombo hence contravenes Lienhardt's (1960: 13) claim that butchering is based on the common interests of the participants. Rather, it resembles Oboler's (1994: 354) account of the Maasai: "[W]hile a variety of individuals hold a variety of different rights in each animal in a herd, no single individual holds total rights of what we would call ownership." Each animal is subject to a multiplicity of claims from a multitude of persons who elicit different parts of its body on the basis of distinct interests and relationships. To paraphrase Gluckman (1959: 755), each animal is subject to a cluster of claims that define and differentiate particular social relationships.

Indeed, Lienhardt (1961: 23) was on the track of this, arguing that "[p]erhaps the clearest example of the way in which cattle represent not only human beings but human relationships may be seen in the division of the sacrificial meat." Similarly, in his only account of how the Nuer share sacrificial meat, Evans-Pritchard (1951: 153–154) states that "[t]he ideal distribution is usually cited in pairs of relationships in the same manner as the ideal distribution of bridewealth, bloodwealth, and elephant tusks is described: 'The right hindleg is the right of the father's brother and the left hindleg is the right of the mother's brother; the right foreleg is the right of the father's sister and the left foreleg is the right of the mother's sister'; and so forth." James (1990: xvi) points out that these categories amount to a double complementary system, which, in the Nuer case, delimits and classifies a person's kinship relations. It is tempting to suggest that just as its four legs hold up an animal, so these relationships support and sustain the person.

The Nuer account provides a clue for the connection between the *uvaha* and the mother's brother. Both contemporary informants and colonial sources claim that life comes from the left-hand side (*kumoosoni*), where the mother originated (Dundas 1924: 129). A person owes her existence to her mother's brother, who has a claim to the animal's left-hand pelvic bone, which enables the animal to stand upright and walk around. The mother's brother makes possible his sister's son's being, and their relationship is recognized by the sister's son presenting his mother's brother with the *uvaha* of each animal that he slaughters. The *uvaha* testifies to and evidences the single-sex character of this particular relationship by being cut from one side of the animal, in contrast to the other shares of meat, which span both the left- and right-hand sides of the animal.[9]

Cutting Language

The process of decomposition may suggest that the animal is a model of social relationships that prescribes an ideal state of affairs with which actual practice may or may not concur. However, this misconstrues the dynamics involved and assumes that the parts of the animal are representations that are separable from the revealed relationships. Such a view entails the 'hierarchism' inherent in social science, which separates out "a realm of interaction which deals with, modifies and above all comments on other realms" and thus "appear[s] to validate the act of describing behaviour as an endeavour separate from the behaviour itself" (Strathern 1985: 112).

However, the butcherer's claim to meat makes clear that this is not the case. The butcherer has a claim to *ksi* and *itingo* because butchering causes pain in the corresponding parts of his body. The butcherer's claim rests upon his engagement in butchering and evinces his relationship to the animal. Through his claim, the butcherer reveals his own activity and capacity, which consists in cutting and creating the different parts of the animal with their appropriate forms. The curiosity is not that the butcherer's claim is based on his engagement in a particular practice, but that this consists in the activity of decomposition, which is revealed in the shares of meat. It means that the butcherer decomposes butchering as a process of decomposition or that he cuts the activity of cutting. The significant fact is that there is no distinction here between the effort involved, the origin of this effort, and its outcome: the expenditure of *horu*, the relationship it involves, and its effect are simultaneous phenomena. Because the activity, the relationship, and the manifestation coincide, the last cannot be a representation of either of the former. The animal body is therefore neither a model *of* nor a model *for* social relationships.

The statements and justifications that are made in the course of butchering appear in a new light on this basis. These statements are not pronunciations of what ought to be done, but instead form part of the processes of elicitation and decomposition. Indeed, it is only when these statements are taken into consideration and at face value that the activity of butchering emerges as a process of this kind. As a consequence, these statements are not rules or norms that aim to bring certain relationships into existence; instead, they form part of the social relationships and the processes of their objectification. The statements afford animals a role as 'figures' that "collect the people through their invitation to inhabit the corporeal story told in their lineaments" (Haraway 2008: 4). Neither the animals nor the statements that surround and accompany their butchering are extrinsic means of communication that symbolize human relationships. Rather, both partake in relations of mutual constitution: "Figures are not representations or didactic illustrations, but rather material-semiotic nodes or knots in which diverse bodies and meanings coshape one another" (ibid.).

It follows from this that butchering is not just a revelatory practice that makes social relationships visible; it is also an articulatory activity that makes those relationships audible. Butchering not only evinces social relationships but enunciates them as well. In the process of butchering, the participants render for themselves the relationships that constitute dwelling and the homestead, including its human and animal inhabitants. It thus provides a perspective from which persons regard each other and a position from which they relate their relationships. Dismembering the animal is an act of membering, in which people mention and become mindful of their relationships. In the process, they carve the world at the joints to render its constitutive relationships. Butchering is a procedure that makes life appear in an event where people "'feel their way' *through* a world that is itself in motion, continually coming into being through the combined action of human and non-human agencies" (Ingold 2000: 155). Butchering is thus "a contact zone where the outcome, where who is in the world, is at stake" (Haraway 2008: 244). Not only does butchering involve the use of a knife, but the event is itself wielded as a knife to allow the world to appear and be talked about in certain ways (Strathern 1990: 41).

The result of this is that the modality of revelation is wider in the case of Rombo than in that of Melanesia and that the relation encompasses more elements. Strathern's analytic elaborates on persons, things, relationships, and actions, yet the role of language remains undertheorized. Her approach and findings obviously presuppose and draw upon vernacular claims and justifications, but language is silenced in, or cut out of, her conceptual deliberations. Strathern's (1990: 36) view of language is partly based on a Melanesian suspicion, which contrasts with Melanesians' attitude toward things and images: "Talk is always part of an effort to manipulate events and relationships, making motivation ambiguous, whereas—like the revelation of gift [...]—in producing images, people produce the effects by which they know what they themselves really are." Language is a slippery medium that does not readily submit to the same kind of analysis as objects and images. In my view, Strathern's (1999: 257) admitted blind spot regarding the revelatory rationale of display activities and the resultant visibility of social relationships stems from her attitude toward language.

The ethnography from Rombo, on the other hand, shows how persons, things, words, and relationships literally articulate and demonstrates the manner in which this is manifested and enunciated in the process of butchering. The expanse of life is thus cut in a different way to allow for an alternative relation to language. In this respect, it is significant that the Chagga notion of *moo* (life), which the flows of *horu* enable and constitute, is a cognate of the Kuria concept of *omooyo*. According to Ruel (1993: 109), *omooyo* designates the gullet or windpipe, which, as a passage for food, breath, and water, is central to a person's life, health, and well-being (*obohoro*). Munday (cited in ibid.: 104), moreover, describes how, for the nearby Luyia, the cognate *omwoyo* refers to a passage for language and verbal communication, as well as breath and food. The idea that life and language flow along the same passageway entails that language participates in the currents of life and well-being. In the case of Rombo, this means that while *horu* is everted from the animal to extend dwelling (*ikaa*) in certain directions, language simultaneously everts life (*moo*) to render dwelling and its enfolded relationships in a particular form. By interweaving with the vernacular specifications, the shares of meat manifest and enunciate the relationships that constitute this particular form of life. Language entwines with *horu* to interdict its flow of similarity and constitute specific relationships. At the same time, the flows of *horu* cut and stop language, as the shares of meat fulfill claims and turn around the persons who have been drawn out of their homesteads to participate in the slaughtering event. The linguistic, material, and practical forms enfold and emerge from dwelling and life, which thus are extended in specific directions. In Ingold's (2000: 186) words, "the forms people build, whether in the imagination or on the ground, arise within the current of their involved activity, in the specific relational contexts of their practical engagement with their surroundings." In the case of Rombo, *horu* and speech enfold to enable and engender a relational form through which life enunciates itself.

The statements that surround butchering are thus 'poetic' in J. Weiner's sense that they reveal the "existential foundations" of the world (2001: 16) and present things "in their spatial, temporal and historical relation to human concerns" (ibid.: 27). The ethnographic description moreover extends out of these statements from which the analysis is everted. The shares of meat, the vernacular specifications, the ethnographic descriptions, and the anthropological analysis are thus lateral extensions of each other that exist on the same level and scale. The description and analysis do not involve the application of external concepts on a given material, but emerge and telescope out of the material, practical, and linguistic forms that the event of butchering entails and generates. In this way, the ethnography reiterates its subject matter to reveal and declare butchering as a mode of revelation and enunciation that lays bare the conditions of life in a particular place. The exploration of the material from Rombo thus combines and divides vernacular and analytical concepts in a different manner to recast the relationship between data and theory and between ethnography and anthropology (Crook 2007: 218). In this way, the concern for language involves a particular form of 'relation-making' (Crook 2009: 105) that affects both vernacular and anthropological phenomena. It cuts the expanse of social life in a manner that allows language to play itself out as the poetic revelation and enunciation of a particular mode of life. At the same time, it cuts and combines vernacular and analytical languages in a way that enables an alternative relation between them.

Conclusion

By discounting the dominant analytic of sacrifice, Ruel's notion of non-sacrificial ritual killing creates space for considering the significance and meaning of the butchering of animals. As I have argued, this phenomenon is commonly mentioned but rarely explored in Africanist anthropology due to the distortive effects of the concept of sacrifice. The idea of sacrifice as a means of communication between the sacred and the profane, along with the bedazzlement occasioned by animal killings, sustains a focus on the substitutability of human and animal life. It emphasizes how livestock are used to represent and regulate social relations in the domain of religion and ritual, as well as that of kinship and marriage (Evans-Pritchard 1953: 189). Sacrifice concerns the animal's life, but this is distinct from its corporeality. The crucial matter is the relationships between persons and groups that are expressed in terms of animals and are altered by their killing.

In contrast, I have shown that the objective of animal killings in Rombo is not the taking of life, but the taking apart of the animal's body in order to cut, reveal, and extend the social relationships that dwelling enfolds within it. These relationships constitute a mode of life that enables and encompasses animals and humans, whose relations are revealed in the division of the animal and extended through the distribution of its meat. In this conception, relationships are the points of origin, and they are made manifest in forms of action that render persons and things as their effects. Processes similar to those described by Strathern from Melanesia are thus recognizable in Rombo, but only when vernacular statements are taken into consideration. For this reason, language must be added to Strathern's concern with persons, things, actions, and objects (Myhre 2012). Indeed, language participates in, and is integral to, the relationships that constitute and ramify sociality. The ethnography of butchering makes possible forms of representation that exist alongside, and extend out of, vernacular specifications (Myhre 2007: 315), which are therefore on a par with their anthropological representations. These representations do not suppose a hidden order to be revealed behind people's language and deeds; instead, they describe the complex relationality that inheres in the vernacular and is enabled by it. By attending to and including language, this Africanist ethnography achieves a distortive transformation of the analytics developed from Melanesia.

Acknowledgments

Versions of this chapter were presented at the 'Afrinesia' workshop and in departmental seminars at the universities of Bergen and Oslo. I thank Ørnulf Gulbrandsen and Christian Krohn-Hansen for their invitations to hold these seminars. I also extend my gratitude to the participants in all of these events for their remarks and questions. I am furthermore grateful to Harri Englund, Adam Reed, Kathleen Marie Jennings, and two anonymous reviewers for their comments and suggestions. Financial support from Oxford University, the Norwegian Research Council, the German Academic Exchange Service, the Institute for Comparative Research in Human Culture, the Nordic Africa Institute, and the University of Oslo, as well as research permits from the Tanzanian Commission for Science and Technology, are gratefully acknowledged.

Knut Christian Myhre is a researcher attached to the ERC-funded project entitled "Egalitarianism: Forms, Processes, Comparisons" in the Department of Social Anthropology at the University of Bergen. Recent publications include articles in *American Ethnologist*, *Anthropological Theory*, *Journal of the Royal Anthropological Institute*, and *Social Analysis*. He previously held research positions at the University of Oslo, the Nordic Africa Institute, and the Norwegian University of Science and Technology (NTNU).

Notes

1. Ruel's move resembles Strathern's strategy as a lipogrammatic attempt to write ethnography without recourse to a particular concept (Reed 2003: 19), in this case, the notion of sacrifice.
2. Fieldwork was conducted in Rombo District of Kilimanjaro Region between April 2000 and September 2001, October 2006 and January 2007, and August and December 2008, with preliminary and follow-up visits in November 1998, April 2002, April 2003, November 2011, and November 2012.
3. Dundas (1924: 134–135), for instance, describes a system of slaughtering from the early twentieth century that strongly resembles the method currently used in Rombo.
4. These contemporary statements are corroborated by Dundas (1924: 141), who describes how bulls were suffocated in this manner in Rombo.
5. Depending on the occasion of the slaughtering, the relationships involved in the different shares of meat may concern the person on whose behalf the animal is slaughtered, rather than the person who conducts it. This distinction applies particularly in the case of slaughterings performed in connection with burials or subsequent ceremonies on behalf of the deceased. However, the distinction makes no difference to my argument, so for the sake of brevity and simplification, I describe these relationships and events from the perspective whereby the person conducting the slaughtering and its subject coincide.
6. *Ihora kaa* is a large ceremony that 'cools the homestead' and ends the mourning period after burial proceedings.

7. Gutmann (1923: 245) describes *ngari* as 'rib association', which obtains between close brothers (*mngari*), who can claim the first three ribs of any slaughtered cattle. According to Gutmann, *ngari* is the second most important relationship of any household head.

8. The link between strength or force and the rib cage is also contained in Swahili, where the phrase 'to use one's ribs' (*kutumia mabavu*) means to use force or to make someone do something that they otherwise would not do.

9. The only other instance that evidences a single-sex relationship is when the right foreleg is included in the *ngari* share to objectify the agnatic relationship of classificatory brothers.

References

Barnes, John. 1954. "Class and Committees in a Norwegian Island Parish." *Human Relations* 7, no. 1: 39–58.

Crook, Tony. 2007. *Anthropological Knowledge, Secrecy, and Bolivip, Papua New Guinea: Exchanging Skin*. Oxford: Oxford University Press.

Crook, Tony. 2009. "Exchanging Skin: Making a Science of the Relation between Bolivip and Barth." *Social Analysis* 53, no. 2: 94–107.

Dundas, Charles. 1924. *Kilimanjaro and Its People: A History of the Wachagga and Their Laws, Customs and Legends, together with Some Account of the Highest Mountain in Africa*. London: Witherby.

Evans-Pritchard, E. E. 1951. *Kinship and Marriage among the Nuer*. Oxford: Clarendon Press.

Evans-Pritchard, E. E. 1953. "The Sacrificial Role of Cattle among the Nuer." *Africa: Journal of the International African Institute* 23, no. 3: 181–198.

Evans-Pritchard, E. E. 1956. *Nuer Religion*. Oxford: Clarendon Press.

Gluckman, Max. 1959. "The Technical Vocabulary of Barotse Jurisprudence." *American Anthropologist* 61, no. 5: 743–759.

Gutmann, Bruno. 1923. "Die Bindekräfte im Banturechte und ihre Bedeutung für den Erhalt afrikanischen Volkstum." *Zeitschrift für Vergleichende Rechtswissenschaft* 40: 241–258.

Gutmann, Bruno. 1924. "Die Ehrerbietung der Dschagganeger gegen ihre Nutzplannzen und Haustiere." *Archiv für die gesamte Psychologie* 48: 123–146.

Haraway, Donna. 2008. *When Species Meet*. Minneapolis: University of Minnesota Press.

Ingold, Tim. 2000. *The Perception of the Environment: Essays on Livelihood, Dwelling and Skill*. London: Routledge.

Ingold, Tim. 2008. "Anthropology Is Not Ethnography." *Proceedings of the British Academy* 154: 69–92.

James, Wendy. 1990. "Introduction." Pp. ix–xxii in E. E. Evans-Pritchard, *Kinship and Marriage among the Nuer*. Oxford: Oxford University Press.

Latour, Bruno. 2000. "A Well-Articulated Primatology: Reflections of a Fellow-Traveller." Pp. 358–381 in *Primate Encounters: Models of Science, Gender, and Society*, ed. Shirley C. Strum and Linda M. Fedigan. Chicago: University of Chicago Press.

Lienhardt, Godfrey. 1960. "The Sacrificial Society." *The Listener* 64, no. 1632: 13–15.

Lienhardt, Godfrey. 1961. *Divinity and Experience: The Religion of the Dinka*. Oxford: Oxford University Press.

Myhre, Knut Christian. 2007. "Family Resemblances, Practical Interrelations and Material Extensions: Understanding Sexual Prohibitions, Production and Consumption in Kilimanjaro." *Africa* 77, no. 3: 307–330.

Myhre, Knut Christian. 2012. "The Pitch of Ethnography: Language, Relations and the Significance of Listening." *Anthropological Theory* 12, no. 2: 185–208.

Oboler, Regina S. 1994. "The House-Property Complex and African Social Organization." *Africa* 64, no. 3: 342–358.

Reed, Adam. 2003. *Papua New Guinea's Last Place: Experiences of Constraint in a Postcolonial Prison*. New York: Berghahn Books.

Ruel, Malcolm. 1990. "Non-sacrificial Ritual Killing." *Man* 25, no. 2: 323–335.

Ruel, Malcolm. 1993. "Passages and the Person." *Journal of Religion in Africa* 30, no. 1: 98–124.

Strathern, Marilyn. 1985. "Discovering Social Control." *Journal of Law and Society* 12, no. 2: 111–134.

Strathern, Marilyn. 1988. *The Gender of the Gift: Problems with Women and Problems with Society in Melanesia*. Berkeley: University of California Press.

Strathern, Marilyn. 1990. "Artefacts of History: Events and the Interpretation of Images." Pp. 25–44 in *Culture and History in the Pacific*, ed. Jukka Siikala. Helsinki: Finnish Anthropological Society.

Strathern, Marilyn. 1992. "The Decomposition of an Event." *Cultural Anthropology* 7, no. 2: 244–254.

Strathern, Marilyn. 1996. "Cutting the Network." *Journal of the Royal Anthropological Institute* (n.s.) 2, no. 3: 517–535.

Strathern, Marilyn. 1999. *Property, Substance and Effect: Anthropological Essays on Persons and Things*. London: Athlone Press.

Wagner, Roy. 1977. "Analogic Kinship: A Daribi Example." *American Ethnologist* 4, no. 4: 623–642.

Weiner, Annette B. 1980. "Reproduction: A Replacement for Reciprocity." *American Ethnologist* 7, no. 1: 71–85.

Weiner, James F. 2001. *Tree Leaf Talk: A Heideggerian Anthropology*. Oxford: Berg.

Chapter 7

THE PLACE OF THEORY
Rights, Networks, and Ethnographic Comparison

Harri Englund and Thomas Yarrow

The New Melanesian Ethnography, a phrase coined over 20 years ago (Josephides 1991), is no longer so new. The reason is the rapid increase, since the 1990s, of anthropological studies that have sought to address topics neglected by this literature. This work has been at the forefront of making the anthropology of Melanesia investigate the effects of colonialism, post-colonialism, nationalism, commodification, Christianity, and so on (see, e.g., Foster 2008; Gewertz and Errington 1999; Knauft 1999; Robbins 2004). As Marilyn Strathern admitted in an interview with *Cambridge Anthropology* in the mid-1990s, she was a 'snob' during her first fieldwork in the 1960s and stayed clear of Christian churches (Czegledy 1992: 5). She did so despite the fact that the Lutheran Church had become established in her research area before she commenced fieldwork there.

Notes for this chapter begin on page 146.

The obvious benefits of expanding the thematic scope of Melanesianist anthropology should not, however, result in throwing the proverbial baby out with the bathwater. A designation used more by its critics than its practitioners, the New Melanesian Ethnography transcended, even as it anticipated, the anthropological auto-critique of the 1980s. Disciplinary certainties about the ethnographer's authority had begun to crumble before *Writing Culture* (Clifford and Marcus 1986) was published, because the ethnographic work by authors such as Wagner (1974) and Strathern (1980) had started to ask unsettling questions about the assumptions that anthropologists had conventionally brought to bear on their study of social groups and gender. Unlike some of the reflexive critique that was to follow, however, the New Melanesian Ethnography presented ethnography as a form of theory, or rather, to put it more directly, refused a straightforward distinction between theory and ethnography. Reflexivity was seen as a function of anthropological fieldwork, not a practice abstracted from it.

The reflexive turn anticipated by the New Melanesian Ethnography has taken several directions in anthropology, but its subtle relationship between ethnography and theory has not received the attention it deserves. Far too often places come to stand for theories, as though 'composite person', for example, represented a theory generated by fieldwork in Melanesia, just as 'segmentary lineage' once appeared as the distinctive contribution of Africanist anthropology (see, e.g., Kuper 2005: 163–178). These two notions are, of course, particularly revealing for the way in which anthropological concepts can and do travel despite their origin in specific ethnographic locations. The concept of the 'dividual', which gave rise to 'composite person', was first coined in the anthropology of India (Marriott 1976) and has been used productively in the ethnographies of East Africa (Sanders 2008) and West Africa (Piot 1999). 'Segmentary lineage', in turn, had appeared in the study of Arabic societies before its prominence in Africanist anthropology (Dresch 1988). This facility by which concepts travel across ethnographic regions must not, however, be confused with the expectation that they stay intact when they do so. The key lesson of the New Melanesian Ethnography was to make explicit the origins of theory. It involved a degree of specificity about the processes of conceptualization and description that a simple application of concepts borrowed from elsewhere can only undermine.

Robbins has suggested that at the heart of the New Melanesian Ethnography was the injunction that "theory be made out of the materials that one finds in the same *place* one finds one's data" (2006: 172; emphasis added). It is worth exploring whether this injunction properly describes the theory-ethnography interdependence. It certainly conveys a sense of situated, reflexive knowledge production for which the New Melanesian Ethnography is justly renowned. Insofar as propositions, claims, and arguments can be recognized as being 'theoretical' only if they afford a perspective on other situations than the one with which they are initially associated, the injunction would also seem to acknowledge the capacity of ethnographically grounded concepts and ideas to travel. But the emphasis on place may inadvertently introduce a measure of cultural relativism into the explication of the New Melanesian Ethnography. Once again, place—and the localized fieldwork it seems to demand—appears as the source of anthropological theory, whereas a close reading of works by authors such as Wagner and Strathern reveals a more complex set of conceptual and pragmatic debts that give rise to fresh theory. Fieldwork is the crucial component of this mode of knowledge production. But Wagner's ([1975] 1981) idea of culture and Strathern's (1988b) work on property and gender necessarily refer to modes of knowing and experiencing beyond the instances they ostensibly enunciate. How else would ideas about personhood described in ethnographies on Papua New Guinea provide a productive standpoint for the study of new reproductive technologies in Europe (see Strathern 1992)?

In this chapter, we seek to reclaim the reflexivity of the New Melanesian Ethnography by exploring its insights into relational knowledge production in the contexts of discourses pertaining to 'relational rights' and 'networks'. After considering how 'Africa' has been the recipient of 'Melanesian' theories without becoming the donor of theoretical counter-gifts, we attend to Robbins's (2010) notion of the rights of relationships and to Riles's (2001) work on the network. In both cases, we insist that the importance of perspectives deriving from the New Melanesian Ethnography is not in the elaboration of theories to be applied to novel African contexts. Rather, the inspiration of those perspectives lies in demonstrating how the development of anthropological ideas necessarily exceeds place-bound theorization. In this understanding, 'place' emerges as an artifact of ethnographic comparison rather than as a stable, empirical reality on which theory is subsequently built. Although skeptical of the way in which 'culture areas' have been demarcated by anthropology and related disciplines, our argument by no means denies the analytical utility of constructions such as 'Africa'. On the contrary, as we discuss in our concluding section, our argument can reinvigorate regional scholarship as anthropology's key means of placing limits on its theories.[1]

Comparisons Compared

For much of the twentieth century, it has been axiomatic in anthropology (and, indeed, within the social sciences more broadly) that while theories change and evolve, fieldwork stands still. Fardon (1990b) notes that Malinowski the fieldworker remains a part of our ethnographic present, even as theories are located in the past as part of an evolving disciplinary history. Despite over two decades of critical deconstruction of stable and bounded conceptualizations of 'the field', fieldwork is still commonly afforded epistemic primacy as the empirical basis on which theories are subsequently built. This conception can be understood as a component of a wider 'multicultural' ontology of a singular 'natural' world that can be multiply (culturally and subjectively) perceived (Viveiros de Castro 1998). While theory is often regarded as more general in its spatial applicability, it is usually perceived as more temporally specific.

Strathern (1990) calls this assumption into question, suggesting that in order to understand the process by which places are assigned essential features, we need to apprehend the analytic framing of regions within wider anthropological discourses. Analytic models, built up through a complex process of synthesis, are localized and regionalized at the moment they are transferred. For example, Mauss's theory of the gift emerged in relation to the potlatch, the *hau*, the Indian gift, and the kula. This complex conceptual history is foreclosed, however, when the ideas are located in relation to different regionalized literatures, and thus we arrive at the idea of the gift as Melanesian. In his discussion of 'gate-keeping concepts', Appadurai (1986, 1988) contends that this process of theoretical regionalization has taken place across a range of spatial and historical contexts. Similarly, Fardon (1990b) notes how regions become exemplars of types, features, and phenomena: lineage in Africa, exchange in Melanesia, caste in India, Aboriginal marriage in Australia, and so on.

If theories have been localized by reference to a range of ethnographic contexts, not all are equally successful. Some theories travel while others stay put. Strathern (1990) accounts for this discrepancy as a matter of the extent to which different regional literatures have been drawn into the rearrangement of the existing canon of anthropological thinking. She refers to this conceptual reordering as a 'negative strategy': anthropological knowledge is extended and reconfigured through encounters that undermine or 'trouble' the very conceptual framework through which comparisons and translations take place.

Therefore, the success of 'African' structural-functionalist descent theory is located in its capacity to trouble existing anthropological concepts and, in turn, a wider set of Euro-American understandings. Although we might now be able to highlight the ethnocentric assumptions on which such theories were based, the elucidation of a distinct relationship between kinship and polity acted to overturn existing ideas about the distinctiveness of family and government. Transported to the highlands of New Guinea, these ideas of descent and linearity initially framed the region as an instance of this conceptual framework. This formulation provided the context whereby later critiques drew on Melanesian conceptions of the gift to invert African understandings of descent. Later still, these ideas were used to question assumptions latent in Marxist understandings of a commodity logic. Thus, Strathern (1990) suggests that anthropologists working in Melanesia have inverted anthropological concepts through the creation of ethnographic artifacts that appear to originate in Melanesia. However, the success of these objects does not straightforwardly derive from the region. Strathern argues that "instead we have to understand that the character of the Melanesian economy is most efficiently grasped through rearranging a particular set of Western concepts, namely those to do with commodification. But the rearrangement can only take place for creative effect when it is seen to be motivated by an external context that stands to it as an *independent* source. For the inversion not to appear as an internal self-referential move ..., it must appear to have been elicited by conditions outside internal construction" (ibid.: 210).

An important implication of this insight is that theory and place cannot be understood as the abstract to the concrete or as the shifting to the stable (Holbraad and Pedersen 2009). Rather, the distinction between theory and place is itself an artifact of the way in which we locate the sources of ideas that, in practice, derive from complex engagements—including with other anthropologists and those whom we meet while doing fieldwork. This view also means accepting that our sense of a world comprised of distinct regions is an artifact of comparison, not the sine qua non from which theory is subsequently built. Places are not the basic units from which comparison proceeds: the concreteness of particular concepts (their location as self-evident facts about particular places) emerges through comparison with other places and through the complex intertextual relations on which any ethnography, as a form of writing, depends.

In light of our discussion so far, we are sympathetic to recent attempts by Africanists to engage with insights emerging from the New Melanesian Ethnography (e.g., Sanders 2008), but we cannot greet with unqualified enthusiasm the basis on which such theories have been analogically extended. A notable example is Piot's (1999) work on the Kabre of Togo, which deploys Strathernian theories of Melanesian sociality to overturn the canon of anthropological thinking on Voltaic peoples and to question key elements of the ways in which Africanist scholars have conceptualized 'society'. Based on structural-functionalist, Marxist, and practice theory, Piot shows how successive theoretical innovations have reproduced prevailing Western understandings. His suggestion is that, throughout these transformations, a fundamental concern with social organization and with the relation between the individual and society has prevailed. In moving beyond this, he argues that the Kabre exemplify a wider African propensity to constitute the person through the dialectical incorporation of various 'outsides'.

The result is a description that interestingly exceeds its theoretical starting point, specifically through its focus on the incorporation of 'outsides'. Piot uses theories derived from Melanesian ethnographies to illuminate aspects of Kabre sociality that might otherwise be overlooked, and this in turn leads to a critical engagement with a broader literature on globalization. However, the comparative framing of the account does not explicitly negate or impose theoretical limits on the 'Melanesian' concepts from which it starts. Hence, while Melanesian theory is used to illuminate African ethnography, there is no theoretical 'return'. The Melanesian theory of the gift constitutes a theoretical gift, so to speak, that remains unreciprocated. To the extent that description and analysis exceed their theoretical point of departure, this excess is descriptively bracketed out as a difference of culture and place. Excess is registered as another instance of ethnographic concreteness rather than as a fundamental extension of anthropology's conceptual apparatus. The image is that of 'Melanesian theory' applied (or extended) to 'African ethnography'.

This effect can be understood as an artifact of the framework by which anthropologists conventionally order their comparisons. Over two decades ago, Holy (1987) made explicit the changing conceptualization of the role of ethnographic comparison (see also Gingrich and Fox 2002; Lazar 2012). Where positivistic anthropologists saw the description of ethnographic 'facts' as a means to enable cross-cultural generalization, Holy (1987) proposed that interpretive approaches entailed the comparison of processes of meaning creation. He noted that since these are different in distinct cultures and societies, they cannot themselves provide the basis for comparison. In his own words: "To carry out comparison, we need a vantage point that is not culturally specific" (ibid.: 13).

For example, the comparison of gift and commodity logics becomes possible through the mediating, external concept of 'the economy'.

Yet as Strathern (1988a) notes, the problem with this formulation is that anthropology's mediating terms produce their own sense of disproportion. If certain regions seem more interesting than others, that discrepancy is not reducible to the nature of the societies being studied. It arises in relation to the placement of regions vis-à-vis analytic problems. In a related way, Mudimbe (1988) points to the distortion that such mediating concepts have with respect to scholarly accounts of Africa. In their 'epistemological ethnocentrism', these studies set up a "silent dependence on a Western *episteme*" (ibid.: x). Mudimbe sees this attitude as reflecting "the belief that scientifically there is nothing to be learned from 'them' unless it is already 'ours' or comes from 'us'" (ibid.: 15).

As a form of conceptual leveling, the New Melanesian Ethnography might appear to provide solutions to this problem, or at least new ways of thinking, and this is what Piot (1999) explicitly argues. Yet we need to be alert to the dangers of the comparative possibilities that these new conceptual frameworks set up. In his subtle analysis of globalization and personhood, Piot's rendering of Kabre sociality is considerably more sophisticated that the straightforward application. Nonetheless, his analysis rests on a conceptual framework in which comparative possibilities are framed by ideas that appear to derive from other parts of the world. Pointing to new forms of personhood and 'dividuality' reinscribes the theoretical importance of Melanesia, providing new versions of ideas that appear to originate elsewhere. Another and perhaps more important implication is that such cross-cultural analysis underscores a basic duality: 'we' construct a conceptual base from which to compare all others. As another 'other', the Kabre do not appear to trouble fundamentally the framework in which 'otherness' is conceived.

While we wish to make explicit the comparative issues that attend this mode of theoretical application, our intention is not to critique the Strathernian theories of sociality on which Piot's account rests. Rather, it is to highlight how Strathern's own approach points to the limits of this kind of thinking. In addressing the theoretical framing of regions and the regional framing of theory, she cautions us not only against the straightforward application of theories to places, but also against the mutually validating role of theory and place in the ethnographic imagination. If Strathern's concern is to elucidate precisely the dynamics by which theories reflexively emerge through place (and vice versa), then it is clear that the straightforward application of theory ('Melanesian' or otherwise) to novel ethnographic contexts will not do justice to this insight. Perhaps a more Strathernian approach might draw less heavily on Strathernian theory.

In highlighting this possibility, we draw from Strathern's observation that one way of avoiding the sense of disproportion that attends cross-cultural comparison would be to aim for comparison while keeping in mind the non-comparability of the phenomena compared. This would entail making comparisons without subordinating either phenomenon to a pre-existing comparative frame. Strathern (1990: 212) outlines how, in this approach, "the anthropologist, unable to represent the one completely in terms of the other, would use his or her Western concepts to mediate between the two in such a way as to give the analytical language the status of a visible third voice. The trick would be to demonstrate the non-comparability of [regionally specific] ideas, *despite* the mediating third language."

We have been arguing that recent anthropological accounts have sought to rearrange our descriptions and analyses of various African realities in line with models of sociality emerging through the New Melanesian Ethnography. By contrast, we suggest that a Strathernian analysis invites us to ask how we might use our descriptions of these ethnographic specificities in such a way as to rearrange creatively the understandings and concepts that are central to metropolitan anthropological theory. To the extent that these theories are now dominated by models of sociality that locate the source of their insight in Melanesia, this would entail a creative reworking of some of the theories we have come to think of as 'Melanesian'.

Relational Rights

The distinction between theory and approach is illustrated by Robbins's (2004, 2010) work, which has emphasized 'relationalism' as the key theoretical contribution of the New Melanesian Ethnography. He has not so much questioned the validity of the New Melanesian Ethnography as used his own version of it to conceptualize radical cultural change among the Urapmin people of Papua New Guinea with whom he worked. Relationalism has, as such, come to stand for theory generated through fieldwork in Melanesia. It is revealing that Robbins (2006: 172) has found the occasion to salute the New Melanesian Ethnography as "a brave, final, and radical stand on the side of cultural difference in the context of an anthropology about to grow tired of detailed explorations of local symbolic worlds in all their particularity."

Note the emphasis on 'cultural difference' as the main preoccupation of the New Melanesian Ethnography. Relationalism theorizes, for Robbins, a culturally distinct world and provides a conceptual foundation for his account of Christian conversion among the Urapmin. Unsurprisingly, the opposite of relationalism is 'individualism', and the emphasis on cultural differences informs Robbins's (2004: 13) desire to carry out an analysis of "the encounter between a relational culture and an individualist one." What is initially surprising is the way in which Robbins has, in his other work, been able to propose universalist aspects in the Melanesianist insights into relationalism. Shifting his attention from radical cultural change to justice and human rights, Robbins (2010: 173) notes the limited appeal of relativism: "[I]t is hard to get an audience even within anthropology, much less outside of it, for a full-blown relativist critique of global discourses of human rights and justice." It is this avoidance of relativism in current discussions about human rights that he identifies as the main reason why he has not previously written about the topic (ibid.: 171). Robbins is concerned to retain an 'anthropological voice' in the efforts to engage the topic of human rights after the appeal of relativism has waned. His answer is to "set aside relativism and play the universalist game" (2010: 173). He gives himself "the constructive task of suggesting potential universals currently unrecognized or unelaborated in global debates" (2010: 174).

Here relationalism, as it is inflected through Melanesianist anthropology, becomes a 'candidate universal', in Robbins's (2010) terms, to qualify the convention by which individuals and groups have been seen as rights-bearers by political philosophers, lawyers, and activists across the world. Where the primary unit of value is relationships, people both actively create relationships and experience them as inescapable. As such, relationships cannot be reduced to this or that individual or group and their particular preferences. Robbins (ibid.: 188) argues that "it is not so much people who have rights to relationships, but the other way around." Drawing on, among other works, Strathern's (2004) account of a human rights NGO's intervention in a dispute where a young woman was supposed to be a part of compensation payment, Robbins (2010: 182–186) highlights contemporary tensions between the relational and individualist models of justice in Papua New Guinea. Noting similarities and differences between relationalism and Honneth's (1996) theory of recognition, Robbins (2010: 187–188) emphasizes the capacity of relationalism to open up fresh perspectives on justice in the contemporary West, a capacity that suggests its potential as a candidate universal.

The jump from distinct cultures to candidate universals seems breathtaking, or at least inconsistent, but the discrepancy may be more apparent than real, a result of the different topics being addressed—that is, radical cultural change in one instance and human rights in the other. Relationalism is only one among many universals, and the tension between different models of justice discussed in Strathern's (2004) account might be seen to indicate the institutional reasons why some models appear to be more universal than others. Backed by transnational NGOs and aid money, the individualist model of justice can be mistaken for a more generally applicable model than relationalism. It is here that Robbins's (2010) argument reveals its anthropological credentials by refusing the easy distinction between generality and particularity that such interventions can entail. What he does not mention, however, is the long history of relational rights as a topic of anthropological theory, from Maine ([1861] 1913) to Malinowski (1926), who both famously emphasized social identity and status as the preconditions of rights. Before the current focus on human rights in discussions about justice, relational rights received an ethnographically and theoretically more sophisticated treatment in the works of mid-century Africanists (see, e.g., Epstein 1954; Gluckman 1965), whose insights continue to be evoked in more contemporary settings (see, e.g., Comaroff and Roberts 1981; Englund 2002; Griffiths 1997; Oomen 2005). In fact, such has the emphasis been in Africanist anthropology on the embeddedness of dispute settlement in kinship rights and obligations that the paradigmatic cases of Robbins's candidate universal might be better located there than in Melanesianist anthropology.

Tempting as this observation might seem for an Africanist to make, however, the theory of relational rights did not emanate from any particular place. The argument between Gluckman (1965, 1969) and Bohannan (1957, 1969) reveals the extent to which working in the same continent and sharing similar analytical interests did not guarantee consensus on the nature and purpose of anthropological comparison. After identifying the importance of debt and obligation to the definition and practice of relational rights, Gluckman could hope for a greater precision about the meaning of debt through a comparative analysis involving material not only from his own Barotse study in present-day Zambia but also from other ethnographies of 'tribal law' and from studies of Roman and early English law. "What is the difference between debt in these contexts," Gluckman (1965: 245) asked, "and the fact that any obligation establishes a state of indebtedness, in another sense of the word, while clearly obligation is basic in any system of law?" The question was skewed neither toward particularity nor generality as such but sought to elicit specificity through a comparative exercise. Gluckman felt, however, frustrated with the cultural particularism of some of his contemporaries working on African ethnography. Bohannan (1957) also emphasized the importance of debt to the idea of justice among the Tiv of Nigeria, but he insisted that the uniqueness of their system could not be examined in terms of the concepts of Western jurisprudence. Each culture has its own folk system, and it would be an error to 'raise' a folk system "to the status of an analytical system" (ibid.: 69). Note the assumption of scaling up when one moves from a folk system to an analytical system: the first is always ranked lower than the second. "Insistence on uniqueness constantly obscures problems," Gluckman (1969: 365) complained, pointing out the many not-so-unique features of Tiv language on justice and debt.

It was the "lack of perspective" in cultural particularism that troubled Gluckman (1965: 251), the inability to identify "similarities within differences" (ibid.: 254) that would permit a more precise understanding of what was specific about the case in hand. To mark his intellectual debts, Gluckman dedicated his book to the jurists of Barotseland and of the Yale Law School. A close ethnographic study of a particular judicial system was, therefore, more than the result of intense fieldwork in Zambia. The locations of the emergence of his insights were more than two,[2] but the point to stress here is the way in which Gluckman understood universals to be specific in their historical scope and therefore the result of careful comparative work. To be sure, his comparison between tribal law and early English law would seem to have denied that the Barotse and the world where he operated outside fieldwork were coeval (Fabian 1983). Yet Gluckman, who pioneered the study of contemporary race and industrial relations in the anthropology of Africa (see, e.g., Gluckman [1940] 1958, 1961), was equally interested to note the nature of justice in contemporary Britain in light of his findings from Barotseland. Again, similarities and differences could be identified. Evoking the importance of property among the Barotse in constituting and maintaining relationships,[3] Gluckman (1965: 266) admitted awareness that "obligations in all personal relations in modern society are expressed in the form of material gifts, and redress for small offences is similarly made." Such "pockets of multiplex relationships in modern society" (ibid.) should not, however, obscure the specific nature that commodities had taken in contemporary Britain. Rather than being vital to the discharging and creation of debts between persons, "[c]ommodities began to develop an autonomous existence, and ... increasingly drew people into impersonal, restricted, ephemeral relationships" (ibid.: 270). Insights from fieldwork in Zambia were crucial to afford this perspective on contemporary Britain. As a comparative exercise, it was no more anachronistic than the gift-commodity and West-Melanesia distinctions that Strathern (1988b) deployed in her exploration of sociality and knowledge practices.

The notion of relational rights, in other words, was the innovation of neither Africanist nor Melanesianist anthropology but the outcome of careful, reflexive comparison. In comparing Melanesian insights with Honneth's (1996) work, Robbins (2010) continues this approach to good effect, although his self-professed relativist impulse (ibid.: 171) has also resulted in an emphasis on cultural distinctiveness in his readings of the New Melanesian Ethnography, as described above. The dispute between Gluckman and Bohannan demonstrates, however, that such analytical predilections do not simply reflect the place where anthropologists have done their fieldwork. Gluckman worked within a tradition of anthropology that adopted as its key interest the description of difference and specificity in human affairs, without shying away from the possibility of using universal categories in that descriptive work. Unlike relativism, it made possible an engaged anthropology in which "the right of the ruling community to a monopoly of moral judgement [was] sharply questioned" (James 1973: 46). This position is all the more striking when its origin is traced to the colonial period, when, for example, Evans-Pritchard (1931) admonished colonial administrators for their ignorance of the distinctions Africans made between different types of witchcraft and sorcery. Yet the approach did not emanate from some distinct 'British School', as Gluckman's (1975: 27–29) identification of a parallel between Leach's structuralist fascination with 'cultural grammar' and South Africa under apartheid made clear.[4] After all, both Bohannan and Gluckman received their training in Oxford. Rather than localizing anthropological knowledge as a function of the places where anthropologists either do their fieldwork or get their training, it seems more pertinent to assess the extent to which they have acknowledged the multiple sources of their insights.

Networks

Networks, like relational rights, have provided the focus for sustained analytic attention that has localized its insights in a range of ways. Tracing some of the debates surrounding the concept, this section explores how Riles's (2001) recent formulation of 'the network', developed in the context of Fiji, prompts reflection on the theorization of networks by various Africanists. While we find utility in Riles's approach, which turns the network from an analytic to an ethnographic concern, we argue that her approach itself precludes the possibility of any straightforward application of her theory. Rather, it begs the question as to the conceptual limits that novel contexts might introduce.

For scholars such as Barnes (1969), Mitchell (1969a, 1974), and Epstein (1969), 'network analysis' provided a counterpoint to the rigid abstractions of structural functionalist approaches. Network theory can thus be seen as a 'negative strategy' in the Strathernian sense: it exposed conceptual limits to structural functionalist thinking when applied to the urban contexts that these scholars were beginning to examine. According to Mitchell (1969a: 9), while in 'traditional' rural contexts, the model of lineage descent continued to provide "a coherent and systematic framework into which nearly all the daily activities of people and their relationships ... could be fitted," structural accounts were inadequate to the realities of urban life. Here the potential of network analysis was seen to inhere in its capacity to reveal how actors were forced to perform multiple roles in order to link domains of life that appeared to be structurally distinct. For network analysts, the network is invoked as an explanation of the dynamics by which actors connect structurally and institutionally distinct domains of life through the contextual negotiation of roles and relations.

On a superficial reading, these accounts might suggest that personal networks are sociologically or ethnographically distinctive features of African sociality. However, network analysts themselves have offered reasons for circumspection. While recognizing a shifting ethnographic focus (away from 'tribal' and 'traditional' societies, toward 'urban' and 'modern' ones) as a significant conceptual stimulus, scholars such as Mitchell, Barnes, and Epstein were at pains to distinguish network analysis from the ethnographic circumstances it described. As an explicitly analytic construct, the network enabled comparison precisely because it stood outside the realities being compared. It should be noted that although many of the initial applications of the concept were in African contexts (specifically Southern Africa), significant developments in the approach arose in relation to studies of Norway (Barnes 1954) and London (Bott 1957). Yet the more fundamental point is that, even in the context of Africa, social and cultural differences emerged as a property of the distinct forms that networks can take. Rather than an explanation or theory, network analysts argued that as a *concept*, the network's capacity to facilitate comparison lay precisely in its externality. Thus, Kapferer (1973: 84) is critical of a tendency to imagine network analysis as a "theory in itself," proposing, rather, that it should be regarded as "a concept ... by which we seek 'to organise human perception'" (ibid.: citing Meehan). Networks, as concepts, are not "natural entities" (ibid.) but a way of organizing the realities that are encountered in the field. Thus, the appeal of the concept can be seen to inhere in its capacity to order complexity by enabling comparison across a range of manifestly diverse ethnographic contexts. Epstein (1969), for example, suggests that as an analytic concept the network enables discernment between behavior that is 'random and haphazard' and that which is 'ordered'.

As one instance of a modernist faith in cumulative knowledge, the network therefore held out the possibility of the incorporation of multiple perspectives in an overarching 'whole'. In this pluralist vision, comparison was a matter of identifying general scales to act as common denominators that aided the movement from the particular to the general (Strathern 1991; cf. Holbraad and

Pedersen 2009). Against this ideal, internal critiques foreground the problems that result from a slippage of scale and from the difficulties entailed in moving from the concrete to the abstract (and vice versa). Barnes (1969: 53), for example, comments on the conceptual confusions that have resulted from the application of network analysis to different ethnographic material: "Perhaps because of the diversity of contexts in which the idea of a network has been applied, there is already a good deal of confusion in the literature, for each analyst … introduces new refinements to suit his own particular problem." Barnes's wider concern is that such 'refinements' end up confusing the concept, so that the basis for comparison is annulled. Related problems emerge with respect to the extent to which network analysis is able to operate independently of actors' own understandings of the relationships that they hold.

Recent work turns these conceptions of the network 'inside out', in Riles's (2001) own terms. Treating the network not as an analytic construct but as an ethnographically significant fact, she shows how, for NGO workers based in Fiji, the network is itself intrinsic to the sociality they inhabit. For these people, 'the network' and 'personal relations' are not mutually explanatory contexts, but "versions of one another seen twice" (ibid.: 26–27; cf. Strathern 1991). Accordingly, Riles (2001: 27) contends that "[n]etworkers in Suva do not make sense of their personal relations in terms of their networks or vice versa; rather, like in the double view of the hologram as described by Baudrillard …, it is in seeing the form of each in turn that both become real." Her own account makes explicit how this ethnographic understanding leads to a reconsideration of the tenets of network analysis. Networkers in Fiji "would insist that personal relationships of the kind social network analysts study are not networks because they are not formal. For networkers in Suva, a network was an entity of a particular *form*. To include a person, an institution, or a project in a network was to formalize it and vice versa" (2001: 66–67). No longer an external (analytic) context, the network therefore emerges as a product of the imaginative practices of her informants.

This account elucidates a theory whose elegance and analytic power might suggest its utility as an explanatory device for other contexts—including in Africa. In line with our broader argument, however, our suggestion is that such a theoretical application should be resisted. Rather than seeking to replicate the theory, recognition of the power of the insight should direct us to the approach that gave rise to it. In particular, the account usefully troubles the analytic place of 'the relation', directing attention to the form in which social relations emerge. In questioning the self-evidence of a distinction between 'personal' and 'institutional' relations, Riles also suggests fruitful possibilities for research that suspends analytic judgment about the ways in which these domains intersect in order to apprehend how such domains are ethnographically configured. As a counterpoint to much contemporary theorization, such approaches might fruitfully lead us beyond the generalized terms in which personal relations, as networks, have been variously apprehended as vectors of corruption and neo-patrimonialism across the continent of Africa,[5] directing us instead to the ethical concerns that surround the intersections of different relational forms. Such a focus might in turn introduce productive limits to Riles's conceptual framework. In Ghana, for example, a study of the ways in which NGO workers understand and practice networks brings to light the specific ways in which personal relations are understood as networks, challenging the universality of Riles's claim that networks, as form, emerge in opposition to (as inside out versions of) personal relations (see Yarrow 2011).

Our wider point is that, as an instance of New Melanesian Ethnography, Riles's insights about the network emerge via a form of reflexivity with epistemological underpinnings profoundly at odds with the comparative framework. If network analysis used the concept of the network to order ethnographic material, Riles reveals how the network as ethnographic artifact, acts to (re)order anthropological concepts. In line with the New Melanesian Ethnography, from which her approach explicitly draws, she effectively makes a virtue of the 'confusion' of ethnography and analysis that Barnes decries. Riles's understanding of the network is an outcome of a form of conceptual displacement—the side effect of taking seriously what her informants take seriously themselves. Here knowledge increases not through the accumulation of contexts within a comparative framework that remains 'untroubled', but through increasing internal differentiation resulting from the conceptual redeployment and reconfiguration that attends ethnographic engagement.

Conclusion: A Place for Africa?

In different ways, both rights and networks emerge as complex intersections of ideas in ways that trouble any straightforward separation between theory and ethnography and that demonstrate the utility of cross-cultural comparison—not as a means to an end of generalization, but as a method of conceptual refinement and differentiation. In both cases we have shown how descriptions and comparisons using these terms ('relational rights' and 'networks') destabilize and complicate the terms themselves, which in turn provides the basis for a descriptive language more finely attuned to the specificities of particular contexts. At once concepts belonging everywhere and nowhere, relational rights and networks can become 'third terms' that mediate insights gained through long-term fieldwork in diverse locations. Patently, some concepts are more specific to their ethnographic context than others, and not all concepts have the potential to become third terms. In this regard, our insistence on keeping application and approach separate in imagining the relationship between ethnography and theory is crucial. Following the spirit of the New Melanesian Ethnography, envisaging relational rights or networks as theories awaiting their application to particular ethnographic cases would do no justice to this approach.

It is worth reiterating our argument that this view of ethnographic comparison marks a departure from the association of anthropological concepts with particular places or regions. As Lederman (1988) has suggested, culture areas were from the outset not just geographical units but theories about the people and environments that pertained there. This mutual validation of theory and place has created problems that persist in certain formulations of regional differences as naturalized and discrete entities. A diversity of people is subsumed to an encompassing logic. While this results in the relation of people and entities who may have little in common beyond geographical contiguity, it also leads to the disconnection of related but geographically discrete people and things. As a framing context, others have pointed out how a regional focus on Africa has at times resulted in an unwarranted sense of coherence and a relative lack of attention to the processes by which the continent connects to people and places beyond it (see, e.g., Chabal 1996; Guyer 2004).

Over the past three decades, the notion of geographically bounded units has come under sustained critical attack in anthropology. The bounded field sites presupposed as the basis of fieldwork by a previous generation of anthropologists have been shown to be artifacts of the very practices through which anthropologists researched and wrote about them (Gupta and Ferguson 1997; Marcus 1998). At the same time, empirical changes, frequently glossed as globalization, have led to a situation in which people and things are imagined to be on the move as never before. In this context, anthropologists have questioned the wisdom of both geographically bounded local field sites and geographically bounded regions. Old habits die hard, however. Even the theoretically most knowledgeable of anthropologists find themselves defending the association of theory with place, specifying copious caveats about the porosity of the place they identify as the origin of theory (see, e.g., Comaroff and Comaroff 2011).

For many of these anthropologists, regional scholarship has been discredited as an outdated relic of previous theoretical frameworks and as an anachronism that fails to reflect the connectedness of the contemporary world we inhabit.[6] Yet scholarship that is emerging from a variety of sources might lead us to question whether a bounded notion of either the field or the region is necessarily problematic, if we recognize the arbitrariness of the terms in which we construct it. Our suggestion draws on Candea's (2007) recent conceptualization of the 'arbitrary location' as a critique of multi-sited fieldwork. His argument is that, in privileging connections and relations between entities, recent formulations of fieldwork have led us to overlook the importance of disconnection and detachment. In recasting this insight at a regional level, we also take inspiration from Mamdani (1996), who insists that establishing the legitimacy of Africa as a unit of analysis does not entail the ascription of any underlying cultural or historical process to that place.

In this vein, we might acknowledge the analytic construction of Africa and its sub-regions while recognizing its analytic utility. As an arbitrary location, Africa forces us to consider both relation and detachment, connection and disjuncture. Ethnographically, this leads us to consider logics and practices that spatially co-exist without relating. Theoretically, this regional framing points to the reflexive decomposition, differentiation, and recomposition of concepts, even as particular analysts disagree as to what might be important—or even the case—about any given place. Anthropologists need to allow places to put limits on their ethnographic and theoretical artifacts even as they recognize their own role in the construction of both.

Acknowledgments

Thanks to Knut Christian Myhre for organizing the workshop that provided the conceptual provocation for this chapter and for his thoughtful editorial help. The chapter has benefited from the comments of Matei Candea, Morten Pedersen, Adam Reed, Marilyn Strathern, Richard Werbner, and two anonymous reviewers.

Harri Englund teaches social anthropology at the University of Cambridge. He has been engaged in ethnographic research among Chichewa/Nyanja speakers in Malawi, Mozambique, and Zambia for over two decades. His current interests include justice, morality, and African-language media. His most recent book is *Human Rights and African Airwaves: Mediating Equality on the Chichewa Radio* (2011).

Thomas Yarrow lectures in social anthropology at Durham University. He has undertaken ethnographic fieldwork in Ghana with a focus on NGOs, development organizations, and, more recently, the ongoing impacts of the Volta Resettlement Project. He is the author of *Development Beyond Politics: Aid, Activism and NGOs in Ghana* (2011).

Notes

1. It goes without saying that our argument is informed by long-term ethnographic engagements in Ghana (Yarrow) and in Malawi, Mozambique, and Zambia (Englund). However, rather than seeking to demonstrate the force of our argument by appealing to our fieldwork, as in much of what we have published, we focus here on other sets of analytic and inter-textual resources in order to put 'place' in its place in anthropological theory.
2. Gluckman did not fail to mention Manchester in his acknowledgments.
3. "The Law of Persons, the Law of Things, and the Law of Obligations are inextricably involved in one another" (Gluckman 1965: 271).
4. Memorably, Gluckman (1975: 29) noted that it was "possible in the cloistered seclusion of Kings College, Cambridge … to put the main emphasis on the obstinate differences: it was not possible for 'liberal' South Africans confronted with the policy of segregation within a nation into which 'the others' had been brought, and treated as different—and inferior."
5. For example, generalizations about personal relations as networks are central to much of the recent work on the post-colonial African state influenced particularly by Bayart (1993).
6. For a more detailed discussion on the discrediting of regional scholarship, see Guyer (2004) and Lederman (1988).

References

Appadurai, Arjun. 1986. "Anthropology: Center and Periphery." *Comparative Studies in Society and History* 28, no. 2: 356–361.

Appadurai, Arjun. 1988. "Introduction: Place and Voice in Anthropological Theory." *Cultural Anthropology* 3, no. 1: 16–20.

Barnes, John A. 1954. "Class and Committees in the Norwegian Island Parish." *Human Relations* 7, no. 1: 39–58.

Barnes, John A. 1969. "Networks and Political Process." Pp. 51–76 in Mitchell 1969b.

Bayart, Jean-François. 1993. *The State in Africa: The Politics of the Belly*. London: Longman.

Bohannan, Paul. 1957. *Justice and Judgment among the Tiv*. London: Oxford University Press.

Bohannan, Paul. 1969. "Ethnography and Comparison in Legal Anthropology." Pp. 401–418 in Nader 1969.

Bott, Elizabeth. 1957. *Family and Social Network*. London: Tavistock.

Candea, Matei. 2007. "Arbitrary Locations: In Defence of the Bounded Field-Site." *Journal of the Royal Anthropological Institute* 13, no. 1: 167–184.

Chabal, Patrick. 1996. "The African Crisis: Context and Interpretation." Pp. 29–54 in *Postcolonial Identities in Africa*, ed. Richard Werbner and Terence Ranger. London: Zed Books

Clifford, James, and George. E. Marcus. 1986. *Writing Culture: The Politics and Poetics of Ethnography*. Berkeley: University of California Press.

Comaroff, Jean, and John L. Comaroff. 2011. *Theory from the South: Or, How Euro-America Is Evolving toward Africa*. Boulder, CO: Paradigm.

Comaroff, John, and Simon Roberts. 1981. *Rules and Processes: The Cultural Logic of Dispute in an African Context*. Chicago: University of Chicago Press.

Czegledy, Andre P. 1992. "(Re)production of the Self: An Interview with Marilyn Strathern." *Cambridge Anthropology* 16, no. 3: 1–18.

Dresch, Paul. 1988. "Segmentation: Its Roots in Arabia and Its Flowering Elsewhere." *Cultural Anthropology* 3, no. 1: 50–67.

Englund, Harri. 2002. *From War to Peace on the Mozambique-Malawi Borderland*. Edinburgh: Edinburgh University Press for the International African Institute.

Epstein, Arnold L. 1954. "Juridical Techniques and the Judicial Process: A Study in African Customary Law." Rhodes-Livingstone Institute Papers Series, No. 23, Manchester University Press.

Epstein, Arnold L. 1969. "The Network and Urban Social Organization." Pp. 77–116 in Mitchell 1969b.

Evans-Pritchard, E. E. 1931. "Sorcery and Native Opinion." *Africa* 4, no. 1: 22–55.

Fabian, Johannes. 1983. *Time and the Other: How Anthropology Makes Its Object*. New York: Columbia University Press.

Fardon, Richard, ed. 1990a. *Localizing Strategies: Regional Traditions of Ethnographic Writing*. Edinburgh: Scottish Academic Press.

Fardon, Richard. 1990b. "Localizing Strategies: The Regionalization of Ethnographic Accounts." Pp. 1–35 in Fardon 1990a.

Foster, Robert J. 2008. *Materializing the Nation: Commodities, Consumption, and the Media in Papua New Guinea*. Bloomington: Indiana University Press.

Gewertz, Deborah B., and Frederick K. Errington. 1999. *Emerging Class in Papua New Guinea: The Telling of Difference*. Cambridge: Cambridge University Press.

Gingrich, Andre and Richard G. Fox, eds. 2002. *Anthropology, by Comparison*. New York: Routledge.

Gluckman, Max. [1940] 1958. *Analysis of a Social Situation in Modern Zululand.* Manchester: Manchester University Press for the Rhodes-Livingstone Institute.

Gluckman, Max. 1961. "Anthropological Problems Arising from the African Industrial Revolution." Pp. 67–82 in *Social Change in Modern Africa*, ed. Aidan Southall. Oxford: Oxford University Press.

Gluckman, Max. 1965. *The Ideas in Barotse Jurisprudence.* Manchester: Manchester University Press.

Gluckman, Max. 1969. "Concepts in the Comparative Study of Tribal Law." Pp. 349–400 in Nader 1969.

Gluckman, Max. 1975. "Anthropology and Apartheid: The Work of South African Anthropologists." Pp. 21–39 in *Studies in African Social Anthropology*, ed. Meyer Fortes and Sheila Patterson. London: Academic Press.

Griffiths, Anne M. O. 1997. *In the Shadow of Marriage: Gender and Justice in an African Community.* Chicago: University of Chicago Press.

Gupta, Akil, and James Ferguson. 1997. "'The Field' as Site, Method and Location in Anthropology." Pp. 1–29 in *Anthropological Locations: Boundaries and Grounds of a Field Science*, ed. Akil Gupta and James Ferguson. Berkeley: University of California Press.

Guyer, Jane I. 2004. "Anthropology in Area Studies." *Annual Review of Anthropology* 33: 499–523.

Holbraad, Martin, and Morten A. Pedersen. 2009. "Planet M: The Intense Abstractions of Marilyn Strathern." *Anthropological Theory* 9, no. 4: 371–394.

Holy, Ladislav. 1987. "Introduction: Description, Generalisation and Comparison: Two Paradigms." Pp. 1–22 in *Comparative Anthropology*, ed. Ladislav Holy. Oxford: Basil Blackwell

Honneth, Axel. 1996. *The Struggle for Recognition: The Moral Grammar of Social Conflicts.* Cambridge, MA: MIT Press.

James, Wendy. 1973. "The Anthropologist as Reluctant Imperialist." Pp. 41–69 in *Anthropology and the Colonial Encounter*, ed. Talal Asad. New York: Ithaca Press.

Josephides, Lisette. 1991. "Metaphors, Metathemes, and the Construction of Sociality: A Critique of the New Melanesian Ethnography." *Man* (n.s.) 26, no. 1: 145–161.

Kapferer, Bruce. 1973. "Social Network and Conjugal Role in Urban Zambia: Towards a Reformulation of the Bott Hypothesis." Pp. 83–110 in *Network Analysis: Studies in Human Interaction*, ed. Jeremy Boissevain and J. Clyde Mitchell. The Hague: Mouton.

Knauft, Bruce. 1999. *From Primitive to Postcolonial in Melanesia and Anthropology.* Ann Arbor: University of Michigan Press.

Kuper, Adam. 2005. *The Reinvention of Primitive Society: Transformations of a Myth.* London: Routledge.

Lazar, Sian. 2012. "Disjunctive Comparison: Citizenship and Trade Unionism in Bolivia and Argentina." *Journal of the Royal Anthropological Institute* 18, no. 2: 349–368.

Lederman, Rena. 1988. "Globalization and the Future of Culture Areas: Melanesianist Anthropology in Transition." *Annual Review of Anthropology* 27: 427–449.

Maine, Henry Sumner. [1861] 1913. *Ancient Law: Its Connection with the Early History of Society and Its Relation to Modern Ideas.* London: Routledge.

Malinowski, Bronislaw. 1926. *Crime and Custom in Savage Society.* London: Routledge and Kegan Paul.

Mamdani, Mahmood. 1996. *Citizen and Subject: Contemporary Africa and the Legacy of Late Colonialism.* London: James Currey.

Marcus, George E. 1998. *Ethnography through Thick and Thin.* Princeton, NJ: Princeton University Press.

Marriott, McKim. 1976. "Hindu Transactions: Diversity without Dualism." Pp. 109–142 in *Transaction and Meaning*, ed. Bruce Kapferer. Philadelphia: ISHI Publications.

Mitchell, J. Clyde. 1969a. "The Concept and Use of Social Networks." Pp. 1–50 in Mitchell 1969b.

Mitchell, J. Clyde, ed. 1969b. *Social Networks in Urban Situations*. Manchester: Manchester University Press.

Mitchell, J. Clyde. 1974. "Social Networks." *Annual Review of Anthropology* 3: 279–299.

Mudimbe, Valentin Y. 1988. *The Invention of Africa: Gnosis, Philosophy and the Order of Knowledge*. Bloomington: Indiana University Press

Nader, Laura, ed. 1969. *Law in Culture and Society*. Chicago: Aldine.

Oomen, Barbara. 2005. *Chiefs in South Africa: Law, Power and Culture in the Post-Apartheid Era*. Oxford: James Currey.

Piot, Charles. 1999. *Remotely Global: Village Modernity in West Africa*. Chicago: University of Chicago Press.

Riles, Annelise. 2001. *The Network Inside Out*. Ann Arbor: University of Michigan Press.

Robbins, Joel. 2004. *Becoming Sinners: Christianity and Moral Torment in a Papua New Guinea Society*. Berkeley: University of California Press.

Robbins, Joel. 2006. "Review of J. Leach and A. Reed." *Contemporary Pacific* 18, no. 1: 171–175.

Robbins, Joel. 2010. "Recognition, Reciprocity, and Justice: Melanesian Reflections on the Rights of Relationships." Pp. 171–190 in *Mirrors of Justice: Law and Power in the Post–Cold War Era*, ed. Kamari M. Clarke and Mark Goodale. Cambridge: Cambridge University Press.

Sanders, Todd. 2008. *Beyond Bodies: Rainmaking and Sense Making in Tanzania*. Toronto: University of Toronto Press.

Strathern, Marilyn. 1980. "No Nature, No Culture: The Hagen Case." Pp. 174–222 in *Nature, Culture and Gender*, ed. Carol MacCormack and Marilyn Strathern. Cambridge: Cambridge University Press.

Strathern, Marilyn. 1988a. "Concrete Topographies." *Cultural Anthropology* 3, no. 1: 88–96.

Strathern, Marilyn. 1988b. *The Gender of the Gift: Problems with Women and Problems with Society in Melanesia*. Berkeley: University of California Press.

Strathern, Marilyn. 1990. "Negative Strategies in Melanesia." Pp. 204–216 in Fardon 1990a.

Strathern, Marilyn. 1991. *Partial Connections*. Lanham, MD: Rowman & Littlefield.

Strathern, Marilyn. 1992. *After Nature: English Kinship in the Late Twentieth Century*. Cambridge: Cambridge University Press.

Strathern, Marilyn. 2004. "Losing (Out on) Intellectual Resources." Pp. 201–233 in *Law, Anthropology, and the Constitution of the Social: Making Persons and Things*, ed. Alain Pottage and Martha Mundy. Cambridge: Cambridge University Press.

Viveiros de Castro, Eduardo. 1998. "Cosmological Deixis and Amerindian Perspectivism." *Journal of the Royal Anthropological Institute* 4, no. 3: 469–488.

Wagner, Roy G. 1974. "Are There Social Groups in New Guinea Highlands?" Pp. 95–122 in *Frontiers of Anthropology: An Introduction to Anthropological Thinking*, ed. Murray J. Leaf. New York: Van Nostrand.

Wagner, Roy G. [1975] 1981. *The Invention of Culture*. Chicago: University of Chicago Press

Yarrow, Thomas G. 2011. *Development Beyond Politics: Aid, Activism and NGOs in Ghana*. Basingstoke: Palgrave Macmillan.

AFTERWORD

Something to Take Back—Melanesia Anthropology after Relationality

Adam Reed

In what follows, my aim is to respond to the general idea of this volume. In particular, I wish to consider what Melanesianists might gain from the example of this exercise, which has been set and enacted by a group of Africanist anthropologists. There is then no attempt to acknowledge the individual worth of each contribution. However, I want to start by saying how much I enjoyed reading these chapters (and hearing the original workshop papers). As an anthropologist whose work may be identified with the second generation of what has come to be known as the New Melanesian Ethnography (Josephides 1991), it is heartening to see the clear descriptive and analytical purchase of some of its ideas and language. The reflexive introduction and extension of categories, such as relationality, dividual, partibility, and elicitation, into African ethnography is exhilarating to observe. What impresses me most of all is the apparent effort-lessness of the transposition. In particular, I am struck by the way in which these authors make the core invitation in the New Melanesian Ethnography— that is, to imagine a place in which humanity is 'immanent' (Wagner [1975] 1981: 87–88; see also Strathern 1988), where relating is taken for granted rather than assumed to be the task of social action—fit without undue violence to their

Notes for this section begin on page 155.

experience of these events and subjects. This may be 'Afrinesia', but to me the analyses still seemed somehow to emerge from their materials.

That being said, I think that there are areas in which all of the contributors can extend and develop this experiment in ethnographic writing. Most pressingly, I felt the lack of an explanation for what animates African subjects as relational persons. Or, put another way, we need to locate an indigenous theory of cause and effect that might inform and nuance the categories imported from the New Melanesian Ethnography. In the latter, the power of a notion, such as the partible or composite person, rests on a prior, almost simple observation about the way that Melanesians are reported to locate the agent. These subjects, Strathern (1988: 272–273) holds, may believe that they act for themselves, but at the same time they tend to assume that the stimulus for these actions lies elsewhere. To draw on my own Melanesian ethnography, when a prisoner in Papua New Guinea sneezes, he immediately interprets the action as an unintentional response to the fact that kin or gang mates outside the jail are thinking of him (see Reed 2003: 12–13). Likewise, his cellmates may interpret a dream as the outcome of events at home or of the presence of God or Satan in their lives. But as Strathern (1988: 273) points out, it is not just that "[a]gency and cause are split" in this fashion. Crucially, Melanesian subjects seem to insist that they always act with someone else in mind. Indeed, it is the identified presence or memory of other subjects that is taken to elicit a certain kind of action. There is, I have suggested, an ethical dimension to these common claims (Reed 2003: 157). Subjects constantly feel the pressure to demonstrate that they act in reference to another person. To appear to do otherwise is to put oneself at risk, to be open to public criticism.

To reiterate, I feel that if the experiment of Afrinesia is to develop further among Africanist anthropologists, they will need to begin to excavate equivalent or alternative starting points for a language of relationality.[1] Focusing on African trajectories of cause and effect may then allow categories such as dividual and partibility to take root and better escape their Melanesianist moorings.

But what can this experiment achieve for me and other anthropologists of Melanesian societies? How can we in turn 'do' or 'speak' Afrinesian? One thing is clear: it is not sufficient for scholars of the New Melanesian Ethnography just to sit back and enjoy the importation of its terms of analysis into African anthropology. We need to look for a return, to determine what, from our perspective, is the point of this exchange. To put the challenge in the language of the New Melanesian Ethnography, we need to identify what Africanists doing Afrinesia can elicit from us and what Melanesianists can elicit from Afrinesia. This involves imagining ourselves acting with African anthropology in mind, exploring, for instance, how it might creatively reanimate the New Melanesian Ethnography. We need to locate or find something inspiring in Africanist descriptions of 'Africa'—a process that necessarily prohibits the straightforward redeployment of the kinds of relational forms that the authors in this volume wish to borrow from us.

By way of a starting suggestion, I put forward the notion of the fetish, a category introduced in one of the workshop papers that is not reproduced in this book. Famously identified by Pietz (1985) as originating from the long history of European contact, trade, and colonization in West Africa, this category or 'problem idea' was deployed by commercial agents and then appropriated by metropolitan scholars as a means of drawing out what they perceived as the distinctive economy of value and material culture in African societies. Implicitly and explicitly worked out in contrast to the emergent and evolving category of the commodity, the fetish impressed as a form that significantly resisted the reduction of things to their instrumental or exchange value. Attention fell on claims to the 'irreducible materiality' of things in the minds of Africans and to the force or power that Europeans believed these subjects attributed to matter (Pietz 1985: 7; see also Pels 1998). Although expressed through countless and diverse iterations, the fetish has a complicated and not entirely central place in Africanist anthropology. Similarly, while its discursive authority in large part rests on a claim to have come out of Africa, the degree to which the fetish belongs to that space is highly contested. As Pietz highlights, this is in part what makes it an interesting category to think through.

From the perspective of the New Melanesian Ethnography, the introduction of the problem and idea of the fetish is intriguing for a number of reasons. Firstly, the category is almost entirely absent from the anthropology of Melanesian societies (but see Bell and Geismar 2009; Foster 1998; Reed 2007). This is an interesting omission, given the crucial role that regional literature is held to have played in the reinvigoration of material culture studies (see Gell 1998; Miller 1987). It would be interesting, I think, to try to reread Melanesian anthropology for evidence of what one might term 'fetishism' in the valuation or attachment to things. I can think of a number of classic ethnographies on materiality[2] that might gain some purchase from such an alternative reading—in particular, from the invitation to locate those moments when Melanesian subjects consider the attraction or untranscended power of matter, when things are taken to do more or less than substitute for persons or index sets of relations.

Secondly, as a category that operates in contrast to the commodity form, the fetish has the potential to disrupt or throw into relief the more usual focus on the opposition between commodity and gift. The displacement of this dichotomy was a key ambition and achievement of the New Melanesian Ethnography. Indeed, I have long wondered what a text like *The Gender of the Gift* might have looked like had Strathern (1988) placed the commodity-fetish opposition alongside the more dominant commodity-gift relationship that exists in anthropological conventions of description. Certainly, the effect of the displacement, and the kind of language or sociality that emerged as a consequence of this action, might have been rather different. For instance, the revelation that Melanesian gifting and exchange might be better read as a form of objectifying or cutting relations and differentiating subjects rather than of making connections and building society would have to be placed alongside the limit on relationality that the category of the fetish presents. Similarly, the claim that Strathern's Melanesians act with someone else in mind would have to struggle against the observation that they also seem to identify material and immaterial forces in the world that resist the split between agency and cause (see Reed 2011). Subjects can register their impact, but they do not necessarily imagine that these 'things' act in reference to them.

All this is important, I think, because the New Melanesian Ethnography has run into a problem. The kind of analysis developed by Wagner and Strathern, which involved deliberate and critical inversions of the dominant conventions of analysis and description, has in its second and third generation of production begun to appear like a new kind of orthodoxy. Indeed, for me, the reinforcement of this realization is one of the effects of reading the chapters in this volume. The difficulty arises because this experimental language has been increasingly presented by New Melanesian ethnographers, myself included, as an ethnographic reality—as if Melanesians themselves really 'do' relationality. As a consequence, it is becoming harder and harder to see what critical work these kinds of descriptions can achieve. In fact, at times they seem to be constraining Melanesian anthropology, or, rather, Melanesian anthropology's depiction of Melanesian societies, with the same power as previous or alternative orthodoxies (e.g., the still pervasive model of socialization). The challenge must be to relocate the experimental ethos in the New Melanesian Ethnography, or, in what I take to be the spirit behind one contribution to this book (see Englund and Yarrow), to actively work to radically re-detach theory from place.

In this regard, the category of the fetish might also operate conceptually as a kind of dark matter, to be made to stand for that part of anthropologists' experience of Melanesian societies that is irreducibly not about relationality. In other words, it might be a way to explore the limit of the relation as the endpoint of analysis. What do persons and things look like if they are not viewed as objectifications of sets of relations? At what moments do subjects envisage themselves not acting with someone else in mind? To me, it seems that we have a number of options for imagining a limit. New Melanesian ethnographers can seek to make the relation appear radical or new again, to show how it can still do work to distance ourselves from conventions of description in Melanesian anthropology and beyond. It is notable, for instance, how conservative the deployment of relationality has been. There is an implicit running assumption that some kinds of relations are more given or central than others. The New Melanesian Ethnography typically starts and ends its narration with the language group and kinship, as if these were more real or authentic relational forms in Melanesian societies than others (such as workmates, Christian denominations, national citizens, or gang mates), or as if they necessarily provided the context for understanding those other forms. This seems, oddly, to restrict the power of a notion like 'immanent humanity' and to predetermine instead the way that the story of Melanesian lives can be told. The other, perhaps more challenging option is to seek to replicate the spirit of the original experiment and to discover a way to write without relationality. Just as Strathern strove to reread parasitically the classic ethnographic texts of Melanesian anthropology in order to make them undermine their own terms of analysis and reveal signs of relational logic, so we would need to reread/rewrite the texts of the New Melanesian Ethnography.

But we should remain cognizant of the dangers of trying to leave the language of relationality behind. Writing without the relation does not mean returning to the conventions of description that preceded it—stories of socialization and relationship making premised on the oppositions between gift and commodity, individual and society, nature and culture. Equally, we must avoid swapping the attachment of theory to place for the attachment of theory to time, that is, the temptation to imagine that the problem is solved by historicizing the state of relationality as though it belonged to the past or quickly changing present of Melanesian realities. If texts like *The Gender of the Gift* teach us anything, it is surely that an alternative language will emerge only through the careful and rigorous deployment of the constraint we choose to impose. In this respect, learning how *not* to describe Melanesia through relational idioms is perhaps the best way of continuing to do what some people term the New Melanesian Ethnography.

Indeed, it may be that the Africanist anthropologists writing in this volume are not really looking to invest African anthropology with the relational language of the New Melanesian Ethnography. Rather, they may be working toward their own moment of radical constraint, seeking to find inspiration in this kind of approach. For them, the idioms of relationality deployed by New Melanesian ethnographers may be useful precisely because they remain unorthodox in the context of African anthropology and deploying them makes one write 'Africa' differently. That can only be a good thing. But it should not be a stopping point in working out what it is that Africanist anthropologists must learn to write without.

Acknowledgments

I wish to thank all of the contributors to this volume and to the workshop that preceded it. In particular, I am grateful to Knut Christian Myhre for the invitation to participate and for his careful editorial comments. I also owe special thanks for the feedback provided by Tom Yarrow and Harri Englund.

Adam Reed is a Senior Lecturer in the Department of Social Anthropology and in the Centre for Pacific Studies, University of St Andrews. His Melanesian work is based on fieldwork conducted in a maximum-security jail in Papua New Guinea and focuses on issues of incarceration, post-coloniality, law, money, narratives of crime, and the urban. He also conducts research in Britain, with interests in the city as a site of anthropological description, literary culture, and ethical campaigning.

Notes

1. By way of suggestive potential, see Rodima-Taylor's account of *omooyo* and Myhre's account of *horu* in this volume.
2. For examples of ethnographies on materiality, see, for instance, the work of Weiner (1988) on pearl shells, Küchler (1985, 1988) on Malangan figures, or O'Hanlon (1995) on war shields.

References

Bell, Joshua A., and Haidy Geismar. 2009. "Materialising Oceania: New Ethnographies of Things in Melanesia and Polynesia." *Australian Journal of Anthropology* 20, no. 1: 3–27

Foster, Robert J. 1998. "Your Money, Our Money, the Government's Money: Finance and Fetishism in Melanesia." Pp. 60–90 in Spyer 1998.

Gell, Alfred. 1998. *Art and Agency: An Anthropological Theory*. Oxford: Clarendon Press.

Josephides, Lisette. 1991. "Metaphors, Metathemes, and the Construction of Sociality: A Critique of the New Melanesian Ethnography." *Man* (n.s.) 26, no. 1: 145–161.

Küchler, Susanne. 1985. "Malangan: Art and Memory in a Melanesian Society." *Man* (n.s.) 22, no. 2: 238–255.

Küchler, Susanne. 1988. "Malangan: Objects, Sacrifice and the Production of Memory." *American Ethnologist* 15, no. 4: 625–637.

Miller, Daniel. 1987. *Material Culture and Mass Consumption*. Oxford: Blackwell.

O'Hanlon, Michael. 1995. "Modernity and the 'Graphicalisation' of Meaning: New Guinea Highland Shield Design in Historical Perspective." *Journal of Royal Anthropological Institute* 1, no. 3: 469–493.

Pels, Peter. 1998. "The Spirit of Matter: On Fetish, Rarity, Fact, and Fancy." Pp. 91–121 in Spyer 1998.

Pietz, William. 1985. "The Problem of the Fetish, I." *RES: Anthropology and Aesthetics* 9: 5–17.

Reed, Adam. 2003. *Papua New Guinea's Last Place: Experiences of Constraint in a Postcolonial Prison*. New York: Berghahn Books.

Reed, Adam. 2007. "'*Smuk* Is King': The Action of Cigarettes in a Papua New Guinea Prison." Pp. 32–46 in *Thinking Through Things: Theorising Artefacts Ethnographically*, ed. Amiria Henare, Martin Holbraad, and Sari Wastell. London: Routledge.

Reed, Adam. 2011. "Hope on Remand." *Journal of the Royal Anthropological Institute* 17, no. 3: 527–544.

Spyer, Patricia, ed. 1998. *Border Fetishisms: Material Objects in Unstable Spaces*. London: Routledge.

Strathern, Marilyn. 1988. *The Gender of the Gift: Problems with Women and Problems with Society in Melanesia*. Berkeley: University of California Press.

Wagner, Roy. [1975] 1981. *The Invention of Culture*. Chicago: University of Chicago Press.

Weiner, James F. 1988. *The Heart of the Pearl Shell: The Mythological Dimension of Foi Sociality*. Berkeley: University of California Press.

INDEX

absence, 4, 13, 36
actor-network theory, 2, 9–11. *See also*
   theory
acts, parliamentary, 43
aesthetic, 46, 90–91, 115, 121
affinal relationships, 60. *See also* network,
   affinal
affines, 27, 31, 60, 70. *See also* co-affines
affinity, 49, 59, 69, 71, 73n3
Africa, 2–7, 9, 12–19, 20n3, 25–27, 31–33,
   35–38, 39n5, 44, 46–48, 50, 53–54,
   61, 71–71, 73n4, 73n7, 74n13,
   76–79, 81, 89–91, 92n2, 95–98,
   102, 105, 110, 114, 128, 133–145,
   146nn4–5, 150–152, 154
Africanist anthropology, 2–3, 9, 12, 78,
   91, 96, 128, 133, 139, 152. *See also*
   anthropology
Afrinesian, 16, 18–19, 151
agency, 7, 9, 61, 79–80, 109, 152
agent, 6, 14–15, 27, 29–30, 102, 105–106,
   108, 110, 121, 151–152
AIDS, 13, 25–27, 31–37, 111n8. *See also*
   HIV/AIDS
AIDS awareness, 32, 37
AISI (African Information Society
   Initiative), 48
alcohol, 100, 103–104, 108
alliance, 31, 60, 79, 82, 84, 86, 88
Amin, Idi, 108
analysis, 2–12, 16–17, 20n2, 20n5, 20n7,
   20n9, 26–27, 29, 37, 47, 49–50,
   78, 92n5, 105, 110, 127, 136–138,

140, 142–145, 151, 153. *See also*
   description; network, analysis;
   situational analysis
analytic, 2–3, 7–8, 13, 15, 18, 110, 116,
   126, 128, 134–135, 137, 141–143,
   145, 146n1
Anderson, Warwick, 27, 30–31, 37
animal, 15–16, 106, 108–109, 111–112n17,
   114–128, 129n5
   killing, 106, 114–115, 122, 128,
   129nn3–5, 130n7
anthropology, 2–9, 12–13, 16–19, 20n6,
   20n9, 26, 53–54, 59, 78, 91, 95–97,
   128, 132–134, 136–141, 145, 151–
   154. *See also* Africanist anthropology; ethnography
arbitrary location, 145
Arens, William, 38n3
arms control, 48
Ashforth, Adam, 26
assemblage theory, 2
autopsies, 29–31, 37

bagaas, 60, 64–68, 73n7. *See also*
   trousseau
Bahaya, 99
banana, 27, 99–100, 105–106, 116–117,
   123
Barnes, John, 3–4, 6–10, 95–96, 142–144
Barotse, 140. *See also* Lozi
Barry, Andrew, 49
Barth, Fredrik, 50
Bastian, Misty L., 55n7

www.ingramcontent.com/pod-product-compliance
Lightning Source LLC
Chambersburg PA
CBHW060042030426
42334CB00019B/2455